Stig Abell is the breakfast presenter on Times Radio, a station he helped to launch, and a columnist for the *Sunday Times*. Before that he has been the editor and publisher of the *Times Literary Supplement*, a presenter on Radio 4's *Front Row* and had a weekly radio programme on LBC. His first book, *How Britain Really Works*, was published in 2018. His favourite book is *American Tabloid* by James Ellroy, and he can't stand audiobook snobs.

Praise for What to Read Next

'Unusual and engaging . . . the whole book is a lucky dip: put in your thumb, pull out a plum, and relish it' Allan Massie, *Scotsman*

'A thoroughly enjoyable saunter through some great, and not so great, works of literature' *TLS*

'Beyond splendid . . . a brilliant idea, beautifully realised' Bill Bryson

'A witty, warm and wonderfully wise celebration of the written word. A huge treat' Lucy Foley

Also by Stig Abell

How Britain Really Works

What to Read Next

How to Make Books Part of Your Life

STIG ABELL

JOHN MURRAY

First published in Great Britain in 2020 as *Things I Learned on the 6.28*
by John Murray (Publishers)
An Hachette UK company

This paperback edition published in 2021

1

Paperback ISBN 978-1-529-33724-2
eBook ISBN 978-1-529-33722-8

Typeset in Bembo MT by Hewer Text UK Ltd, Edinburgh
Printed and bound in Great Britain by Clays Ltd, Elcograf S.p.A.

John Murray policy is to use papers that are natural, renewable and
recyclable products and made from wood grown in sustainable forests.
The logging and manufacturing processes are expected to conform
to the environmental regulations of the country of origin.

John Murray (Publishers)
Carmelite House
50 Victoria Embankment
London EC4Y 0DZ

www.johnmurraypress.co.uk

For Nadine, the perfect partner in quarantine

Contents

Autumn

Read in order to live.

Gustave Flaubert

I never travel without my diary. One should always have something sensational to read on the train.

Oscar Wilde, *The Importance of Being Earnest*

I'm a writer. I'm supposed to understand what makes people tick. I don't understand one damn thing about anybody.

Raymond Chandler, *The Long Goodbye*

Preface

'You're so lucky,' my wife Nadine said to me once, in that hazy space sometime between our first and second child, 'having that commute every day. You get to sit by yourself, listen to music and read a book. It must be heaven.' And she was right. I moan, like most people, about the diurnal trudge of the working day, its colourless symmetry, the routine that always feels like a rut. But I do get time to myself as I travel, quite a lot of it, and tend to spend it happily, questioningly, improvingly engaged in the act of reading. You can get through an awful lot of books if you spend almost an hour every day of the working week doing little else. This one book is testament to that.

The average commute, to and from work taken together, is around fifty minutes in both the US and the UK, so I set myself the challenge of reading for that period on every working day of the year. Picture me then, if you can, sitting in the same corner of a scuffed and featureless train carriage, rattling through suburbs, those blood-orange seats, the indifferent horde of commuters pressing upon me, headphones on to shut out the world, quietly reading, in my own world and a world created by another.

I wrote this book in the year 1 BC (Before Coronavirus), but if some travel habits have changed as a result of fear of contagion, the importance of a regular relationship with books has not. Here are some things you probably need to know about me at the time of writing: I was thirty-nine, awoke each day with the bodily ache of middle age and the existential dread of failure, and went to work as the editor of the *TLS*, a cultural magazine of some heritage. Every week, I also presented *Front Row*, a cultural magazine show on BBC Radio 4; and talked about politics late at night on Sky News. It was – and is – a profoundly anti-heroic existence. On my commute from a minor London suburb, I left behind Nadine, Nelly (ten), Teddy (seven), our latest, and surprise final,* addition, Phoebe (one) and – for the beginning of the year at least – our dog Biscuit too. My family and my work will crop up from time to time in the diary, so it is as well that you have them in mind from the beginning.

Each month I read a different type of book: English classics, comic fiction, crime writing, poems, Shakespeare and so on. And then I wrote about them, and any other thoughts about what might be broadly termed culture, in the diary. So one way of you using this book would be to spend a year reading along with me, and get – like me – a broad literary education from Anthony Powell and Marcel Proust, Nancy Mitford and Oscar Wilde, Lord Byron and Zora Neale Hurston, and the like. I hope some of you try that, but don't worry if that does not appeal. For each month's category, I also recommend a further twenty-odd books, so you could instead pick one area and spend the year reading just in that particular world: a year of American classics or a year of modern literary fiction, for example. Or you could just read this one book, perhaps buy a couple more for your friends, and leave it at that.

You don't need to be a commuter to do this. I am simply advocating spending a happy chunk of time on regular reading.†

---

* Not to over-share, but the cauterised tubes in my testicles now bear eloquent witness to the unplanned nature of Phoebe's arrival.

† And that means listening to audiobooks too. There should be no snobbery about that. Personally, I prefer reading texts to hearing somebody else read them, but that is simply personal taste. Almost all the books I read this year can be experienced as audiobooks too.

I think it is a boon to mental health, and an act of self-improvement. The world has changed since I began my diary; but in essence it is the same: a place of uncertainty and anxiety, in which escape into the words of others is more necessary than ever. If, when you finish my book, you have found one or five or twenty-five more books (previously unknown; possibly intimidating) to read, then I will be very happy. Please do tell me on Twitter what you're reading: talking about books is, after all, one of the few pleasurable and joyful things about that cloacal place. Indeed, one of the central pleasures in life is sharing what you've read, finding common ground, pressing a heartfelt recommendation upon somebody else. If nothing else, I hope this commuter's guide will offer some new suggestions for you.

A word on the canon, and this book's relationship to it. I have picked books throughout – and there are references to more than five hundred in the pages that follow – that I think are important, are meaningful to me, and I feel I know something about. This is inevitably conditioned by who I am, and where I grew up. There can never be an exhaustive list, and it will omit – by accident and ignorance – writers who have been historically undervalued, even as it tries to identify some of them. My overall list will skew towards European males, because they have dominated much of the literary discourse over the centuries. But over the course of the year, I will read books written in broadly equal numbers by men and women, and will think about the question of diversity and write about it quite a bit. Identity is an important issue, though it is not – and I think this point worth emphasising amid today's culture wars – the only one.

Without wishing to overstate it, reading for me is one of the central facets of existence. I cannot spend a day without a book.*

---

* 'One does not love breathing,' said Harper Lee about how she once undervalued the act of reading. Imagine books taken away from you, forbidden by the state, and you will see what she meant.

I have – in common with everybody – regular moments of mental unrest, roiling disquiet, uncertainty and anxiety. I manage them with a sedative, an analgesic: the escape into worlds created by other people. The invention of the novel, it seems to me, is one of the true triumphs of human endeavour. It codifies something magnificent within all of us: the act of empathy. When we read, we forge a connection with an author, and often then a common culture or tradition that is greater than us. Reading is an act of enlarging, of expansion. It makes our 'I' bigger than just ourselves; it stretches our sense of identity and experience.

Reading is also, of course, a diversion, about which I shouldn't get too breathy and serious.* This year of commuting for me has been, above all other things, fun. And you do not hear that very often. I experience a tingle of expectation as I approach the train platform in the watery morning light, even more so when I know I am starting a new book, which may or may not turn out to be something I remember for ever. All this literary work has given me joy, distraction, meaning and – above all – repose. It was a troubled year, 2019, especially in politics (though, as we now know, it had nothing on 2020). As in an Austen novel, world events will loom and hover in these pages, but never quite obtrude. Brexit is mentioned, as is Donald Trump, but soon passed over.

So here it is, a year in the life of a commuter, a year in books that encompasses continents and millennia, compressed into a few hundred pages. 'I guess there are never enough books,' said John Steinbeck. He was right. But this is an account of a few to be getting on with.

---

* So glad I side-stepped that landmine.

WINTER

January

Crime

Rebecca (1938) by Daphne du Maurier
The Tiger in the Smoke (1952) by Margery Allingham
Watchmen (1987) by Alan Moore and Dave Gibbons

The first journey of January is always burdened by gloom. I sit in an empty train carriage, well before daybreak, with night seeping away. London in the dank dark always reminds me of Dickens. This is from *Oliver Twist* (1839): 'Morning drew on apace. The air became more sharp and piercing, as its first dull hue, the death of night, rather than the birth of day, glimmered faintly in the sky. The objects which had looked dim and terrible in the darkness, grew more and more defined, and gradually resolved into their familiar shapes.'

At such moments, it's easy to feel weighed down by the elements, as if life were dissolving into one giant pathetic fallacy. Anthony Powell (who we'll meet later) once wrote that 'Early morning bears with it a sense of pressure, a kind of threat of what the day will bring forth.' He, like me, was susceptible to a bit of 'cosmic gloom'. But gloom is just gloom, isn't it? Just darkness decaying into light; unconnected to what we feel inside.

Have you noticed that history books often begin with wintry weather? It is as if the past, as Powell also noted, is somehow signified by the sensation of cold. Perhaps historians want us subconsciously to be reminded of times when we were less removed from the elements, were not surrounded by the warm prophylaxis of modern comforts.

Elmore Leonard's first rule of writing was 'Never open a book with weather', and he is right that it has become a cliché. The forgotten novelist Edward Bulwer-Lytton began a novel in 1830, *Paul Clifford*, with this clunker: 'It was a dark and stormy night; the rain fell in torrents.' And it has now become the epitome of bad, weather-based opening lines.* There is even a contest in his name in which writers compete to offer atrocious openers. This was the winner in 2018, by seventeen-year-old Tanya Menezes:

> Cassie smiled as she clenched John's hand on the edge of an abandoned pier while the sun set gracefully over the water, and as the final rays of light disappeared into a star-filled sky she knew that there was only one thing left to do to finish off this wonderful evening, which was to throw his severed appendage into the ocean's depths so it could never be found again – and maybe get some custard after.

The first book on my reading list has one of the most famous opening lines in English literature: 'Last night I dreamt I went to Manderley again.' A bit better, I think we can all agree.

Rebecca begins my month of crime fiction, although there may be a debate about whether it should be classed in this genre

---

* Can we agree that 'The first journey of January is always burdened by gloom' is not a weather-based opening line? Just checking.

at all. I think it shares many characteristics of a crime novel: fast-moving plot, a sense of mystery, a threatening atmosphere, a pulpish pleasure in the act of storytelling itself. In common with many crime novels, as we shall see, it was undervalued by critics too.

Back in 1938 the *TLS*, with its common high-handedness,* dismissed *Rebecca* as a 'low-brow story with a middle-brow finish', but then rather helplessly went on to show why it has gone on to be so successful as an 'ingenious, exciting and engagingly romantic tale'. The review's conclusion is magnificent in its snobbery: 'It is fair, no doubt, to call this type of fiction "dope". But it is no good pretending that everybody would read Tolstoy or Proust if there were no dope literature.'

And I love dope literature unequivocally: books that energise, or sedate, make the pupils dilate, or soothe the spirit; are filled with the narcotic of compulsive narration. Genre novelists have been undervalued because they are thrilling; and du Maurier certainly felt this: 'You don't know how hurtful it is to have rotten, sneering reviews, time and time again throughout my life. The fact that I sold well never really made up for them.' *Rebecca* sold more than 3 million copies by 1965, and its total global sale today is closer to 30 million. We'll see if we can understand why.

6 January

Today I feel anxiety, like a chill, deep within me. Sometimes, I can control it by pushing my feet into the ground, so I can feel a physical sensation that must be real, but today I find it hard to manage. Dread is not an uncommon feeling for me; my first emotion is worry about the future, about fucking up a life upon which my family, their home and wellbeing rely. I carry it like a

---

* In 1938 that is. Now it is a paragon of far-sighted fairness.

weight inside. Reading is an escape from it. And *Rebecca* is a novel about impostor syndrome, about being judged a failure, about impossible expectation. It is also a fantasy, I know. But it is not very soothing at seven thirty in the morning as a means of managing existential dread.

It certainly had a difficult beginning. It was du Maurier's fourth novel, and she was trying to write it in Alexandria, where her soldier husband Frederick 'Boy' Browning* had been posted. She was missing her beloved Cornwall 'like a pain under the heart continually', and struggling to transmute that pain into prose. She wrote an apology to her publisher, saying that 'the first 15,000 words I tore up in disgust and this literary miscarriage has cast me down rather', and even when the manuscript was completed was concerned that it was 'a bit on the gloomy side' with an ending 'a bit brief and a bit grim'.

The gloominess, the Gothic tinge, is at the heart of its charm. The story is told by a nameless narrator – 'You have a lovely and unusual name,' says Max at one point; but nobody tells the reader what it is – who begins the novel far away from home, missing Cornwall intensely. There she meets a Byronic man called Maxim de Winter, who is mourning his mysterious dead wife Rebecca.

7 January

Manderley is really one of the main characters in *Rebecca*. I try to think of other fictional houses that impinge on our consciousness

---

* He was a hero, who won the DSO in the First World War for an action where he was the only surviving officer of seventeen involved. He fought in the Second World War too, and was played by Dirk Bogarde in *A Bridge Too Far*, the film about the Battle of Arnhem. His later life was filled with depression and drinking; Daphne du Maurier called him 'Moper'.

quite as much. There's Darcy's beautiful home in *Pride and Prejudice* (1813). Elizabeth Bennet is asked, near the end, when she had fallen in love with him and answers, with enough truth in it to be funny: 'It has been coming on so gradually, that I hardly know when it began. But I believe I must date it from my first seeing his beautiful grounds at Pemberley.' There's Miss Havisham's Satis House in *Great Expectations* (1861), which is based on a real place in Rochester,* or Bleak House. I've always been fond of Gardencourt, the country mansion owned by the Touchetts in *The Portrait of a Lady* (1881) by Henry James: 'A long gabled front of red brick, with the complexion of which time and the weather had played all sorts of picturesque tricks, only, however, to improve and refine it, presented itself to the lawn, with its patches of ivy, its clustered chimneys, its windows smothered in creepers.'

We first see it in a perfect afternoon, when 'the flood of summer light had begun to ebb, the air had grown mellow', and it has stood – as it is supposed to – in my mind for ease and comfort. Other places that occur on my journey, although I am sure you could add many of your own: Gatsby's mansion ('a colossal affair by any standard – it was a factual imitation of some Hôtel de Ville in Normandy, with a tower on one side, spanking new under a thin beard of raw ivy, and a marble swimming pool, and more than forty acres of lawn and garden'); Thoreau's cabin by Walden Pond (a real place, I suppose, so it may not count); Blandings Castle, as populated by Wodehouse's kindly gang of aristocrats and servants; Baskerville Hall, once Sherlock Holmes has cleared out that pesky hound (I could live there at the

---

* Apparently the name dates back to a visit from Queen Elizabeth I, who was asked if she had been comfortable and acidly replied, 'Satis.' Estelle explains it in the novel: 'which is Greek, or Latin, or Hebrew, or all three – or all one to me – for enough'.

weekends, and spend the weekdays at 221B Baker Street, smoking shag tobacco and taking cocaine).

I put my phone in my bag while I read. In a thirty-minute journey, I take it out twice, first to tweet something desultory and strikingly whimsical, and second to gauge the world's minimal reaction, and use it somehow to calibrate my ongoing account of self-worth. I have my phone out as the doors of the train open at Waterloo, because it would be a shame not to inconvenience people behind me with my walking and screen-watching, even as I harrumph at the slowness of those in front, themselves preoccupied elsewhere.

Reading presents a pause and a break, and an opportunity to escape. Howard Jacobson once referred to the 'infinite distractions' of a screen, 'so deceptively alluring compared to the nun-like stillness of the page, whose black marks you can neither scroll through nor delete'. And the stillness of books – Proust happily called them 'children of silence' – is what makes them appealing, and has always done so.

I don't eat breakfast, so I'm always hungry when I'm reading on the train. *Rebecca* doesn't help. Here is high tea at Manderley: 'Those dripping crumpets, I can see them now. Tiny crisp wedges of toast, and piping-hot, floury scones. Sandwiches of unknown nature, mysteriously flavoured and quite delectable, and that very special gingerbread.' I can see them too, alas. Descriptions of food were especially evocative in the first half of the century, becoming more so when the impact of war meant that fantasy nourishment was all that was available. Evelyn

Waugh talked about *Brideshead Revisited* (1945) in that context: 'A bleak period of present privation and threatening disaster – the period of soya beans and Basic English – and in consequence the book is infused with a kind of gluttony, for food and wine, for the splendours of the recent past, and for rhetorical and ornamental language, which now with a full stomach I find distasteful.'

I think of some of my favourite acts of consumption in literature: the chowder at the beginning of *Moby Dick* (1851) ('made of small juicy clams, scarcely bigger than hazelnuts, mixed with pounded ship biscuits, and salted pork cut up into little flakes; the whole enriched with butter, and plentifully seasoned with pepper and salt'); the ice-cold wine 'tasting faintly of rust' in Hemingway's *The Sun Also Rises* (1926); the picnics, the sweet cocoa, in Enid Blyton (and how disappointing it was when I tasted cocoa for the first time, my expectations raised by reading dashed by the bitter sludge); the cooking of French chef Anatole in the Jeeves and Wooster stories by P.G. Wodehouse ('Consommé aux Pommes d'Amour, Sylphides à la Crème d'Écrevisses, Mignonette de Poulet Petit Duc', and so on). Food in real life to me has become little more than the concealed threat of ill-health, calories to be worked off or despised; it is healthful to think of a time when that sort of mentality was little known and ignored. The truly guiltless meal exists only in the pages of a book.

13 January

Rebecca's characters are boldly drawn, and unforgettable. The narrator stands for every awkward teenager, 'the raw ex-schoolgirl, red-elbowed and lanky-haired', desperately in love with someone who (quite wrongly) is judged to be her superior. She is mordant, and thus very modern, on her own feelings of inadequacy: 'the wind blowing my dull, lanky hair, happy in his silence yet eager for his words'. Max himself is anti-modern, the very model of a Gothic bastard; here he is in one of the narrator's fond imaginings: 'He would stare down at us in our new world from a long-distant past – a past where men walked cloaked at night and stood in the shadow of old doorways, a past of narrow stairways and dim dungeons, a past of whispers in the dark, of shimmering rapier blades, of silent, exquisite courtesy.'

We can hear the masochistic tremble, the simplistic romanticism of bad movies and airport fiction, which *Rebecca* never truly escapes. But the sexual tension remains suppressed and largely unresolved, so it enlivens the novel throughout. Max's proposal is perhaps the most charmless in all fiction. Sitting in a bleak, empty hotel at breakfast ('all the while he ate his tangerine, giving me a piece now and then'), he says this: 'No, I'm asking you to marry me, you little fool.'

This sets the tone for much of the relationship: older man and infantilised wife: 'I was like a child brought to her first school, or a little untrained maid who has never left home before.' Max treats her like an inferior, to be petted ('Good dog then, lie down, don't worry me any more') or disciplined: 'And now eat up your peaches, and don't ask me any more questions, or I shall put you in the corner.' There is the sense of unwholesomeness, even paedophilia, as when Max tries to dress her up like Alice in Wonderland with a ribbon in her hair.

It is acutely done, perhaps not least because of du Maurier's complicated relationship with her own father, and with her sexuality. Gerald du Maurier was an actor-manager,* who clearly

---

* His father, George, wrote the bestselling novel *Trilby* (1894), which gave the world both the name of the hat, and – in the sinister hypnotist character – the term 'Svengali'.

felt an uncomfortable closeness to his daughter. He died after her second novel, *The Progress of Julius* (1933), was published – the year after she got married – and it is actually about a father who drowns his daughter rather than losing her to another man. It has descriptions like this of him watching her play the flute, aware of 'an odd taste in his mouth, and a sensation in mind and body that was shameful and unclean'.

Du Maurier's marriage to Browning, though long-lasting, was not entirely happy. They both had affairs, both with women. Du Maurier today may have been described in more fluid gender terms than was possible in the 1930s: she called herself a 'half-breed', outwardly female 'with a boy's mind and a boy's heart'. And it is striking that the narrator of *Rebecca* says to Max:[*] 'I'll be your friend and your companion, a sort of boy. I don't ever want more than that.'

All that sense of unrewarded, unrewarding sexual longing gives the book its suppressed tension, its prolonged sense of agony.[†] It is indicative that, in the du Maurier family, the slang word for attractiveness was 'menacing', a neat conflation of desire and recoiling fear. The most overt expression of love in the novel is terrifying in its passion, and occurs between two women: Mrs Danvers for the dead Rebecca. The former is the star of the novel, with her 'dead skull's face', and controlled contempt. At one point she confronts the narrator with some of Rebecca's possessions, and commits metaphorical assault: she 'forced the slippers over my hands, smiling all the while,

---

[*] Rebecca herself is said to look 'like a boy in her sailing kit, a boy with a face like a Botticelli angel'.

[†] Manderley is a place of postlapsarian sexuality, its driveway 'twisted and turned like a serpent', the garden full of all that 'bitter fruit'. You don't need to be a psychoanalyst to see what is lurking here either: 'the beeches with white, naked limbs leant close to one another, their branches intermingled in a strange embrace'.

watching my eyes . . . I shall never forget the expression on her face, loathsome, triumphant. The face of an exulting devil.'

14 January

I come to the end of *Rebecca*, and reflect on its unsubtle virtues. It values atmosphere over realism, in a way that resolutely looks back to the extravagance of Gothic fiction. Rebecca is a madwoman in the crypt* rather than the attic, a figure of exuberant sexuality not allowed her place in life, nor peace in death. When evidence of her murder is uncovered, the plot quickens relentlessly: information comes from telephone messages,† there's a coroner's finding, a trip to London, an uncovering of medical records. It is the combination of narrative movement and wallowing in atmosphere that makes *Rebecca* so eminently readable; all the action is surrounded by moments of pause and reflection. It begins and ends with a dream, and the narration is often in the conditional mood, reflecting on how things might be, but are not: 'We should grow old here together, we should sit like this to our tea like old people'; or 'We would have children. Surely we would have children.'

They do not. We know from the opening that the de Winters are childless and rootless, staying in foreign hotels, shifting about without joy. He is a murderer, she an accomplice after

---

* *Rebecca*'s debt to *Jane Eyre* is obvious. Rochester, like Max, was 'dark, strong and stern', although rehabilitated in the end. Bertha Mason, Rochester's first wife, was wrongly silenced and accused of mania in a similar way to Rebecca herself. And the fire of Thornfield Hall imaginatively provides the spark for the immolation of Manderley.

† I think the first ever telephone in fiction is in the Sherlock Holmes book *The Sign of Four* (1890). Conan Doyle, in this as in so much else, the trailblazer. Proust, by the way, was the first to make reference to the camera-phone, in *À l'ombre des jeunes filles en fleurs* (1919): 'le photo-téléphone de l'avenir'.

the event; there is no real resolution. That is relatively rare for a crime novel, which tends to end with revelation and answers, but it is one of the crucial complicating factors that makes *Rebecca* impossible to dismiss, as the *TLS* did, or Alfred Hitchcock did when he said it was merely representative of 'a whole school of feminine literature of the period'. His movie version famously ducks the real moral dilemma, as his Max only kills Rebecca accidentally. In the book, not only do we know his guilt, it is actually the one thing that brings husband and new wife together in passionate embrace, 'feverishly, desperately, like guilty lovers who have not kissed before'. *Rebecca* is a novel without a true hero or heroine, of difficult sexuality, of narrative daring and authorial unease, and thus a novel well worth reading in the twenty-first century.

15 January

There has always been snobbery about genre novels, and it has been applied to crime fiction especially, because of its violence, the guiltiness of its pleasure (all that sensation, the thrill of the transgressive) and the standardisation of its form (puzzle being met by solution). The forebears of detective fiction arrived in the nineteenth century in Edgar Allen Poe and Charles Dickens. Dickens was a writer who liked big reveals, but also – as Edmund Wilson put it – 'invested his plots with a social and moral significance that made the final solution of the mystery a revelatory symbol of something that the author wanted seriously to say'. Dickens arguably wrote the first literary detective, Inspector Bucket, in *Bleak House*, and then inspired his friend Wilkie Collins to write a book with such a figure nearer to its centre, Sergeant Cuff in *The Moonstone* (1868). T.S. Eliot called it 'the first, the longest, and the best of the modern English detective novels in a genre invented by Collins'.

Eliot loved crime fiction, and indeed once told Virginia Woolf he might be described as 'a person who specializes in detective stories and ecclesiastical history'. Like everyone else, he recognised that Conan Doyle's Sherlock Holmes series at the turn of the century marked both the formation of the genre and its high watermark: stories whose sole point was to introduce a mystery, and then to have somebody clever solve it. After Holmes came the so-called 'Golden Age of detective fiction', which stretches from the 1920s to the 1960s with writers such as Georges Simenon in Belgium, Raymond Chandler and Dashiell Hammett* in America, and the great British exponents Agatha Christie and Dorothy L. Sayers. And Margery Allingham, whose *Tiger in the Smoke* I'm now reading.

It is striking how their genre has sparked so much debate, as snobs wrestle with its status. Are the books literary enough? Do they embrace thrills over quality? Edmund Wilson wrote two pieces in the *New Yorker* in the 1940s on the subject (with the exasperated titles, 'Why Do People Read Detective Stories?', and, lampooning Christie, 'Who Cares Who Killed Roger Ackroyd?'), concluding that reading them 'is a vice that, for silliness and minor harmfulness, ranks somewhere between crossword puzzles and smoking'.

W.H. Auden also conceded the narcotic delight of the genre ('For me, as for many others, the reading of detective stories is an addiction like tobacco or alcohol'), but then tried to dress up his delight in rather too flashy literary terms: 'The interest in the thriller is the ethical and eristic† conflict between good and

---

* Interesting that the great Americans are men, and the British are women: American detective fiction was deliberately more macho, more brutal and more urban; the British more considered, baroque and class-ridden.

† Don't worry, I had to look it up: it means combative or oppositional. It is essentially unnecessary in this sentence.

evil . . . The interest in the detective story is the dialectic of innocence and guilt'; 'the detective story probably should, and usually does, obey the classical unities'. Such froth of pretension perhaps conceals his sense of disquiet about taking simple pleasure in rather simple pleasures.

The detective story attracted many attempts to rationalise and compartmentalise it. The novelist S.S. Van Dine called the genre a 'game', and in 1928 wrote twenty rules for it, including things like 'There must be no love interest in the story. To introduce amour is to clutter up a purely intellectual experience with irrelevant sentiment'; and 'A detective novel should contain no long descriptive passages, no literary dallying with side-issues, no subtly worked-out character analyses, no "atmospheric" preoccupations.' In the same year, another author called Ronald Knox, also a Catholic priest, offered his own 'ten commandments', including the perhaps understandable 'the detective must not himself commit the crime' and the frankly baffling 'no Chinaman must figure in the story'.

16 January

I immediately want to take issue with Van Dine's contention that detective fiction should not concern itself with 'atmosphere' or character. The *Sherlock Holmes* canon, as Chandler put it, 'is mostly an attitude'; and *The Tiger in the Smoke* has its force thanks to the sense of dank, concealed, creeping violence.

The story is complicated and rather weak: an army major hides treasure during the war and leaves it for his wife (aptly described as a 'Queen Nefertiti in a Dior ensemble'); one of his men, the villainous Jack Havoc, tries to track it down, killing as he goes. We know *whodunnit* almost from the beginning; the *howdunnit* is the interesting part. And the context is key: a post-war London immured in vile fog that conceals a multitude of sins.* The climate is – as in Dickens – a central character of the novel itself: 'the ancient smell of evil, acrid and potent as the stench of fever, came creeping through the gentle house to him, defiling it as it passed'; the fog that 'crept into the taxi where it crouched panting'† or 'slopped over its low houses like a bucketful of cold soup'.

Havoc himself has an 'extraordinary atmosphere', as does his fellow conspirator, Mrs Cash, of whom it is said: 'The air is always a little cooler where she is.' As we shall see, this is less a detective novel than a villain novel: they are the unforgettable figures that lurk in the imagination. Mrs Cash, 'looking like a pottery figure designed to hold mustard', is a usurer, who preys on the impoverished and hoards their valuables 'like petrified morsels hacked out of living pain'. They are joined by a band of street musicians, freaks and cast-offs, the 'rags of humanity', led by an albino caperer called Tiddy Doll. Havoc is a genius of sorts: he escapes prison by falling sick on the thirteenth and twenty-seventh of every month ('thirteen letters in twenty-seventh') until his behaviour attracts the attention of a doctor whom he can bump off. But he is also a tortured, attenuated figure, almost painful to perceive. This is him dropping into the lair of the street band: ' "Dad's back," he said, and his voice was smooth and careful. Only the shadow flitting like a frown across his forehead, and his pallor, which was paperlike, betrayed his weariness. His spirit danced behind his shallow eyes, mocking everything.'

---

* This was the smog that, in the winter a year later, was to kill 12,000 Londoners in just five days, leading to the first Clean Air Act being passed by Parliament.
† Compare the beginning of *Bleak House*: 'Fog in the eyes and throats of ancient Greenwich pensioners, wheezing by the firesides of their wards; fog in the stem and bowl of the afternoon pipe of the wrathful skipper, down in his close cabin; fog cruelly pinching the toes and fingers of his shivering little 'prentice boy on deck.'

18 January

On the way home from work, I read Raymond Chandler's 'The Simple Art of Murder', first published in 1944. It is his response both to the maundering, highbrow criticism of detective fiction, and the rather staid English tradition within the genre itself, books 'with such a title as *The Triple Petunia Murder Case* or *Inspector Pinchbottle to the Rescue*'. He does a pitch-perfect pastiche of the country-house murder:

> It is the same utterly incomprehensible trick of how somebody stabbed Mrs Pottington Postlethwaite III with the solid platinum poniard just as she flatted on the top note of the 'Bell Song' from Lakmé in the presence of fifteen ill-assorted guests; the same ingénue in fur-trimmed pajamas screaming in the night to make the company pop in and out of doors and ball up the time-table; the same moody silence next day as they sit around sipping Singapore slings and sneering at each other, while the flatfeet crawl to and fro under the Persian rugs, with their derby hats on.

That burn still scorches seventy years later.* Chandler prefers writers like Dashiell Hammett, because – like all novelist-critics – his criticism is actually making the case for his own art. After all Hammett, like Chandler himself, 'took murder out of the Venetian vase and dropped it into the alley'; and created the macho hero who sneaked seamlessly into Hollywood too: 'Down these mean streets a man must go who is not himself mean, who is neither tarnished nor afraid.'

Chandler is prone to parody himself. Anyone with such a sense of style is. But I have a chapbook of Chandler's best lines, which I dig out when I get home. What other writer could produce a book

---

* Here's another good one: 'The English may not always be the best writers in the world, but they are incomparably the best dull writers.'

of cracks and quotations like this? I wonder. I can think of Wilde, Shakespeare and Dorothy Parker, and nobody else. Here are a few lines to roll around the mouth, like cheap Scotch:

- 'It was a blonde. A blonde to make a bishop kick a hole in a stained glass window.'
- 'He was a guy who talked with commas, like a heavy novel.'
- 'I was as hollow and empty as the spaces between the stars'; or 'The sunshine was as empty as a headwaiter's smile.'
- 'I'm a writer. I'm supposed to understand what makes people tick. I don't understand one damn thing about anybody'.

20 January

Margery Allingham's books feature, like so many of the period, an amateur sleuth: Albert Campion. But he is absent for much of *The Tiger in the Smoke*, which seldom shifts its attentions towards the act of detection itself. When the forces of the law are required, they come in the form of 'a living question-mark', Inspector Charlie Luke, whose 'diamond-shaped eyes' or, later, 'diamond eyes live as coals' glint amid the penetrating murk. Havoc's murderous mission is destined to destroy itself, so there is little necessary focus on the operation laid against him.

The *TLS*, needless to say, didn't love *The Tiger in the Smoke* when it was first published, likening it to an 'unevenly baked cake in which there are too many different kinds of fruit'. I nearly understand what it means: the story is rather shapeless and messy; things loom and then shrink, dwindling like presences in the fog. But that is what has made it linger so long. It is not a trite piece of plotting that could meet certain preordained rules; it is a post-war treatment of angst and uncertainty. Life then, as Allingham noted, was a 'sea of muddles and unsatisfying things'. Campion lived in an age 'which had never known illusion, the grimly humorous generation which had both expected and experienced the seamier side'. Allingham is closer to Chandler's mean streets than she gets credit for; and a fine companion for our own unsatisfying, muddled age.

21 January

To *Front Row* today, where we'll be debating whether the representation of sex is changing in culture. There is very little sex in crime fiction, which is probably a good thing. This was Marlowe's response to a romantic offer in *The Big Sleep* (1939): 'The imprint of her head was still in the pillow, of her small corrupt body still on the sheets. I put my empty glass down and tore the bed to pieces savagely.'

In general there is very little good sex on the page. Perhaps because it is mostly men who have chosen to write about sex and who cannot do so without letting intrusive fantasies pervade the prose. The blood tends to go to the wrong organ as they write. As women take more creative control in the various industries, we will get more sex without the male gaze – perhaps more honest, more sceptical; or perhaps eventually more prone to their own distortions too.

Each year the Bad Sex in Fiction Award is dominated by men; last year it was all men. The winner, James Frey, had one scene which featured ejaculate eight times (always a telltale sign of prose getting out of control). Here's a sample, as it were: 'Blinding breathless shaking overwhelming exploding white God I cum inside her my cock throbbing we're both moaning eyes hearts souls bodies one. One. White. God. Cum. Cum. Cum. I close my eyes let out my breath. Cum. I lean against her both breathing hard I'm still inside her smiling.'

If we are being charitable, we can see what he is trying to do here: capture an essence, a rush, a feeling of inescapable overwhelming. It's just that repeating the word 'cum' isn't a very good way to do it. People say and do things during sex that might seem embarrassing when the moment has faded; committing them to the unfading memory of prose is a dangerous thing to do. We see this with Hemingway too, in *For Whom the Bell Tolls* (1940), in the famous 'did the earth move for thee?' passage:

> For him it was a dark passage which led to nowhere, then to nowhere, then again to nowhere, once again to nowhere, always and forever to nowhere, heavy on the elbows in the earth to nowhere, dark, never any end to nowhere, hung on all time always to unknowing nowhere, this time and again for always to nowhere, now not to be borne once again always and to nowhere, now beyond all bearing up, up, up and into nowhere, suddenly, scaldingly, holdingly all nowhere gone and time absolutely still and they were both there, time having stopped . . .

Again, we see the rhythmic repetition, that grasp towards something ineffable (the nonsense sequence 'suddenly, scaldingly, holdingly' is particularly jarring). And the argument should perhaps be that if it is ineffable, the best thing to do is not to effing try to say it. So many books would be improved with a simple, factual reference to sex, and then the story moving on. But for some reason the lure to explain, to anatomise takes over. John Updike* is guilty of this especially. I once reviewed a book of his called *Villages* (2004), with lines like 'her dear known sex in its gauzy beard of fur', 'that rosy badge of her authority to

---

* Norman Mailer has his narrator say in *Tough Guys Don't Dance* (1984) that 'the best description of a pussy I ever came across was in a short piece by John Updike' and that he really wanted 'to have him guide me through the inside of a cunt'. And some people call Mailer ridiculous. Updike actually wrote a limited edition chapbook of poetry in 1974 called *Cunts*, which I have almost no interest in reading.

service the male', 'those livid wrinkles looking like lava folds'. Or this on ejaculation: 'an astonishing release, a clench that took him back to infancy, its tight knit of newness before memories overlaid the bliss of being'.

Jonathan Gibb, writing on the subject in the *TLS*, once quoted James Salter as describing a man ejaculating 'like a drinking horse': 'so falling foul of *Gibbs's Law of Reversible Similes*: if you can describe something as being like something else, then that comparison should work equally well in reverse. I am yet to see a horse drink "like a man coming", and hope I never will.' Similes and sex are a hard combination to manage.

I shouldn't criticise too much. The first sustained piece of creative writing I ever wrote were pornographic stories* for my wife: there the detail and the passion were serving more than just an artistic purpose, though. And yes, I hope they never surface anywhere.

23 January

I have been inside the houses of three authors on my reading list, and only one of them invited me in. Charles Dickens and Henry James had me over in the capacity of casual tourist, prodder of stationery and fond imaginer of ghostly genius. Dave Gibbons, illustrator of *Watchmen*, once welcomed me to his 'Dave Cave', a drawing studio crammed with books and memorabilia, when I made a radio programme on the rise of comic book movies.

It is inescapable that the world of comic books has gone mainstream in the last decade, especially thanks to the efforts of Hollywood. Dave told me that, as a child in the 1950s, American comics were frowned upon and seen as subversive in the UK.

---

* I also wrote her parodies of detective stories starring a young, mixed-race couple called Wabblepussy and Cont, who solved crime in a hard-boiled version of London. I'm very lucky to have her, I know.

They were confiscated at his school and burned before his eyes, a formative experience if ever there was one.

Gibbons went to America in the 1980s and met fellow Brit Alan Moore, a beaver-bearded anarchist, occultist and comic book writer of genius. Together they revolutionised the form. *Watchmen* – in common with the other breakthrough title of the era, *The Dark Knight Returns* (1986) by Frank Miller – turned the medium in on itself: it reflected upon the very nature of heroism, costumes and comic book writing; they grounded fantasy in hard-boiled grim reality.

With still a week to go before February, I have time to read all of *Watchmen*, my first proper experience of a graphic novel.

25 January

Watchmen is set in an alternative version of America in the mid-eighties, in which Richard Nixon stays President for more than three terms and the war in Vietnam was won. Masked superheroes have been present for half a century, but gradually whittled away, and in 1977 formally banned by the government. This is a summary of their current plight: 'The first Nite Owl runs an auto-repair shop. The first Silk Spectre is a bloated, ageing whore dying in a Californian rest resort. Captain Metropolis was decapitated in a car crash back in '74. Mothman's in an asylum up in Maine. The Silhouette retired in disgrace, murdered six weeks later by a minor adversary seeking revenge. Dollar Bill got shot. Hooded Justice went missing in '55.'

The point throughout is that heroes all have feet of clay. Dollar Bill, for example, was killed in a bank robbery: 'his cloak became entangled in the bank's revolving door and he was shot dead at point-blank range before he could free it.' Only a few have remained active. That includes Doc Manhattan, a naked blue figure who was the result of a nuclear experiment gone awry, and the only person in the whole book to have actual superpowers. He can control all matter, and experiences time 'in a quantum fashion', with past, present and future all available to him simultaneously. It is thanks to him that Vietnam was a victory, and that the US remains in control of the Cold War: 'The Superman exists,' someone observes, 'and he's American.'

Doc Manhattan is on the government payroll, as is the Comedian, a sociopathic, rapist vigilante who 'saw the face of the twentieth century and chose to become a reflection, a parody of it'. Off the reservation completely is Rorschach, an unsanctioned vigilante, who gets many of the best lines. He is the type of bad good guy, who escapes the control of his creator and becomes the charismatic focus of the story: think Milton's Satan.

28 January

Moore called *Watchmen* 'a superhero *Moby Dick*; something with that sort of weight, that sort of density'. And it is hugely ambitious: a nine-panel grid of grim dystopian drawings, punctuated by journal entries, book extracts, an entire meta-comic and other cultural clutter. The tone is recognisably butch and noirish from the very beginning: 'Dog carcass in alley this morning, tire tread on burst stomach. This city is afraid of me. I have seen its true face. The streets are extended gutters and the gutters are full of blood and when the drains finally scab over, all the vermin will drown.'

It is easy to dismiss the violence of *Watchmen*, but there is both self-conscious humour and cleverness at play to lighten and deepen it. The first Nite Owl is aware of the perilous relationship between reality and fantasy, and can pinpoint the ridiculousness of 'all of us choosing to dress up in gaudy costumes and express the notion of good and evil in simple, childish terms while over in Europe they were turning human beings into soap and lampshades'. *Time* magazine put *Watchmen* in its top 100 novels since 1923, and it was the only comic to make the list. I can see why. But I also come to realise how unvisual my brain is: I struggle to follow a story in panels, struggle to identify characters and to pursue the chain of the conversation. I love prose, the orderly array of sentences advancing a narrative; on each morning of reading a comic, my tired eyes and mind feel the lurid jumble of narratives slowing the storytelling down.

30 January

I think very little about the train I get on each morning, from the same spot on the same platform, glowering at my fellow commuters. But as a mode of transport it has shaped the country, indeed the world, over the last 200 years: the sudden annihilation of distance and space meant that people, goods and capital became more mobile in the nineteenth century, and the economic system we now know became possible. Trains created the concept of Europe too, perhaps. At least that is the argument of a book by Orlando Figes called *The Europeans*, published in 2019, which tells the tale of the shrinking of the Continent in the 1840s, as capital cities became connected, and everybody was able to listen to the same music, watch the same plays, and read the same books all at the same time. These are the words of the German poet Heinrich Heine in 1843: 'Space is killed by the railways . . . I feel as if the mountains and forests of all countries are advancing on Paris. Even now, I can smell the German linden trees; the North Sea breakers are rolling at my door.'

Solid rails actually existed in Europe 2,000 years ago: there was a track built across the Isthmus near Corinth, used to move heavy goods. But the nineteenth century was the revolution: the age of mobility; the age of connectedness; the age of trains.

Think of Turner's painting *Rain, Steam and Speed: The Great Western Railway* in 1844, or *The Gare St-Lazaire* by Monet or *Landscape with a Carriage and a Train* by Van Gogh, who called the train a sign of 'desperately swift passing of things in modern life'.

Trains in novels are familiar things: possibly because they bring people together in proximity, move people with speed, but also allow moments of pause for plot to develop. I think immediately of Holmes and Watson in a first-class carriage, surrounded by mountains of newspapers, smoking and gleaning and planning. Or of the 'excellent' train from Paddington to Blandings, with the Earl of Emsworth snoring stertorously, his octopus-like legs manspreading with nonchalance. Or Agatha Christie's *Orient Express* and the improbable conclusion of its mystery, or – involving the same train – Bond fighting an assassin in *From Russia With Love* (1957). There's Hannay leaping off a moving train in both *The Thirty-Nine Steps* (1915) and *Mr Standfast* (1919); Mr Toad escaping; the adventures of *The Railway Children* (1906); and so on and on.

How about Dickens, who was himself to survive a train crash in 1865, in which ten were killed and forty injured, and Dickens spent time at the scene tending the wounded.* He had written beautifully about the thrilling, damaging cost of the new technology in *Dombey and Son* (1848). Look at (listen to) the mimetic thundering of the prose here:

> Away, with a shriek, and a roar, and a rattle, from the town, burrowing among the dwellings of men and making the streets hum, flashing out into the meadows for a moment, mining in through the damp earth, booming on in darkness and heavy air,

---

* He died exactly five years to the day later, and some believe he never recovered from the shock.

bursting out again into the sunny day so bright and wide; away, with a shriek, and a roar, and a rattle, through the fields, through the woods, through the corn, through the hay, through the chalk, through the mould, through the clay, through the rock, among objects close at hand and almost in the grasp, ever flying from the traveller, and a deceitful distance ever moving slowly with him: like as in the track of the remorseless monster, Death!

Then we must remember Anna Karenina and her final act of oblivion too: 'And all at once she thought of the man crushed by the train the day she had first met Vronsky, and she knew what she had to do. With a rapid, light step she went down the steps that led from the tank to the rails and stopped quite near the approaching train.'

That's enough trains – ed.

~

Further Reading

The Complete Sherlock Holmes (1887–1927) by Arthur Conan Doyle

The Amateur Cracksman (1899) by E.W. Hornung

Mr Standfast (1919) by John Buchan

The Maltese Falcon (1930) by Dashiell Hammett

Murder Must Advertise (1933) by Dorothy L. Sayers

Murder on the Orient Express (1934) by Agatha Christie

Brighton Rock (1938) by Graham Greene

The Big Sleep (1939) by Raymond Chandler

The Killer Inside Me (1952) by Jim Thompson

Kiss Me, Deadly (1952) by Mickey Spillane

The Talented Mr Ripley (1955) by Patricia Highsmith

Black Money (1966) by Ross MacDonald

In Cold Blood (1966) by Truman Capote
The Godfather (1969) by Mario Puzo
The Choirboys (1975) by Joseph Wambaugh
A Morbid Taste for Bones (1977) by Ellis Peters
Harlot's Ghost (1991) by Norman Mailer
The Secret History (1992) by Donna Tartt
American Tabloid (1995) by James Ellroy
Death in Holy Orders (2001) by P.D. James
The Girl with the Dragon Tattoo (2008) by Stieg Larsson
An Uncertain Place (2011) by Fred Vargas

February

English Classics

The Female Quixote (1752) by Charlotte Lennox
A Question of Upbringing (1951) /
A Buyer's Market (1952) by Anthony Powell

I burrow into a book, as ever, to escape reality, and it's an unfamiliar one: *The Female Quixote* by Charlotte Lennox. The novelty of the name feels appropriate for my new project in this still new year.

The eighteenth century, when Lennox was writing, was the primordial period of the novel in Britain. It was a giant, fizzing, burping, enswamping soup of ideas waiting for its moment to be given form. Print was getting cheaper, the social order was slowly beginning to relax, and there was an opportunity for writers to rise up and grab attention.

They were mostly men, of course. And the big beasts of the period wrote big intimidating novels: Henry Fielding, Thomas Sterne, Samuel Richardson and Tobias Smollett (what a name redolent of his century old Tobias has). These novels today manage to feel both archaic – they are filled with ramshackle punctuation, seemingly random capitalisation of nouns, and sentences allowed to spread unchecked – yet very new-fangled:

the eighteenth century brought us postmodernism before modernism even existed. All the authors, a bit like the playwrights of Shakespeare's generation, were incredibly conscious of the novelty of the form, so they kept mentioning it, musing on it, playing with it. It can get tiresome, but it is also rather thrilling. Sterne's *Tristram Shandy* (1759), which Ezra Pound thought was the only novel in the language equal to Joyce's *Ulysses* (1922), is perhaps the most obvious example. It is full of digressions, sharp turns, its footing laid in the very rubble of the fourth wall it has destroyed. At one point, it leaves a blank page and asks the reader to draw a version of a character, 'as like your mistress as you can – as unlike your wife as conscience will let you'.

3 February

The second day of reading *The Female Quixote*, and I am starting to get into the swing of the prose already. That is the thing to do with 'difficult' or archaic writing, as we will see with Shakespeare: read into the pace and feel of it, and it gets more comfortable each day.

Charlotte Lennox was one of the leading writers of her time, but died in penury, struggling to earn money as an author and freelance journalist. Though born in Gibraltar, she spent much of her childhood in New York State, before the death of her soldier father, and so has been dubbed – disingenuously – the first ever American novelist. When she came to live in England, she married badly to a man who seems to have been something of a shit (she called him 'a most unnatural father', which could conceal a whole multitude of sins) and flung herself into literary life.

Lennox was welcomed by no less a figure than Samuel Johnson, the great man of letters of his age. He supported her work, and when her first novel, called *The Life of Harriet Stuart* (1751), was published, held a party at the Devil Tavern for her, including a 'magnificent hot apple-pye' served with bay leaves.* A year later, at the age of just twenty-four, she produced *The Female Quixote*, which is agreed to be her most striking and best work.

We do not know much more about Lennox of significance. Horace Walpole said she was a 'poetess and deplorable actress', and she launched a magazine called, like something out of Wodehouse, *Lady's Museum*. It was a hodgepodge of stories and letters, edited by Lennox in the persona of a woman who is 'young, single, gay, and ambitious of pleasing'. Lennox also had the supreme self-confidence to take on Shakespeare in a book that was less than reverent, criticising him for his 'Poverty of Invention' and 'want of Judgement'. Johnson, speaking oddly in the manner of a twenty-first-century tweeter, said that she had 'demolished' the playwright, and promptly nicked her idea in the *Preface to Shakespeare* he went on to write.

Other ambitious women seem to have sniffed at Lennox: Frances Burney,[†] with neat cattiness, noted that 'Mrs Thrale says that though her Books are generally approved, Nobody likes her.' That, at least, was not true: both Johnson and Samuel

---

* Johnson was not an unequivocal feminist, it must be said. He is the author of this: 'a woman's preaching is like a dog's walking on his hind legs. It is not done well; but you are surprised to find it done at all.' But also this: 'It is a paltry trick indeed to deny women the cultivation of their mental powers and I think it is partly a proof we are afraid of them.' I can hear the teeth-rattle of women nodding in agreement with that last bit.

† Another woman lost largely to posterity. She was a novelist and satirist who inspired Jane Austen (a passage from her book *Cecilia* (1782) gave Austen the title of *Pride and Prejudice*), and whose lively diaries of the period have over-shadowed her fiction. Mrs (Hester) Thrale was another notable diarist and patron of the arts, perhaps best known for her friendship with Johnson.

Richardson liked her a lot. And although Lennox could clearly be what even then was described as a 'difficult woman' – her only entry in the legal record is a court case against her for beating her servant – she was also regarded fairly widely as part of the new generation of female intellectuals. *The Female Quixote* remains the only novel Samuel Johnson ever reviewed.

It is a giant satire of French romances, the precursors to the novel in English. Those books featured heroines with names like Clelia and Mandana, who undergo 'Adventures' in exotic settings, normally involving them being courted by a series of idealised lovers. Madame de Scudéry was the most successful author of the genre, and she has the probable distinction of writing the longest novel ever: *Artamène ou Le Grand Cyrus* (1649), coming in at a slab-like two million words.[*]

The central character of *The Female Quixote* is Arabella, a young heiress with one 'Foible': she believes such romances to be real history, and that her life follows a similar path, that she is a heroine in her own love story. So every stranger she meets is a vexed Lover, an undercover Prince, a malign ravisher, and so on:

> She often wondered, indeed, that she did not find her Name carved on Trees, with some mysterious Expressions of Love; that he was never discovered lying along the Side of one of the little Rivulets, increasing the Stream with his Tears; nor, for three Months that he had lived there, had ever been sick of a Fever caused by his Grief, and the Constraint he put upon himself in not declaring his Passion.

Much 'Confusion' occurs as a result of this disappointed expectation.

---

[*] The longest in English seems to be *Clarissa* (1748) by Samuel Richardson, which doesn't quite scrape a million words.

7 February

I press play on my music seconds before I get on the train. I've always worked and read with music as a background. It dates to the time I used to do homework with my dad on Sunday mornings. We'd sit at either end of the dining room table, scarified with pencil impressions and compass scratches until my mum insisted on a padded covering. And, while he did his work, I did mine to the accompaniment of bands he liked: Jethro Tull, Genesis, Black Sabbath, Iron Maiden. I look back with great affection to those mornings, gas fire on, a sense of tacit communion, getting to grips with the achievable. Fast-forward twenty-five years, and it is old rock music in my headphones still. I'm on my own, though, and things seem less readily achievable than getting to the end of an essay; reading is less work, more escape.

The Female Quixote is saturated in bookishness. Its title and plot is a play on Cervantes's *Don Quixote* (published more than a hundred years before, in 1605), about a well-drubbed nobleman who shared a similar delusion, and spent his days careening around Spain believing he was a knight. Martin Amis once said that 'While clearly an impregnable masterpiece, *Don Quixote* suffers from one fairly serious flaw – that of outright unreadability.' He called 75 per cent of it 'inhumanly dull'. I would put the figure at no more than 30 per cent.

Lennox's version, thank God, is better than that. It is a little intimidating still, and has many of the ticks and tricks of its age. Freckled with the Needless Capitalisation of every Noun, each chapter comes with its own little summary: 'In which our Heroine is suspected of Insensibility'; 'Contains several Incidents in which the Reader is expected to be extremely interested'. And each gloomy day, I am indeed interested, not always extremely, but enough.

Arabella, the character, is a distinct pleasure to meet on the train. Towards the end, I realise that *The Female Quixote* is about impossible standards of expectation, especially for women. Arabella's central disappointment is that life is not as orderly or certain as literature; we all wish we could be in control of the narrative of our own existence. She hides away in stories, because they provide a sense of conclusion.

Take her reaction to the death of her father: 'Cruel Destiny! . . . Has robbed me of the only Parent I had left, and exposed me, at these early Years, to the Grief of losing him, who was not only my Father, but my Friend, and Protector of my Youth!' Arabella is at once knowing in her use of romantic cliché, but also genuinely consoled by it; she is taking refuge in the orderly exclamation of it all. There is a shape to the family tragedy, a 'Destiny', and a sense that others in the past have shared the experience. That way lies consolation.

Lennox surrounds Arabella with characters that add some – but not quite enough – texture to the tale: Glanville, her cousin and lover, desperate to protect her from humiliation in society by those who think she is 'a little wrong in the Head'; his sister, a catty false friend, who fears both the brains and beauty of her rival; Sir Charles, their father, who becomes legally responsible for Arabella (and whom she accuses of fancying her); and Sir George, a wily rake, who pretends to like romances as much as she does to try to get beneath her corset.

This sounds like the beginning of a plot by Jane Austen, and it is clear that Lennox is an important literary precursor to her: Arabella is closely related to Catherine Morland,[*] of *Northanger Abbey* (1817), who was obsessed with Gothic novels and 'in

---

[*] She also prefigures the romantic, novel-inflected daydreaming of Madame Bovary.

training for a heroine'. As with *Pride and Prejudice*, the plot of *The Female Quixote* hinges on an entail of the estate: Arabella must marry Glanville to keep her father's property. Miss Glanville is as mean-spirited and shallow as Miss Bingley, and she is no advocate of the sisterhood, as she does not 'think it possible one Woman could praise another with any Sincerity'. Miss Glanville accompanies Arabella to Bath, where two Austen novels were to be set (*Northanger Abbey* and *Persuasion*, 1817), and is a regular attendee at the 'stupid parties' condemned by Austen in her diaries.

It is at Bath that we see the strength of Arabella's character. She may be determined to copy the 'Manners of the Heroines' of her novels, but that does mean she 'follow'd no Fashion but her own Taste'. She stands out from the crowd, and is fearless in doing so. Later, back in London, she spies a woman dressed as a boy (clearly a prostitute) at a society event, and supports her when she is assailed, because Arabella's delusions are based on an equality of approach, a sense of fairness. Finally, she must learn the difference between fantasy and reality, that 'nothing is more different from a human being than Heroes or Heroines'. Arabella recognises that idealism and story-making must give way, and in doing so she can reach her own happy ending with Glanville.

Is Lennox worth reading now? I think so. Arabella is a little bit like a minor Austen character – the girl who likes books too much – pushed centre-stage, with one trick to display. At the same time, she manages to be more than that; the charm of her character, her 'Wit and Vivacity', shine out. *The Female Quixote* is good at judging the fake morality of society and is wise to the fact that we cannot expect the behaviour of past centuries to stand up to the scrutiny of the modern age: 'Heroes of Antiquity' can be 'Bad Men', and we must come to terms with it, without negating the achievements of the past. All this is relevant today.

But we do not always turn to literature for relevance; we turn to it for intelligence, originality and distraction. *The Female Quixote* has all of these as well.

There's a piece on the *Daily Mail* website today about how women can avoid having a 'man-repellent' home. Apparently, books can be one of the problems. The article quotes an interior-design expert who warns against the danger of displaying 'novels with depressing titles', and indeed having books at all in the bedroom. Intimidating to male dates, apparently.

I am intrigued by the idea of books as repellents. Are there any books that would put you off a prospective partner?* I'm not sure there are. Booklessness, though, would be a huge warning sign. A house empty of ideas and warmth; it would be hard to get past that. The novelist Linda Grant once told me that she could not trust a man who did not read fiction. And I understand what she meant: if someone cannot empathise with another person's story, how could they empathise with me?

Another week of especially unsettling politics, as the Brexit wranglings in Parliament begin what may or may not be their tireless, year-long crescendo, filled with rhetorical, bloviating references to the Second World War and things like 'Blitz spirit'.

---

* It would be easy to say Ayn Rand, but my wife actually owned two books by her, and liked them growing up (and she is basically normal). Or, snobbishly, Jeffrey Archer, but I read them as a child and kind of liked them too. Paulo Coelho with his whimsy dressed up as wisdom? A whole shelf of self-help books, screaming out like a horizontal distress flare? I honestly think that almost anything is forgivable.

Solace can be found in books written at a time when the circumstances of war were in recent memory, but rendered without hysteria. John Buchan's Richard Hannay novels for example, or *A Dance to the Music of Time*, the series of twelve novels by Anthony Powell, the first of which was published in 1951, and set in 1921. That will be my commute book for the rest of the month, *A Question of Upbringing*.

15 February

A couple of years ago, we ran a review in the *TLS* under the headline 'Who still reads Anthony Powell?'. And it remains a good question. *A Dance to the Music of Time* was produced, with new instalments at intervals of two years, between 1951 and 1975. Only after the fifth volume was it clear that they would form a complete arc of twelve books. And Powell took that decision because of an unexpected bequest from his father, worth about £1.5 million in today's money, which meant he had the financial security to keep on writing. Read in 2019, the books are – almost parodically – the product of a certain sense of privilege. They tell the largely footling tales of people pitched somewhere between posh and bohemian over the middle years of the twentieth century. The narrator, Jenkins, is a bit like the author (schooled at Eton, dull wartime service, career in publishing), and the characters are often the author's friends transmuted into fiction.*

Powell apparently wanted his narrator to be 'colourless', so that his personality would not interfere with his role as observer of the people and events that surround him. 'You are thought cold,' Jenkins is told at one point, 'but you possess deep

---

* The impecunious Julian Maclaren-Ross, for example, is faithfully translated into the novelist X. Trapnel.

affections, sometimes for people worthless in themselves.' And that sense of worthlessness, of minor-key incident, is at the centre of the whole series.

16 February

I wasn't home from work at Sky News until 1 a.m. last night. I fell asleep to be woken by Biscuit barking and slept on the sofa with him until six so he wouldn't wake the baby.

On the train this morning, I struggled to keep my eyes open despite Powell's valiant efforts. In truth, the gentle world of private school and independent wealth, people called Tuffy and Le Bas and Widmerpool, is not especially good at shocking you into wakefulness. I drowse, allowing schoolboy tales to slip into my mind like a half-remembered dream, before starting and looking around suspiciously. I open a jostled bottle of fizzy water, spraying my clothes, and that livens me up for the last ten minutes.

A Question of Upbringing has, it must be said, very little activity. School is highlighted by a 'rag' in which the boys pretend to police that their housemaster is a man wanted for fraud; Oxford is characterised by 'prolonged, lugubrious stretches of Sunday afternoon'. Even a car crash is immediately construed as an 'inconvenient occurrence' and an 'uncomfortable situation'. It was caused, we discover allusively, by one of the men groping a girl: he 'had disturbed her sensibilities in some manner, so that she had drawn herself unexpectedly away from him'. We should, perhaps, not expect much more empathy than that: that the car was crashed is unfortunate; that a woman was assaulted is not even considered.

Jenkins is an apt recorder of events, but his 'colourlessness' means we do not really ever feel them. He is a peculiarly British figure, who imagines what love might be like, but cannot truly experience it. This is the closest he gets to genuine stirrings in that organ of desire: 'I was not yet old enough to be aware of the immense rage that can be secreted in the human heart by cumulative minor irritation.'

In fact, *Dance* is a series of the 'cumulative' and the 'minor'. Powell once noted that 'One of the most difficult things to realize when one is young is that all the awful odds and ends taking place round one are, in fact, the process of living.'

18 February

I read, today, some awful odds and ends about Charles Dickens, including his abysmal treatment of his wife. I knew he had left Catherine to pursue an affair with Ellen Ternan in 1858, acting terribly towards her in the process, including making the false claim that she 'does not – and she never did – care for the children'. It turns out he went further. Newly discovered letters show he approached a doctor to have Catherine committed to a lunatic asylum, because, as his neighbour put it, 'she had borne ten children and had lost many of her good looks, was growing old in fact.' Elizabeth Barrett Browning said: 'What a crime, for a man to use his genius as a cudgel . . . against the woman he promised to protect tenderly with life and heart.'

So does the cruelty impact on our assessment of the genius? It is a common question now, and one that will come up again and again in my year of reading. How much do the sins of the writer matter to an appreciation of the writing? And, perhaps more acutely, what happens when we read a book with references to a person's gender or sexuality or race that are unacceptable, but were permitted in the past? When John Buchan writes of 'nigger musicians' who look like monkeys, or Hemingway says in *The Sun Also Rises* that Robert Cohn had 'a hard, stubborn, Jewish streak'?

So what do we do about good art from bad people? Last night I saw a new Michael Jackson documentary in which two men make specific and detailed claims of sexual assault against him. If we believe them, should we stop listening to his music? The initial answer seems, simply, no. Art can ever be separated from artist. Caravaggio was a murderer (he may have killed a man by castrating him), so was Ben Jonson. T.S. Eliot was an anti-Semite, as was Ezra Pound, and they are still part of the canon of poetry. But here we enter murky waters. What if the art touches upon the moral failings of the artist? Is *Alice's Adventures in Wonderland* (1865) tainted because it rises from Lewis Carroll's questionable obsession with under-clothed young girls?

Again, I think we can be robust. We can judge the art and artist in parallel, and hold competing, even uncomfortable, views in our minds at once. But this is straightforward when the artist is comfortably dead. Pound doesn't benefit from our commercial patronage, nor does Dickens. Living artists (or the recently deceased, with active estates) do, and should they be subject to the legitimacy of individual personal boycott? If you disapprove of the conduct of a bank or a supermarket (or a newspaper), you can stop buying it, vote with your feet, register an economic objection.

Is there anything wrong with doing that to Michael Jackson, or the singer R. Kelly (charged this week with ten counts of assault)? Artists are not saints, but perhaps we should not want to see rapists get rich either.

Happily enough, I stumbled today on an article in the *New York Review of Books* on a row precisely about Ezra Pound and his place in the canon. In 1945 *An Anthology of Famous English and*

American Poetry was set to be published by Random House, and Pound was to be excluded. The publishers were clear on it: they 'flatly refused at this time to include a single line of Mr Ezra Pound. This is a statement that the publishers are not only willing but delighted to print.' One of their authors was not so sanguine. Auden was so incensed by the act of censorship, he said he would leave Random House, offering this explosive sentiment:

> The issue is far more serious than it appears at first sight; the relation of an author to his work only one out of many, and once you accept the idea that one thing to which a man stands related shares in his guilt, you will presently extend it to others; begin by banning his poems not because you object to them but because you object to him, and you will end, as the Nazis did, by slaughtering his wife and children.

Auden more or less despised Pound's poetry as poetry, but clearly felt strong enough to indulge in an almost grotesque overstatement on the matter of principle. Art and artist were separate, and the art is all that matters. In a later letter, he offered this further (and sensible) distinction: 'There are works of fairly high aesthetic value which present attitudes which are poisonous, and they present a problem to a publisher, and he has to decide whether the public are grown up enough to enjoy the first without harm because they are sufficiently aware that the second is poison.' Content, and context, is key.

Auden won in the end. Random House reconsidered, published Pound, and Auden stayed with them for the rest of his life.

Dance is a tribute to painting, to artistic rendering, which might help account for its lack of the pulsing hum of real life. Its title comes from an image by Poussin, described by Powell like this:

> The image of Time brought thoughts of mortality: of human beings, facing outward like the Seasons, moving hand in hand in intricate measure: stepping slowly, methodically, sometimes a trifle awkwardly, in evolutions that take recognisable shape: or breaking into seemingly meaningless gyrations, while partners disappear only to reappear again, once more giving pattern to the spectacle: unable to control the melody, unable, perhaps, to control the steps of the dance.

I think this epitomises the whole first novel, a sense of the awkward and clumsy treated in the elevated tone of high art. The *TLS* review in 1951 noted that 'in composing long sentences Mr Powell has skilfully avoided the morass of circumlocution into which Mr William Faulkner has lately floundered', but the more apt comparison is surely Henry James. Powell has similar fastidiousness of language, the endless attenuation of sub-clauses. But he is more painterly in his approach. Indeed, his descriptions keep returning to works of art as reference points: 'Stringham took a step forward, and, without moving farther into the room, stood for a moment looking more than ever like Veronese's Alexander'; Jean Dupont, whom Jenkins loves, reminds him of a 'girl smoking a hookah in Delacroix'; London is memorably like 'one of those clusters of tumble-down dwellings depicted by Canaletto or Piranesi'.

I'm off today to record a discussion about female painters, in light of an opportunistic Sotheby's auction selling work by women between the sixteenth and nineteenth centuries. A quick test: can you name five female painters now? I'm not sure it is that easy. At home, we have a book called something like *1001 Paintings to See Before You Die*, and one of our mild amusements was for the whole family to have a go at re-drawing them in crayons. I know. But at one point, as we laboured – tongues peeking out of the side of our mouths – over a Velasquez or Van Gogh, Nelly asked this: 'Why are all the famous painters men?'

And it remains a good question. There seems to be a combination of answers when we look back on the history of painting: women were not allowed access to life drawing, for fear of the impropriety of nudes; they were often not allowed to be taught one-on-one by male instructors. And the market was a patriarchal one for centuries: work by women would not have been promoted or collected, or any value attributed to it. The painters I am set to discuss tonight (Artemisia Gentileschi, Vigée Le Brun, Angelica Kauffman) are not as famous as they might be.

That is changing for the better now. I have been thinking about balance when writing this book: am I focusing on deserving authors whatever their gender; am I skewed towards male authors because of education and centuries of canon-shaping? Another troubling question: is it culturally inevitable that, as a man, my favourite authors largely are men too?

25 February

The painterliness of *Dance* has got me thinking about my own relationship with viewing art. Nobody has ever told me or taught me how to visit an exhibition and get something out of it. At school, we learn how to read novels and poetry, how to experience plays (perhaps), but not how to appreciate art in a museum or gallery.

I put that to the formidable critic Waldemar Januszczak, who gave me some tips about attending exhibitions: find a few things that grab your attention; read about them on the captions so you understand the context; plant yourself there and give it time; zigzag your attention from the top left to the bottom right; and move on when you have had enough; don't be bored and dutiful.

Poussin's sense of time is, inevitably, critical to Powell's artistic conception. The series of novels has three time zones: the historical period of art and artefacts; the action of the narrated present; and the distant perspective of the narrator, recalling those events from an unspecified period in the future. Jenkins's descriptions are themselves recollections, we must realise. Here is a good example of that time structure, when Jenkins is telling the story of Widmerpool and his recent female acquaintance: 'Widmerpool was still staring rather wildly at Gypsy Jones, apparently regarding her much as a doctor, suspecting a malignant growth, might examine a diseased organism under the microscope; although I found later that any such diagnosis of his attitude was far from the true one.'

We soon learn that Gypsy ends up with a growth inside her, a baby, which Widmerpool judges – with characteristic and despicable narcissism – as unwanted and 'malignant'. And Jenkins knew this as he introduced the metaphor into the narration: it points to his own shaping artistic presence. Widmerpool arranges a silent abortion, and is momentarily reflective of his moral lapse: 'You know, I've never even committed a technical offence before – like using the untransferable half of somebody else's return ticket or driving a borrowed car insured only in the owner's name.'

The *New Yorker* called Widmerpool 'one of the greatest creeps in all of literature', but he is creepy because he is so low-key, so insidiously hard to notice. We meet him at the very beginning of the first novel, emerging from the fog, and are told that he 'had his being, like many others, in obscurity'. His 'legend' at school is based on his overcoat, which was 'a slight deviation from normal'; his relaxation is to 'drive golf balls into a net'; his father is in the 'liquid manure' business; the two most exceptional things that happen to him in the first two novels are a hurled banana aimed at his face, and a bowl of sugar upturned on his head. And yet this creepy, pompous, slight figure spends the next twenty years consumed with a 'quest for power'.

If you are not interested in the fate of a character like Widmerpool, then Powell's novels are probably not for you. They make a virtue of quiet complexity, tamped-down ferocity, of minor things happening and then being recalled.

26 February

There is a show on Netflix called *Tidying Up with Marie Kondo*, in which a 'decluttering expert' sorts people's houses out.[*] Which seems laudable: I moved house this year, and threw away so much, knowing Cnut-like that the wave of plastic rubbish for my children would fill the spaces once more. But Kondo also suggests that hoarding books is not a good idea, and that we should limit those we keep in our house to about thirty.

Which seems preposterous to me: at any one time, I am reading several books, browsing others. My commute book is distinct from my bedtime book and my bath book and so on. And one of the joys of a book collection is rediscovering old friends or overlooked purchases, and browsing. Powell called one of the *Dance* novels *Books Do Furnish a Room*, and that feels indisputable. Sitting in a room crowded with books, shelved neatly and then spilling into tottering piles is to feel comforted and cosy.

---

[*] I am unsurprised to report that, in follow-up to this project, Kondo launched an online shop selling what amounts to cluttering crap: 'leather room shoes' for $206, a 'brass kitchen utensil holder' for $275 and so on. Modernity in general – and 2019 in particular – is nothing if not predictably awful.

I do think it can be risky to over-fetishise books, and I am always suspicious of people who want to preserve them in sterile perfection. I constantly scribble on or bend or drop in the bath things I am reading. And I don't mind seeing the surface damage of prior readings. Sylvia Plath would not agree. She once lent someone a book, and got it back a bit torn. This was her diary entry: 'It was so horrifying and it was as if my children had been raped or beaten by an alien.' Which we can all agree is an over-reaction, I think.

Book collections can be ostentatiously used to imply intelligence. The phenomenon of the 'shelfie', the posted image of your bookshelf, is yet another manifestation of pathological narcissism caused by social media. But could you be friends with a person who owned no books?* I always smile at fellow commuters who are reading; and when I bring out Anthony Powell, I feel warmth from a few people, who seem happy to see a bit of literature in this otherwise bleak and functional space. Perhaps I am imagining it.

27 February

Snow has fallen, which always leads to nostalgia. Even now, an adult who spends his life in offices, who only experiences bad weather as a professional inconvenience or personal discomfort, I feel that momentary tingle of excitement at the prospect of snow.

That Robert Frost poem drifts, snow-like, into my head, even though it is set in evening not morning, the one about

---

* I have a word for all this: 'shelf-analysis', the importance of bookshelves to your sense of who you are. There's a great example of it in the papers this week, from a rueful government minister: 'If you knock on a door and they have books on their shelves, you can be pretty sure these days they're not voting Tory.'

woods that are 'lovely, dark and deep'. Nelly had to memorise it for school last month, and I memorised it too,* taking my own pleasure in its knowing repetition, the use of factotum, simple adjectives ('lovely, dark and deep', the 'lovely' slightly suggestive of the 'lonely') given resonance by the rhythm.

The beginning of *Dance* links snow to significance, to portent and meaning:

> For some reason, the sight of snow descending on fire always makes me think of the ancient world – legionaries in sheepskin warming themselves at a brazier: mountain altars where offerings flow between wintry pillars; centaurs with torches cantering beside a frozen sea – scattered uncoordinated shapes from a fabulous past, infinitely removed from life; and yet bringing with them memories of things real and imagined.

This is very Powellian: a long, lingering sentence that starts to melt away, like snow, into something soggy if you examine it too closely.

As the month ends, I keep considering the question: should we read Powell now? The broadcaster Malcolm Muggeridge asked the question in a review:† will posterity be 'less amenable' than contemporary critics, will it 'see in his meticulous reconstruction of his life and times a heap of dust? Despite a strong

---

* Thanks to my children, I now can recite 'The Owl and the Pussycat' and Sonnet 18 by Shakespeare among others. An unheralded benefit of parenting.

† This really was an act of treachery, for which he was never forgiven. Powell and Muggeridge were friends, but that 'personal partiality' did not stop him sticking the boot in. Perhaps Muggeridge suffered from the Gore Vidal syndrome: 'Whenever a friend succeeds, a little something in me dies.' I know I do. As it happens, if Powell is a bit more obscure now than he once was, Muggeridge is a total nonentity in the cultural memory.

personal partiality, honesty compels me to admit it might.' The dryness, the dustiness of *Dance* is notable, and perhaps may indeed make it off-putting now. But let's consider a far wetter analysis, from Powell's friend Evelyn Waugh: 'In the *Music of Time* we watch through the glass of a tank; one after another various specimens swim towards us; we see them clearly, then with a barely perceptible flick of fin or tail, they are off into the murk. That it is how our encounters occur in real life.'

Waugh was intoxicated by the 'permeating and inebriating atmosphere of the haphazard which is the essence of Mr Powell's art', that sense again of the 'odds and ends' of life being randomly collected, then subtly shaped. Do we not demand more pertinence, more poignancy? I wonder. It is not clear how Powell fits into modernity, or post-modernity, at all (even less, say, than Charlotte Lennox who pre-dates him by 200 years).

28 February

Although he has a reputation for being the laureate of aristocracy, I come to realise that *Dance* is actually not that posh. A.N. Wilson, who knew Powell, said once that 'a huge proportion of the characters in *Dance*, whether titled or not (very few are) are the sort of people you might meet at the *TLS* summer party, rather than at a shooting party at Belvoir Castle, let us say.' And I sort of know what he means, not least because I have now hosted a *TLS* party: slightly shabby, prickly, clever, gauche, unfulfilled, bohemian. Powell is a chronicler of mild resentment, of damp wallpaper and soggy kippers, of overcoats and railway timetables, of boils and blocked drains. There is privilege, but it is decaying; there is etiquette, but it is sometimes abandoned.

When Kingsley Amis finished *Dance* in 1975, he experienced a feeling 'like the sadness that descends when the last chord of a great symphony fades into silence'. I read the first two novels of the sequence, and finished them with quiet pleasure and a hungry eye towards reading Shakespeare in March. They are good on a wet, cold morning on a commuter train, where – to quote Powell – 'work and play merge indistinguishably into a complex tissue of pleasure and tedium'. We all feel like that sometimes.

~

Further Reading

Oroonoko (1688) by Aphra Behn
Robinson Crusoe (1719) by Daniel Defoe
The History of Tom Jones, a Foundling (1749) by Henry Fielding
The Life and Opinions of Tristram Shandy, Gentleman (1759) by
    Laurence Sterne
Pride and Prejudice (1813) by Jane Austen
Frankenstein (1818) by Mary Shelley
Wuthering Heights (1847) by Emily Brontë
Jane Eyre (1847) by Charlotte Brontë
Vanity Fair (1848) by William Makepeace Thackeray
Bleak House (1853) by Charles Dickens
The Woman in White (1860) by Wilkie Collins
Middlemarch (1871) by George Eliot
Tess of the d'Urbervilles (1891) by Thomas Hardy
The Picture of Dorian Gray (1891) by Oscar Wilde
Heart of Darkness (1902) by Joseph Conrad
Mrs Dalloway (1925) by Virginia Woolf
Lady Chatterley's Lover (1928) by D.H. Lawrence
Brave New World (1932) by Aldous Huxley
1984 (1949) by George Orwell
The Prime of Miss Jean Brodie (1961) by Muriel Spark
The Golden Notebook (1962) by Doris Lessing
Wide Sargasso Sea (1966) by Jean Rhys

March

Shakespeare

Shakespeare's Sonnets (1609)
Titus Andronicus (1590)
Henry V (1599)
Hamlet (1600)
The Winter's Tale (1612)

I want to get my theory on Shakespeare out of the way first. Never in the history of our species has there been such a productive combination of hack and genius in one body. Shakespeare was compelled by economic necessity, and professional custom, to produce thousands of lines of dramatic poetry. It was a feat of luck that he was a master craftsman of the sort that occurs hardly ever in any millennium, and further fortunate that he was alive at a time when the English language was in flux, growing year by year in its power, range and resourcefulness. Twelve thousand new words entered the English language between 1500 and 1650, and Shakespeare coined more than 2,000, such as madcap, majestic, lustrous, zany, tranquil, generous, bloodstained and monumental. If that wasn't exciting enough, he even came up with 'excitement' as well.

The felicitous combination of personality, occupation and era that met in Shakespeare has never been matched before or since.

Genius, we might imagine, so often becomes focused on the unproductive impossible, or hides itself away from the vulgarity of common life. We think of it as stingy with its gifts, which are the product of aching, restless wrangling. Not for Shakespeare, who was steeped in common life, compelled to use his skill to tell stories over and over again* for money. So we are left with thirty-eight plays (give or take a *Cardenio*), some sonnets and narrative poetry, which compare favourably with everything that has been published before or since.

I once read every play by Shakespeare on the commute to work, so I know it can be done. It takes a bit over six months, if you also read the introductions in the Arden editions. That's all the plays, stretching alphabetically from *All's Well That Ends Well* to *The Winter's Tale*, or with some sense of chronology from *The Two Gentleman of Verona* (about 1593, although like everything else this is a matter of dispute) to *The Two Noble Kinsmen* (about 1613). This month I am going to read the major non-dramatic work (the *Sonnets*), and then however many plays I can squeeze in.

The thing about Shakespeare is that, however familiar he has become, he remains somehow unknowable. And that is because so much about his life (1564–1616) is lost for ever. We don't know which was his first play, the order of his plays, every play he is said to have written (in 1598 we get a tantalising reference

---

* Michelangelo is another alternative candidate for genius compelled to earn a living, who therefore never turned off the tap of his wondrous ability. He lived until ninety, and so left decades of work as a painter (the Sistine Chapel ceiling and altar), sculptor (*David*, the *Pietà*) and architect (St Peter's Basilica). I spent a couple of weekends this year reading the mesmerisingly banal *The Agony and the Ecstasy* (1961) by Irving Stone, which dutifully charts Michelangelo's life, and forms a rather handy compilation of his great works. Stone pretends Michelangelo wasn't gay for some reason, as many Shakespeareans do about their genius.

to *Love Labour's Won*, which has not survived; and later to *Cardenio*, also lost), even which plays he wrote alone or in collaboration. We don't know how much he revised his plays once they were written. We don't know for certain his religion or his sexuality. We don't know what he was doing between leaving Stratford in 1585 and popping up in London in 1592. We don't know if he ever left the country.

We don't know what his name was, as it is always spelled differently (including as William Shagspere in his marriage bond).* The one spelling he did not use, typically, was the one by which he is now known, 'Shakespeare'. We don't know, really, what he looked like. There are three images of him that form the basis for all others: the so-called Chandos portrait from the turn of the seventeenth century; the Droeshout engraving, which adorned the first Folio edition of his plays in 1623; and his statue in Holy Trinity Church in Stratford from about the same time, which shows him, in the words of Mark Twain, with 'the deep, deep, subtle expression of a bladder'. The Chandos painting may not be Shakespeare at all, and the latter two were made after his death by practitioners who were not especially expert, to say the very least.

We do know that he had a child called Hamnet, who died three years before he wrote a play called *Hamlet*; that he left his wife his 'second best bed' in his will; and that his writing will be for ever remembered as the product of an unmatched mind so long as English-speaking human beings are alive.† Some people want to cheat us even of that. There is an 'anti-Stratfordian'

---

* Only fourteen words in his handwriting exist: his name in various ways, and the phrase 'by me' in his will.

† I once called Shakespeare the greatest playwright in a script for *Front Row*. A lovely producer told me that I needed to say he was 'arguably' the greatest. 'So who is possibly greater?' I asked. A long pause. 'Alan Bennett?' He is not even the greatest playwright called Alan.

lobby who insist, ad nauseam, that Shakespeare cannot have written the plays attributed to him: he was too common, too provincial, too poorly travelled to do it. As a fellow Midlander of unpropitious descent, I refuse to accept this. Also because it is bollocks.

A couple of non-Shakespearean Shakespeares have emerged over the years.* There is Francis Bacon, the scientific philosopher, who had no connection to the theatre other than occasionally to say he thought it worthless. There is Edward de Vere, the Earl of Oxford, himself a footling playwright and poet. But he died in 1604, years before, say, *King Lear* (1605) or *Macbeth* (1606) or *The Tempest* (1611) appeared. The argument of 'Oxfordians',† and I am not making this up, is that such plays were already written before his death, stored in a drawer, and then released slowly thereafter. Forget that *Macbeth* clearly refers to the Gunpowder Plot of 1605, or *The Tempest* to a shipwreck in Bermuda of 1609. Forget that Ben Jonson wrote about Shakespeare's genius in private and public, where there could be no possible reason to lie. Forget that, in 1623, the collection of Shakespeare's plays was published to a literary world (the so-called First Folio), which clearly recognised his authorship without complaint. Anti-Stratfordians are the anti-vaxxers of the literary world; fake news merchants and propagandists of pap.

The Folio edition of Shakespeare that preserved his works is a monumental feat of publication, perhaps the greatest in the history of our language. It was put together by John Heminges

---

* Although, notably, not over the first 200 years of the post-Shakespearean period. It is almost as if those with the proximity to Shakespeare's life were able to accept his responsibility for its poetic output.

† It pains me to say that Keanu Reeves, the hero of great action movies (*Speed, Point Break, John Wick* and so on), the handsome and seemingly likeable man with a beard – and dress sense – I like to emulate, believes the Earl of Oxford wrote the plays of Shakespeare. So that's ruined popular culture for me.

and Henry Condell, colleagues of Shakespeare when he was alive, as an impossible attempt to produce an accepted text to set against all the 'stol'n and surreptitious copies, maimed and deformed by frauds and stealths of injurious impostors'. Without it, almost half of Shakespeare's plays would never have survived at all.* Bill Bryson, my own modest literary hero as it happens, calls Heminges and Condell 'unquestionably the greatest literary heroes of all time', and who is to argue with him?

3 March

I have never previously read the sonnets, even at university, so I come at them fresh. And what a surprise they are, not always in a good way. Today is my second day, and I am not into the swing yet.

First, a quick definition of the poetic form. The concept of the fourteen-line verse was invented in thirteenth-century Sicily, and perfected almost immediately in fourteenth-century Italy by Petrarch and his *Songbook*, 366 poems in praise of an idealised woman called Laura. The poems are structurally split into two sections: one of eight lines (with a rhyme scheme abba, abba); one of six (with a varying pattern, like cde, cde). Shakespeare changed things: his sonnets are in fourteen pentameter† lines with this rhyme scheme: abab, cdcd, efef, gg; so three four-line chunks and then a concluding couplet.

Beyond these technicalities, his sonnets are steeped in mystery from the beginning, and have an odd publishing history. The

---

* As it stands, 38 of the 250 plays that survive the period are by Shakespeare, an incredibly high percentage.

† Five beats to the line. You can count this by tapping your leg on every emphasised syllable, although I feel a bit self-conscious doing that on the train.

first mention of them comes in 1598 in a book called *Palladis Tamia*, or *Wits Treasury*, by Francis Meres, in which he said that 'the sweete wittie soule of Ovid lives in mellifluous and hony-tongued Shakespeare'. A year later a pirate edition of Shakespeare was published called *The Passionate Pilgrime*, which contained twenty poems, some falsely attributed to Shakespeare. This looks very much like a cash-in on Shakespeare's popularity as a playwright (in which enterprise it succeeded), and was probably something he tried to block.

Ten years later came the text we use today, a collection of 154 sonnets, which Shakespeare seems to have casually author-ised. It is hard to say why. Perhaps the ravages of the plague, which closed the playhouses for months on end in this period, made him seek some ready cash. In any event, he seems to have sold the poems to a publisher (Thomas Thorpe, or T.T.) and scarpered out of town, leaving the text unproofed. It is here the mysteries deepen further. The book, famously, has this dedication:

TO.THE.ONLIE.BEGETTER.OF.
THESE.INSUING.SONNETS.
Mr.W.H. ALL.HAPPINESSE.
AND.THAT.ETERNITIE.
PROMISED.
BY.
OUR.EVER-LIVING.POET.
WISHETH.
THE.WELL-WISHING.
ADVENTURER.IN.
SETTING.
FORTH.
T.T.

The poems themselves are then split into three sections: 1–17 are a formal series of verse urging a man to marry and have children; 18–126 are to a man with whom the speaker is in love, known as the 'fair youth' or 'lovely boy'; and 127–154 are to a woman, known to posterity (though not in the poems) as the 'dark lady'.

We don't know much more for certain. It is likely that many of the poems were already written before 1598 (especially the dark lady sonnets), but some probably came later, and all may have been rearranged and edited just before publication. There is a reference in Sonnet 107, perhaps, to the accession of James I to the throne in 1603 ('Incertainties now crown themselves assured, / And peace proclaims olives of endless age'), which might confirm some later composition. But Shakespeare's sonnets are like cryptic crosswords in verse, playfully and archly developing scenarios and ideas, none of which may be entirely connected to reality.

And yet we demand biography in first person verse, and all the gaps in Shakespeare's biography spur us to look for clues here. Helen Vendler, the critic, once said that the sonnets work like a 'lightning rod for nuttiness', and she was right. She was following Auden, in fact, who said: 'Probably more nonsense has been talked and written, more intellectual and emotional energy expended in vain, on the sonnets of Shakespeare than on any other literary work in the world.'*

Questions leap out: who was WH in the dedication; was he the same as the fair youth; who was the dark lady; why was Shakespeare, a married man, writing such passionately gay poetry? Answers abound, but don't always convince.† WH could

---

* Challenge accepted!

† This is James Shapiro, one of the greatest living writers on Shakespeare: 'Who is the only begetter of these sonnets? There's a very easy answer to that – we have no idea. And anybody who tells you otherwise is lying.'

be William Himself (after all he did 'beget' the sonnets by writing the damned things); it could be a misprint for WS, William Shakespeare. He could be Henry Wriothesley, the Earl of Southampton (with initials reversed), a patron of Shakespeare to whom *Venus and Adonis* (1593) had been dedicated in the last decade.* He could be William Herbert, another patron, to whom the Folio edition of the plays was dedicated in 1623. Oscar Wilde wrote a story suggesting that WH was a boy actor, called Willy Hughes, who left Shakespeare's company to join another. An identifying pun pops up in the most sexual of sonnets, 20, that apparently nods to him:

> A man in hue, all hues in his controlling,
> Much steals men's eyes and women's souls amazeth.

The dark lady has been variously identified as the Italian poet Emilia Lanier, Aline Florio, the wife of a prominent translator, or a sex worker called Black Luce. We will never know.

4 March

Much of the sonnet sequence is about fame, and permanence and failure. In one of those curious mental associations, I spend my journey trying to think of a passage about the triumph of trying. I can't recall who said it; it's like a prose version of the Kipling poem *If*.

My wife texts and mentions something about my son, Teddy, and the synapses fire. It is the 'Man in the Arena' speech given by Teddy Roosevelt, one of the great Americans and one of the

* Wriothesley was known to be fond, romantically, of men and women alike. When in Ireland, he bunked up with a companion officer whom he would 'hug in his arms and play wantonly with'.

reasons we gave my son his name in the first place. Here is the key bit from a much longer piece of oratory he gave in Paris in 1910:

It is not the critic who counts; not the man who points out how the strong man stumbles, or where the doer of deeds could have done them better. The credit belongs to the man who is actually in the arena, whose face is marred by dust and sweat and blood; who strives valiantly; who errs, who comes short again and again, because there is no effort without error and shortcoming; but who does actually strive to do the deeds; who knows great enthusiasms, the great devotions; who spends himself in a worthy cause; who at the best knows in the end the triumph of high achievement, and who at the worst, if he fails, at least fails while daring greatly, so that his place shall never be with those cold and timid souls who neither know victory nor defeat.

Magnificent. The speech – which is Shakespearean in its heft, its readiness to tackle large issues – has entered the culture: it was quoted by Kennedy, Obama and, less appetisingly, Nixon; Nelson Mandela gave it to the South African rugby captain, Francois Pienaar, ahead of the 1995 World Cup Final.

Teddy Roosevelt was a figure of action, of family, of admirable masculinity. This was him giving a speech after, and I mean immediately after, an assassination attempt in Milwaukee in 1912:

Friends, I shall ask you to be as quiet as possible. I don't know whether you fully understand that I have just been shot; but it takes more than that to kill a bull moose. But fortunately I had my manuscript, so you see I was going to make a long speech, and there is a bullet – there is where the bullet went through – and it probably saved me from it going into my heart. The bullet is in me now, so that I cannot make a very long speech, but I will try my best.

I first came across Roosevelt properly in Caleb Carr's magisterial and creepy crime novel *The Alienist* (1994), which you simply must read, where he features in his real-life role as the reforming New York City Police Commissioner. We'll have to leave him on one final, human, tragic note. On Valentine's Day 1884 he lost both his mother and his wife; his diary entry is terribly and succinctly eloquent, especially for such a big talker:

X
The light has gone out of my life.

It's hard to read that without being moved.

5 March

Shrove Tuesday today, and I left the house amid the bustle and steamy sweetness of pancakes being made. It made me realise that, growing up, we understood the tradition of pancake-eating on this particular day to be an injunction not to eat pancakes on *any other* day of the year. So the tradition and the sensations of that annual event have become for ever fixed in my mind: the batter, glossily smooth as paint; the same pale blue mug, with Tom and Jerry on it, used to delve out a portion (and for nothing else during the rest of the year); the acid sting of lemon and the clumped sweetness of white sugar. It is a Proustian 'madeleine moment' for me, and I am restored to the kitchen of my childhood. This was Proust:

No sooner had the warm liquid mixed with the crumbs touched my palate than a shudder ran through me and I stopped, intent upon the extraordinary thing that was happening to me. An exquisite pleasure had invaded my senses, something isolated, detached, with no suggestion of its origin. And at once the vicissitudes of life had become indifferent to me, its disasters innocuous, its brevity illusory – this new sensation having had on me the effect which love has of filling me with a precious essence; or rather this essence was not in me it was me.

I know this extract even though I have not yet read *Swann's Way* (1913), an omission I aim to set straight in August.

6 March

I manage about ten or twelve sonnets each day on my journey into work, and I feel my brain working differently as I sit picking through them. These are densely worked lines: the first read-through feels shallow and liable to bafflement, and then I have to pore over each couplet again, weighing up words, looking at explanatory notes. Some still defy meaning even then:

> But why thy odour matcheth not thy show,
> The soil is this, that thou dost common grow.
>
> (Sonnet 69)

There is clearly a botanical metaphor at work: the lover like a flower, concealing some aspect of his inner essence; but what role 'the soil' plays in all this is unclear however many times I read it.

The first poem after the marriage sequence is the most famous:

> Shall I compare thee to a summer's day?
> Thou art more lovely and more temperate:
>
> (Sonnet 18)

How many readers think of this as the beginning of a great, impassioned poetic plea from one man to another? Not that many, I suspect; it has slid into a heterosexual canon with scarcely a murmur. Just two sonnets later, we get the most explicit imagery of homosexual love:

> A woman's face with Nature's own hand painted
> Hast thou, the master-mistress of my passion.

The sonnet concludes with this section:

> And by addition me of thee defeated,
> By adding one thing to my purpose nothing.
> But since she pricked thee out for women's pleasure,
> Mine be thy love and thy love's use their treasure.
>
> (Sonnet 20)

The subject here is how 'Nature' has defeated the speaker by adding a penis to his lover, and making him a man. 'Nothing' here implies a vagina (see the joke in the title of *Much Ado About Nothing*);* Nature has chosen (or 'pricked', with another obvious pun) instead to make the love object a man not a woman. As a result, the speaker gets the romance of real love, but another woman gets the publicly acceptable use of their dangly bits. None of this is especially subtle, and Shakespeare seldom refused the temptation to slip in an erotic pun. But the fact remains that he was writing verse exuberant in its gayness, a celebration of same-sex love, and publishing it at a time when he was a married man.

For centuries people have tried to straighten this out, to pretend that this is somehow not happening: but it is there

* I didn't say it was a funny joke.

unequivocally, to my mind, on the page.* So when you are at a church wedding, in a temple devoted to the exclusion of same-sex marriage, and you hear someone starchily invoking, 'Let me not to the marriage of true minds / Admit impediments,' you can thrill to the fact that they are citing the most famous strand of gay poetry in the English canon.

9 March

The sonnets are, almost parodically, obsessed with ageing: the damage it can do, its slackening grasp on flesh and memory. Shakespeare writes about 'time's furrows', 'time's injurious hand', 'confounding age's cruel knife' and so on. Indeed, he connects overtly the 'lines and wrinkles' of ageing skin with the 'beauty in these black lines' of poetry. But it is not a great start to a day when I, thirty-eight and bedraggled, read this:

> When forty winters shall besiege thy brow,
> And dig deep trenches in thy beauty's field,
> Thy youth's proud livery, so gazed on now,
> Will be a tattered weed, of small worth held.

(Sonnet 2)

None of us feel great in the morning, but it is hard to be reminded endlessly of a time in life when there is 'Sap checked with frost, and lusty leaves quite gone, / Beauty o'er-snowed and bareness everywhere' (Sonnet 5). My favourite sonnet

---

* This is the poet Don Paterson, in support of my position: 'The Sonnets have to be read as a narrative of the progress of love . . . Oh come on, people. The guy's in love with a bloke.' This is the neatly poised counter-argument from critic Stephen Booth: 'William Shakespeare was almost certainly homosexual, bisexual or heterosexual. The sonnets provide no evidence on the matter.'

extends the metaphor of wintry landscape to explore the effects of time, with rather muted beauty:

> When yellow leaves, or none, or few, do hang
> Upon those boughs which shake against the cold,
> Bare ruined choirs, where late the sweet birds sang.
> In me thou see'st the twilight of such day
> As after sunset fadeth in the west,
> Which by and by black night doth take away,
> Death's second self, that seals up all in rest.
>
> (Sonnet 73)

There is real self-pity here, of which more shortly, but this carries with it a moving sense of mortality, the tugging feeling of sadness I experience at dusk, when the gloom descends and the vitality of existence seems muted. 'Bare ruined choirs' is deftly, irresistibly Shakespearean: in three words we are reminded of what is there (cold, lifeless trees) and what has gone (the exuberant, noisy birds that would have filled them).

13 March

A minor news story crops up on my phone. They are removing envelopes from those notional shopping baskets that calculate the rate of inflation. Such stationery* is no longer seen as integral to our everyday lives, in contrast to things like Amazon Echo devices and Fitbits.

The demise of the letter can raise concerns about the decline in civilisation: all of us sending off emails and texts, instead of thoughtfully composing prose essays to distant companions.

---

* I only remember how to spell 'stationery', not 'stationary', thanks to thinking of the 'e' in 'envelope'.

Simon Sebag Montefiore's *Written in History* (2018) celebrates great examples of correspondence, like Aaron Burr and Alexander Hamilton's confirmation of their duel, or Anaïs Nin writing notes – seething with carnality – to Henry Miller. Montefiore takes the opportunity to have a pop at emails, which 'make life feel more transient while letters make it feel enduring', one of those sentences that seems to mean something but in fact does not. Montefiore conjures a 'golden age' of letter-writing, of folk with tongues sticking slightly out of their mouths, labouring romantically beside flickering candlelight: 'a physically exhausting duty and a pastime'.

This is the nostalgia of the fusty aesthete. Emails have their problems: unlike letters, they can be hacked, sent in haste, pinged off to the wrong recipient.* And my emails – unlike my spoken words – have become a nauseating thicket of exclamation marks: 'Hi! Thanks! Sounds Good!' and so on. Exclamation marks, those miniature distress flares of chumminess, are awful, I know they are awful, and yet the medium seems to compel their usage.

But I am sure there are beautiful emails, just like there are beautiful letters. And the world will not end because envelopes go the way of the telegram. We are always what we write, whatever the medium. Flaubert was a great correspondent, and a massive show-off: 'I write a love letter,' said he, 'to write, and not because I love.' He never did get married. He provides us with a motto for Shakespeare, perhaps: maybe he wrote sonnets to *write*, and not because he loved.

* For reasons I won't go into now, I once sent an email including the phrase 'anal fucking' to the wrong David in my contacts: the recipient was the editor of one of Scotland's most conservative newspapers.

Shakespeare's sonnets, it seems to me, are often exercises in playing with types, in the exploitation of the familiar. The extended metaphors he uses are deeply traditional ways of exploring the effects of love. So we get sleeplessness: 'But then begins a journey in my head, / To work my mind, when body's work's expired' (Sonnet 27). Or the paradox of conflicting emotions: 'For sweetest things turn sourest by their deeds; / Lilies that fester smell far worse than weeds' (Sonnet 94). None of this is especially memorable.

Indeed, I'm struck by how unromantic, how anti-romantic the whole sequence is. This is not rapturous love poetry, it is not generous or sweet. It is the poetry of a stalker, creepy and unhinged, whiny and obsessive, desperate for attention. There is plenty of self-pity from a speaker 'made lame by fortune's dearest spite' (Sonnet 37); there are interminable maunderings about his own poetic status: 'Why is my verse so barren of new pride, / So far from variation or quick change?' (Sonnet 76).

For consolation, I remind myself that this is a dramatist writing. He could be inventing the role of the lovelorn sonneteer as a character to play with, helplessly voluble, pathetic and full of doubt. The speaker is, in fact, a bit like Hamlet, the self-conscious perma-student, endlessly pondering mortality. Indeed, when death is described as 'that fell arrest / Without all bail shall carry me away' (Sonnet 74), you cannot help but think that Hamlet said, 'fell sergeant, death, is strict in his arrest'. The speaker also talks, like Hamlet, about the rot of decomposition: 'the dregs of life, / The prey of worms, my body being dead, / The coward conquest of a wretch's knife'. This is not the poetry of a lover, but a tragic hero. Or even a tragic villain. This bit sounds more like the schemer Iago, from *Othello*:

> 'Tis better to be vile than vile esteemed,
> When not to be receives reproach of being,
> And the just pleasure lost, which is so deemed
> Not by our feeling but by others' seeing.
>
> (Sonnet 121)

Read it slowly and you get the sense: it is better to be bad than to be wrongly thought bad; and people will always condemn you whatever you do, so you might as well take the pleasure of the naughtiness.

And so we come to the dark lady poems. They are surprisingly sexual, carnal and unsophisticated, full of 'lust in action'. And utterly misogynistic:

> All this the world well knows; yet none knows well
> To shun the heaven that leads men to this hell.
>
> (Sonnet 129)

The old 'vagina-hell' metaphor establishes this part of the sequence as the very opposite of love poetry. The mistress is a dark-skinned figure who is loathed more than she is loved: she has a 'foul face', reeking breath, wiry hair and the like; the speaker notes 'a thousand errors' and seems to enumerate them all. We also get persistent, painful references to the stings of STIs: 'a thousand groans', 'this false plague', 'Only my plague thus far I count my gain, / That she that makes me sin awards me pain' (Sonnet 141). The whole sequence, this famed series of love poetry, ends with a gag about the hot bath used to cure the pox: 'Love's fire heats water, water cools not love.'

What are we to make of this? First, that this section feels like an early attempt to explore and subvert the form. There is a puerility to the punning, which can take the breath away in its imbecile squirms:

> Whoever hath her wish, thou hast thy Will,
> And Will to boot, and Will in overplus;
> More than enough am I that vex thee still,
> To thy sweet will making addition thus.
> Wilt thou, whose will is large and spacious,
> Not once vouchsafe to hide my will in thine?
>
> (Sonnet 135)

'Will' here has three meanings: the name of the author, his penis and his lover's vagina, which he is describing as 'large and spacious'. One of the poems seems to reflect the courtship of Anne Hathaway, Shakespeare's wife, which took place in the 1580s, and pops up in an effortful pun too: '"I hate" from hate away she threw, / And saved my life, saying "not you"' (Sonnet 145).

I think of Anne quite often on my journeys. A wife who probably couldn't read married to the world's greatest writer, whose thoughts on love – outside that one early poem – are turning from her, not only to female rivals, but more urgently, more passionately, towards men. Did someone ever tell her about this sentiment, voiced to another man?:

> You are my all-the-world, and I must strive
> To know my shames and praises from your tongue:
> None else to me, nor I to none alive.
>
> (Sonnet 112)

Did she know that this was just the intellectual play of a dramatist?

We want a Shakespeare who is kind, loving and admirable. But that is not the speaker of the sonnets. And it may not be the man himself. Much is made in a film called *All is True* (2018), by Kenneth Branagh, of how Shakespeare returned home to Stratford to rekindle his love for Anne at the end of his life. Much is made of the death of his son Hamnet, and its terrible impact on his loving father. Maybe Shakespeare's grief drove him to write this part of *King John*, also about the loss of a son:

> Grief fills the room up of my absent child,
> Lies in his bed, walks up and down with me,
> Puts on his pretty looks, repeats his words,
> Remembers me of all his gracious parts,
> Stuffs out his vacant garments with his form.

But soon after Hamnet's death, Shakespeare was writing *The Merry Wives of Windsor* (1597). Maybe he was unmoved, preoccupied with life in London, able to slip easily into his most exuberant comedy, because the death of a child was a distant thing scarcely to be considered.

15 March

Shakespeare exists for us in Britain romantically: he is a figure of majesty and identity (said to have been born and to have died on St George's Day, though this is almost certainly not true); the man who gave voice to the very essence of our collective exist-ence. But his sonnets, to me on a rumbling train that carries me to and from work each day, are clever and highly wrought, but unmoving, self-indulgent and sometimes silly.

That's what Keats thought: 'I never found so many beauties in the sonnets – they seem to be full of fine things said uninten-tionally – in the intensity of working out conceits.' And, along-side the fine things, are some crude thoughts too. I'm glad I've finally read them; I'm glad I know them better; but if they were all we had of Shakespeare, he would be scarcely more remembered than the other poets of the period, Philip Sidney, Samuel Daniel and the like.

Before we leave sonnets, I was once challenged to write one about a personal subject for Radio 4. I went for the Shakespearean form and used it to mark the birth of my baby daughter, Phoebe, the surprise third addition to our family. The theatrical metaphor is a traditional conceit, as we know, but I inverted it: in a Caesarean birth, surgical drapes are held up concealing the operation, and then drop to reveal the baby. So the falling curtain is a symbol of beginning rather than end. Anyway, here it is:

> That feat of mingling we called 'surprise'
> And thought we were too old to make.
> All changed when we saw with our new eyes
> This squirming form with outstretched hands to take.
>
> The curtain fell, but you came on stage
> Arms out, hot lights, transfixed in glare.
> More life than yet could be caught on page;
> Such life that stops all, makes all stare.
>
> And now each day that hum and wail
> Spreads through our home like joyful air.
> Joy, but each sound reminds I cannot fail
> Because, for now, for all, you need our care.
>
> Phoebe: your moony name and lunar skin,
> Eyes black, loves back. More than we can take back in.

18 March

I spend quite a lot of time at weekends with my children involved in their consumption of words and ideas. I help Nelly with her comprehension homework, say, or talk about books with Teddy, or we all watch films together. This weekend was *Jaws*, which was a bold move on my part. I'd read the novel a few years ago (by Peter Benchley, who also wrote the screenplay), and it was a much more psychological and political book than I'd expected, about incompetence and corruption. Brody, the police chief, is constantly troubled by the infidelity of his wife. The sex in it is rather furtive and aggressive, and the first cover image looked a little like a giant *vagina dentata*.* The film moves slowly, menacingly, with plenty of moments of pause and reflection. My children coped with it, jumped in all the right places, but were full of questions during the leisurely initial exposition. I find this impatience in their approach everywhere: they crave explicitness and clarity; they are impatient at blurred edges and implication. That is one of the reasons why books of my child-hood, like Richmal Crompton's *Just William* series, do not appeal to them, despite my self-conscious prodding. The world is not explained, it is built up, and you have to take it on trust that clarity will emerge from the thicket of phrases. I am not sure how readily my children manage that.

This to me is the product of the internet age more perni-cious than the decline of concentration span. Our collective consumption is about instant gratification, rather than a steady accumulation of knowledge and awareness. But in the latter lies not only wisdom but enjoyment. Keats once pondered 'what quality went to form a Man of Achievement, especially

---

* The phrase is Freud's, meaning toothy vagina, but the myth of the dangerous female reproductive organ has a long history in patriarchal societies. It has been plausibly argued that the culture of rape in India has connections to a societal fear of women and their genitalia. The feminist Camille Paglia once said: 'The toothed vagina is no sexist hallucination: every penis is made less in every vagina, just as mankind, male and female, is devoured by mother nature.' I'm not sure how we got on to this.

in Literature, and which Shakespeare possessed so enormously – I mean Negative Capability, that is, when a man is capable of being in uncertainties, mysteries, doubts, without any irritable reaching after fact and reason.' And this gets to the heart not only of the brilliance of Shakespeare, but how we should approach reading him (or anybody else worth reading, for that matter). Embracing negative capability, relishing doubt and complexity, with the confidence that there will be a valuable outcome at the end. I need to find a way to convince my kids of this too.

19 March

I try to read for the rest of the month chronologically, to keep a sense of the shape of Shakespeare's career. As you might expect, his youthful work is scrappier, more formulaic, and sits more comfortably within the framework of its age.

Titus Andronicus (probably first written in 1590, before being subsequently revised) is an example of the revenge tragedy genre. This had classical roots and was much loved by the Elizabethans: people are wronged, they seek vengeance, it all ends horribly. *Hamlet* is a revenge tragedy, but much more than that: he spends the whole time *not* getting vengeance, distracted instead by thoughts of such philosophical greatness that they dominate the whole play, indeed the whole of Anglophone culture.

Titus is not like that. It is gruesome, ugly and sometimes silly, filled with 'murders, rapes and massacres, / Acts of black night, abominable deeds, / Complots of mischief, treason, villanies / Ruthful to hear, yet piteously performed.' Our hero is a garlanded veteran who returns to Rome with Gothic prisoners from the wars, including Queen Tamora and her two sons, Chiron and Demetrius. Tamora ends up married to the new emperor, Saturninus; Titus's daughter, Lavinia, gets married to the emperor's brother, Bassianus, and from then on chaos ensues: Bassianus is murdered by Chiron and Demetrius, who blame Titus's sons, who are then executed; Lavinia is raped and mutilated by Chiron and Demetrius; Titus eventually kills Chiron and Demetrius and serves them in a pie to Tamora;[*] he then kills Tamora and Lavinia, and is killed by Saturninus.

Did you follow all that?

21 March

Some more staid commentators felt that the carnage of *Titus* was too unseemly for Shakespeare, and pretended he did not write the play at all. *Titus* certainly has the most shocking stage direction in all of Shakespeare: 'Enter DEMETRIUS and CHIRON with LAVINIA, ravished; her hands cut off, and her tongue cut out.' And it still shocks with its overwhelming revelling in bloody evil: the men who want to rape a woman on the corpse of her husband ('his dead trunk pillow to our lust'), encouraged to do so by their mother: 'let my spleenful sons this trull deflower'.

Much of the evil is orchestrated by Tamora's black servant, Aaron, who is – let us be clear – exceptionally bad news:

---

[*] He does this while dressed as a chef. He also says this, which is fairly blood-curdling:

> I will grind your bones to dust
> And with your blood and it I'll make a paste,
> And of the paste a coffin I will rear
> And make two pasties of your shameful heads,
> And bid that strumpet, your unhallowed dam,
> Like to the earth swallow her own increase.

Oft have I digged up dead men from their graves,
And set them upright at their dear friends' doors.

I think we can all agree that this is a bit on the gratuitous side. As is the whole play, really. At one point, Aaron convinces Titus that he can save his sons if he agrees to chop off his own hand. Titus obliges, and then is given a present of his sons' heads and his severed hand back, which leads him to say this:

Come, brother, take a head;
And in this hand the other I will bear.
Lavinia, thou shalt be employed: these arms!
Bear thou my hand, sweet wench, between thy teeth.

This scene on the page is ridiculous, and would be surely unplayable in the theatre: a woman stumping off stage with a bloodied hand in her mouth. But here we are beginning to get to the strange power of the play: it is actually *about* the conflict between destructive violence and the ability to make sense of it.

All tragedy is, in fact. If you think about it, the most visceral reaction to death is simply a shriek, unformed and meaningless; the most structured is a highly wrought piece of poetry. Shakespeare's tragedies explore the spectrum between these two responses: sense and senselessness. *Titus* looks ahead to *King Lear* and this critical line: 'The worst is not / So long as we can say "This is the worst"'; if you can put it into words, it cannot be that bad.* Indeed, Titus himself says more or less the same thing at one point:

---

* This is such an important philosophical truth, stated with such economy. It is an answer to war and terrorism, sudden death or illness. If we can find a rational response, we are always capable of raising ourselves up once more. We'll come back to this in June, and Greek tragedy.

> If there were reason for these miseries,
> Then into limits could I bind my woes.

Lavinia, of course, can no longer put anything into words or 'limits': she cannot speak or signal; her 'martyred* signs' are, for most of the play, meaningless. In the end, she carves a single word in the sand: 'stuprum' or rape. And that is the catalyst to justice, of sorts, being done.

23 March

It is striking how many of Shakespeare's plays end with a future glance to the story being re-told; they dramatise our very need to understand things in the form of stories. So Hamlet makes sure Horatio is there to tell:

> Of carnal, bloody, and unnatural acts,
> Of accidental judgments, casual slaughters,
> Of deaths put on by cunning and forced cause,
> And, in this upshot, purposes mistook
> Fall'n on the inventors' heads.

Tragedy makes casual slaughters causal: it gives them shape, without reducing their destructive force. Othello, before he dies, craves that narrative structure too: 'When you shall these unlucky deeds relate, / Speak of me as I am.' And his own death merges with the tale he wants to tell about himself:

---

* The play makes much of the word 'martyr', whose root is in the Greek for 'witness'. A martyr has to testify to something larger; the tragedy for Lavinia is that she cannot testify to anything.

And say besides, that in Aleppo once,
Where a malignant and a turban'd Turk
Beat a Venetian and traduced the state,
I took by the throat the circumcised dog,
And smote him, thus.

That 'thus' enables Othello to end his own life with a sword stroke, like a dramatic full stop. It doesn't soften the sense of the tragic (he is killing himself after jealously* killing his own wife, after all), but it shows his desire to give shape to the carnage he has created.

Much of this self-conscious sophistication is foreshadowed in *Titus Andronicus*, which is – oddly, given its bloodthirstiness – one of the most literary plays by Shakespeare. It contains direct quotes from Seneca, and Lavinia reads her Ovid on stage, telling the relevant story of Tereus and Philomela, in which the former brutalises the latter. Titus, a man driven mad by his daughter, looks ahead to *Lear*, and the pitiless shriek of madness and grief so memorable in that play. At one point, Titus begins to laugh in his wild fury:

MARCUS ANDRONICUS: Why dost thou laugh? it fits not with
  this hour.
TITUS ANDRONICUS: Why, I have not another tear to shed:

This is acute, and echoed later in *Lear* when Edgar observes that 'the worst returns to laughter': some events are so destructive that a helpless, gasping guffaw is all that remains. Shakespeare was mercilessly interested in that thin line between laughter and slaughter: all his plays flirt with the blackly comic amid the elevated tragedy.

---

* The phrase 'green-eyed monster' was invented by Shakespeare for this play.

The key figure in *Titus* is, in fact, Aaron the Moor, who is far more than an unsophisticated stage villain, and indeed is seen to be sometimes sinned against as well as sinning, the victim of a racist society. When he has a child with Tamora, it is dismissed – in terms even more shocking to a modern ear – as 'a joyless, dismal, black, and sorrowful issue: / Here is the babe, as loathsome as a toad.' It is here that he finds mild redemption, refusing to disregard his 'beauteous blossom', his baby. The play ends with him, still wild and vile, but still a father keen to protect his child.

So amid the gore and the silliness there is sophistication and strength. People say *Titus* is not Shakespearean, but they are wrong: it is early Shakespeare, sometimes unsubtle Shakespeare, but it looks ahead to much that is wonderful to come.

24 March

I pick *Henry V* next, written around 1599. It begins one of two unimaginable runs by Shakespeare, feats of compositional brilliance that have been unmatched in any art at any other point. Around 1599–1600 he gave the world *Henry V*, *Julius Caesar*, *Twelfth Night* and *Hamlet*. That's arguably our language's greatest history play, Roman play, comedy and tragedy in one year. At the end of 1604, under a different monarch, Shakespeare went on another roll of *Othello*, *King Lear*, *Macbeth*, *Antony and Cleopatra* and *Coriolanus*. Taken together they represent the period in which Shakespeare went from the greatest writer of his epoch and language to the greatest writer of any epoch and language.

Henry V shows a dramatist capable of running two conflicting storylines at the same time with huge aplomb. There is the lionisation of the national hero, Henry the speechmaker and battlewinner; and the interrogation of the hollowness of that very myth even as it is being created. The play was possibly written for the new Globe* (or at least revised when it was opened), and it begins – famously – with the Chorus talking about the 'wooden O' of the theatre. But that flamboyant theatricality is not only a neat dramatic trick, it is the key to the play. Shakespeare is showing how Henry V was a man desperate to create a role for himself, like an actor: that of the great king, a position that might itself turn out to be no more than propaganda and greasepaint.

For many, Henry's path is a straightforward one: reckless youth, noble man, king and conqueror. And the play has its goosebump moments: not only the famous Harfleur ('Once more unto the breach, dear friends, once more') and St Crispin's Day ('We few, we happy few, we band of brothers') speeches. Like when the Dauphin of France sends him tennis balls as a 'merry message' of contempt in response to Henry's claim to his throne, and Henry's words swell with rage:

> And tell the pleasant prince this mock of his
> Hath turned his balls to gun-stones; and his soul
> Shall stand sore charged for the wasteful vengeance
> That shall fly with them: for many a thousand widows
> Shall this his mock mock out of their dear husbands;
> Mock mothers from their sons, mock castles down;
> And some are yet ungotten and unborn
> That shall have cause to curse the Dauphin's scorn.

* On a wintry night in December 1598, the Lord Chamberlain's Men – a group of players including Shakespeare – dismantled their old theatre (called, unimaginatively, the Theatre), shipped it across the Thames, and rebuilt it. They did this to avoid a dispute about ownership, the sort of direct action you could get away with in the sixteenth century.

That gleeful play on 'mock', energetically rising to the emphatic couplet is beautifully poised. But let us look around these set-piece moments and see what else Shakespeare wants us to think. The play begins, like a snappy drama on American TV, with politicians walking and talking: the Bishop of Ely and the Archbishop of Canterbury promising to support a war simply to stop Henry taxing the Church too much. This is dodgy dossier territory. We are supposed to question the validity of the conflict from the beginning, to question whether Henry is as purely heroic as he seems, and to recall his father's words from a previous play that he should 'busy giddy minds / With foreign quarrels'.

At Harfleur, Henry is willing to license the slaughter of innocents to achieve his perhaps questionable aims:

> I will not leave the half-achieved Harfleur
> Till in her ashes she lie buried.
> The gates of mercy shall be all shut up,
> And the fleshed soldier, rough and hard of heart,
> In liberty of bloody hand shall range
> With conscience wide as hell, mowing like grass
> Your fresh-fair virgins and your flowering infants.

This noble king is content for his soldiers to 'defile the locks of your shrill-shrieking daughters', simply to enable him to capture a minor town in France. Later, in the Battle of Agincourt, the French seem to be rallying ('have reinforced their scattered men') and so Henry simply orders 'every soldier kill his prisoners'. This act has led some to call him a war criminal, but – even if that is an anachronism – it is still the work of bloody treachery by the standards of the age.

And what of those English soldiers, that band of brothers, encouraged to 'remember with advantages' their role in this great battle, to be part of an elite group able to live off their bravery for life? Well, as soon as Agincourt is over, Henry makes it illegal to show off at all, under pain of death:

> And be it death proclaimed through our host
> To boast of this or take the praise from God
> Which is his only.

Shakespeare, at his best (which is the part of his career we are approaching), was resistant to over-simplification. He wants people to question, to puzzle, to poke at ideas. And this play of statecraft and war has its own share of common soldiers to reveal the cost of battle: some of the gang from the earlier plays, who hung out with Falstaff and Hal and got up to no good. But they are brutally treated: Bardolph is executed for theft, Nym and the boy are killed, and Pistol – a man who could start a quarrel alone in the dark – is left to pursue his own malign ends feebly and without hope ('To England will I steal, and there I'll steal').

Shakespeare famously kills off Falstaff without him appearing in *Henry V* at all, and we have to reflect why he chose not to bring his most famous and beloved creation to Agincourt.[*] Perhaps because he wanted to emphasise something soulless and unforgiving about his king? We simply hear that 'the King has killed his heart': there is no place for comedy, or humanity, in the role of a warlike ruler.

---

[*] Falstaff loomed large in the two *Henry IV* plays, and was granted his own spin-off, *The Merry Wives of Windsor*. The epilogue of *Henry IV Part 2* promised a final appearance, too: 'If you be not too much cloyed with fat meat, our humble author will continue the story, with Sir John in it, and make you merry with fair Katharine of France: where, for anything I know, Falstaff shall die of a sweat, unless already he be killed with your hard opinions.'

26 March

Henry V is a delightfully rereadable play, but it is not quite Shakespeare at his peak. The courtship of Katharine of France is rather joyless, which makes the final act unmemorable.* Shakespeare, as we have seen in the sonnets, was pathologically incapable of resisting sex jokes, so Katharine unhilariously confuses the word 'gown', meaning 'dress', with 'coun' meaning 'cunt'. Or the French Lord Burgundy talks about Henry and Katharine getting it on, 'if you would conjure with her, you must make a circle', which is another typical Shakespearean conceit about a vagina. Elsewhere, the characters of the Captains are rather too broad: literally an Englishman, Scotsman, Irishman and a Welshman, complete with ethnic blurts.† So I have moments of joy, but also moments of wistfully looking out at the familiar scenery too.

27 March

Thinking about Shakespeare is a lifelong act (and there are few other writers you can say that about), and I see I have gone on too long about him already. I have read *Hamlet* probably twenty times in my life, at school, at university, on trains and planes. It is one of his longest plays, has a hugely confusing textual history, and is filled with Shakespeare's greatest poetry. It is both a tale of murder and ghosts and family angst, but also a meditation on mankind, destiny, love and death. It is filled with unanswerable questions. Why does Hamlet delay killing his stepfather? Why

---

* It's a bit like *The Lord of the Rings*: the final victory is won, and then Tolkien spends 150 pages leisurely tying up loose ends.

† Fluellen, the Welshman, is the most prominent: he talks constantly about things like leeks, daffodils and Monmouth, and says 'look you' every third sentence. This play also contains the phrase 'weasel Scot', which makes you realise that Shakespeare is a true English figure, not a British one.

does he put on an 'antic disposition', and does he become actually deranged while only pretending to be? Why did he not save Ophelia? Is Hamlet a man of thirty or a young student?

Shakespeare was so creative at this point, so apt at coining phrases (they sprinkle the text like gold dust: 'primrose path', 'murder most foul', 'more in sorrow than in anger' and on and on), he even crams two in one sentence:

> Though I am native here
> And to the manner born, it is a custom
> More honoured in the breach than the observance.

He also clatters together metaphors in a way that should not work, but does. That idea of taking 'arms against a sea of troubles' is an odd combination of fighting and sailing, for example, but it embodies Hamlet's sense of futility perfectly.

More than anything, though, I reflect – in this sprawling play, this vast treasury of ideas – on Shakespeare's sheer economy of expression, his ability to say things in few words. When Claudius says, 'May one be pardoned and retain the offence', he conveys his guilty conscience about benefiting from evil, even as he wants to seek forgiveness for it: a complex concept told in eight words. When Hamlet tells the rather involved story of child actors winning plaudits, he notes that they 'exclaim against their own succession': if they prosper, it will mean all actors will need to be children in the future, so this generation of children will be out of work when they become adults. That is achieved in five words. Claudius mulls over Hamlet's popularity and says that he cannot punish him for murdering Polonius because 'the offender's scourge is weighed / But never the offence': the public would blame the person doing the punishing, not the person punished. I'll stop now before my own prolixity is condemned, but you see what I mean.

28 March

Shakespeare, like Radiohead, got bored with his own straight-forward success, and became determined to experiment with the form for which he had become famous. The later plays are odd things, sad stories with broadly happy endings, but neither comedy nor tragedy. I end the month with *The Winter's Tale*, a romance about jealousy, in which an envious husband, Leontes, believes he has murdered his child, Perdita, and his wife, Hermione.

It is a hugely dense play, filled with caveats and parentheses, wordplay and intricate thought. It has the most famous stage direction in the history of theatre: 'Exit, pursued by a bear.' That concerned the luckless Lord Antigonus, and may have – on the stage – involved a real bear, perhaps even a polar bear (one was kept nearby). That economy of ideas is there, too. Here is my favourite line:

> He makes a July's day short as December,
> And with his varying childness cures in me
> Thoughts that would thick my blood.

Leontes is talking about his son, and I feel that way about my children. When my blood thickens, when the gloom descends, I picture them and their 'varying childness', and all is well for a while.

29 March

On this, my last day of Shakespearean commuting, I get the chance to interview the writer and actor John Kani. He lost a brother, and an eye, to the malign forces of apartheid South Africa. His new play, *Kunene and the King*, is about how an old white actor, played by Anthony Sher, and an old black nurse, played by Kani himself, struggle to live together in the shadow of twenty-five years of post-apartheid change.

It is a beautiful play, and contains much Shakespeare: Sher's character is set to play Lear, and treats Kani's character like the Fool. Shakespeare was a part of colonial education in South Africa, and black children were encouraged to learn the folly of rebellion revealed in *Julius Caesar*. Kani grew impassioned when I suggested that the decolonisation of the curriculum may be seen as progress by some. He demurred: Shakespeare was a universal presence, his words and ideas the symbol of how experience can cross the boundaries of race and geography. Decolonisation should never mean the silencing of such voices; voices like Shakespeare should ring out, but be joined by others to reflect a broader cultural ancestry. Amen to that.

~

Further Reading

Henry VI, Part II (1591)
Henry VI, Part III (1591)
Henry VI, Part I (1592)
Richard III (1592)
The Taming of the Shrew (1592)
Venus and Adonis (1593)
The Two Gentlemen of Verona (1593)
The Comedy of Errors (1594)
The Rape of Lucrece (1594)
Love's Labour's Lost (1595)
A Midsummer Night's Dream (1595)
Richard II (1595)
Romeo and Juliet (1595–6)
King John (1596)

The Merchant of Venice (1596)
Henry IV, Part I (1597)
Henry IV, Part II (1597)
The Merry Wives of Windsor (1597)
Much Ado about Nothing (1598)
As You Like It (1599)
Julius Caesar (1599)
Twelfth Night (1600)
Troilus and Cressida (1602)
All's Well That Ends Well (1603)
Measure for Measure (1604)
Othello (1604)
King Lear (1605)
Macbeth (1606)
Antony and Cleopatra (1606)
Timon of Athens (1606)
Coriolanus (1607)
Pericles (1608)
Cymbeline (1610)
The Tempest (1611)
Henry VIII (1613)

SPRING

April

American Classics

Moby Dick (1851) by Herman Melville
Their Eyes Were Watching God (1937) by Zora Neale Hurston

Today, we had to give up our dog, Biscuit. He had leaped, unprovoked, on baby Phoebe, who had been wriggling and squalling on the other end of the sofa. He had his mouth on her face, and – while he did not bite down – he snarled and left a scratch. This is not his first act of aggression against a child. As a puppy he bit a girl who had jumped on him from behind on a hot day at a park; and since then he snapped at children who came too close.

We thought we could manage the situation, and keep him and the baby apart, but we recognised – at some level – that it was a forlorn, unrewarding hope. We had no choice in the end. My parents knew, remotely, a couple in Lincolnshire in their sixties with a big house and land, desperate for a dog, and so they took him, leaving us bereft.

I was never a dog person, and was faintly baffled at other people's disproportionate loyalty and love for an animal. Until I had one. There is something atavistic about sitting in silent communion with a dog, content to exist in each other's company.

There is something spirit-stirring about watching your dog run in aimless directions, following his instinct and his nose. It is a living, chastening contrast to the laboured complexities of modern life. Dogs are often idealised in literature* – White Fang, say, or Lassie – but they do, I think, represent an ideal we should not ignore.

Byron's dog, Boatswain, died of rabies, nursed to the end by the poet, who carved this epitaph on his tomb: 'Near this spot / are deposited the Remains of one / who possessed Beauty without Vanity, / Strength without Insolence, / Courage without Ferocity, / and all the Virtues of Man without his Vices.' That last line is a little bombastic, and perhaps overstates the point. Elizabeth Barrett Browning had a dog called Flush, about which – oddly – Virginia Woolf wrote a biography in 1933, saying, 'A dog somehow represents – no, I can't think of the word – the private side of life – the play side.' I feel the same: my dog was something and stood for something. And although he is alive, he is no longer in my life, and that makes me sad.

3 April

In February 1849 Herman Melville read Shakespeare for the first time, and recorded his own, typically fevered reaction:

> Dolt and ass that I am I have lived more than 29 years, and until a few days ago, never made close acquaintance with the divine William. Ah, he's full of sermons-on-the-mount, and gentle, aye, almost as Jesus. I take such men to be inspired. I fancy that

---

* They are occasionally the enemies of it, too. Half of the original manuscript for *Of Mice and Men* was eaten by John Steinbeck's setter pup. Steinbeck was philosophical: 'I was pretty mad but the poor little fellow may have been acting critically.'

this moment Shakespeare in heaven ranks with Gabriel, Raphael and Michael. And if another Messiah ever comes 'twill be in Shakespeare's person.

When Melville encountered Shakespeare he saw God. And we can see the impact of his Damascene conversion on his prose, in *Moby Dick*,* the novel he published just a couple of years later. Shakespeare's influence was not unequivocally a helpful one. Melville's masterpiece certainly borrowed some ambition and sense of metaphysical drama, some of its heft, from Shakespeare, but that may have unbalanced the novel more than a little.

As published, *Moby Dick* is a vast, crazed, encyclopaedic account of a captain's obsession with a 'sperm whale of uncommon magnitude and malignity', who once bit off his leg;† Ahab is a figure who combines the madness of Lear, the arrogance of Coriolanus and the misguided faith in fate of Macbeth.

It was a publishing failure. Reviewers were baffled by its eccentricity, with one verdict putting it a little less delicately than that: 'maniacal – mad as a March hare – mowing, gibbering, screaming, like an incurable Bedlamite, reckless of keeper

* The book was originally called *The Whale* when it was published in England, but Melville instructed his brother to change the title for the American edition to *Moby-Dick*. The hyphenated word actually only appears once in the text, so it is unclear why it was hyphenated in the title. My book has *Moby Dick* on the front cover, and *Moby-Dick* inside. As with everything else with this novel, there is a creeping sense of madness at work.

† The whale is named for a real creature called, brilliantly, Mocha Dick, an albino who lived near Mocha Island off the coast of Chile, which was the subject of a magazine article by Jeremiah Reynolds in 1839. And, of course, the coffee references don't stop there: when a couple of Seattle entrepreneurs wanted to name their coffee shop, they believed that words beginning with 'St' were powerful, and someone recalled Starbuck, the chief mate in the novel, with 'flesh as hard as a twice-baked biscuit'. A franchise was born.

or waistcoat'. It did not sell out its first edition, and the remaining copies were accidentally destroyed in a warehouse fire. Melville went on to produce an even more disregarded novel, *Pierre* (1852), and ended his life in obscurity, working in a New York customs house, a failed novelist and poet,* a drunk and probably a wife-beater. 'Though I wrote the Gospels in this century,' he once said to his fellow novelist Nathaniel Hawthorne, 'I should die in the gutter.'

Before *Moby Dick*, Melville had experienced some literary success with his highly spiced tales – based on his own experience, artfully exaggerated – of seafaring adventures in Polynesia: the novel *Typee* (1846) and its sequel *Omoo* (1847). In fact, when he got married in 1847 he was too famous to do so in church, for fear of crowds coming along to disturb the spectacle. He recognised that he would be for ever known as the 'man who lived among the cannibals', but for several decades afterwards was denied even that notoriety. The *New York Times* called him Hiram Melville in an article a week after his death.

When Ernest Hemingway looked back on the American tradition he ignored Melville entirely, stating: 'All modern American literature comes from one book by Mark Twain called *Huckleberry Finn*. American writing comes from that. There was nothing before. There has been nothing as good since.' Henry James omitted Melville too and was heavily influenced by Hawthorne instead.† It took the centenary of Melville's birth in 1919 to begin the resurrection of this figure: his final novel *Billy*

---

* He wrote an 18,000-line epic poem called *Clarel*, which he said was 'eminently adapted for unpopularity' and whose readership was once estimated at one.
† Melville was entranced with Hawthorne himself, writing him stalkerish letters while mopping his own hot brow. *Moby Dick*, in its British incarnation, was dedicated to him 'in token of my admiration for his genius'.

Budd was published for the first time in 1924; and his homo-erotic prose, the incredibly male world of his stories, were celebrated by figures such as E.M. Forster, Auden and Benjamin Britten. D.H. Lawrence struggled with *Moby Dick* a bit ('it reads like journalism. It seems spurious . . . it won't do'), before coming out in firm favour with an opinion that has helped to shape the novel's future reception: 'one of the strangest and most wonderful books in the world'.

6 April

It is a thrill to sit here today with this strange, wonderful book and contemplate it again, open it out on my empty train and tentatively tuck in. I read *Moby Dick* once in the summer holidays before my third year at university. I had won a prize, worth a couple of thousand pounds, for my exam performance the previous year, so did not need to earn anything over those months. I decided to devote time to reading great books.* I remember reclining on a sofa, sun pouring hungrily through the window, balancing *Moby Dick* on my chest, ready to absorb its brilliance. Each day I began, each day I fell almost immediately, and satisfyingly, asleep.

I came to feel about *Moby Dick* like John Updike felt about *Tristram Shandy*, a novel with whose baggy weirdness it shares some similarities. He talked about the 'boredom that pours in waves from the chirping pages', and I remember being similarly stultified and sedated that summer. I'm not sure I ever finished it; and that made me determined to do so now. Mark Twain once called a classic book 'something that everybody

---

* And spending the evenings getting stoned while playing cards with my friends. Which may account for my sleepiness.

wants to have read and nobody wants to read';* and a little part of me has harboured that ignoble thought about *Moby Dick*. Let us see.

So, first things first: the opening words of *Moby Dick* are not 'Call me Ishmael.' The book begins, happily revealing its own eccentricity, with an 'Etymology – supplied by a Late Consumptive Usher to a Grammar School'. The first line is, then, actually: 'The pale Usher – threadbare in coat, heart, body, and brain; I see him now.' But the novel proper gets going with Ishmael, a worthy stand-in for the author, for whom (as for Melville) 'a whaleship was my Yale College and my Harvard'.

Ishmael is one of the great voices in literature, warm and wise, interrogative and thoughtful, someone who muses constantly about whales and humans; 'the problem of the universe,' as he puts it, 'revolving in me'. The first 100 pages of *Moby Dick* are quite different from the following 350, which were written after Melville got obsessed with Shakespeare and Hawthorne and allowed his ambition to swell. We get an almost Dickensian beginning, in which Ishmael tries to find a ship to sail in, and ends up in a busy inn, where he is forced to share a bed with a harpooner. He is reluctant at first:

> No man prefers to sleep two in a bed. In fact, you would a good deal rather not sleep with your own brother. I don't know how it is, but people like to be private when they are sleeping. And when it comes to sleeping with an unknown stranger, in a strange inn, in a strange town, and that stranger a harpooneer, then your objections indefinitely multiply.

---

* Probably. As with all Twain quotes, there is some dispute, because so much has been credited to him without basis. Another version of the line is that a classic is 'a book which people praise but don't read'. This also works for *Moby Dick*.

That harpooner is Queequeg, 'George Washington cannibalistically developed', a tattooed Islander, who spears rare steaks for breakfast using his harpoon.* And the two men happily bunk-up in one of the more homoerotic pages of American literature: 'Thus, then, in our hearts' honeymoon, lay I and Queequeg – a cosy, loving pair ... We had lain thus in bed, chatting and napping at short intervals, and Queequeg now and then affectionately throwing his brown tattooed legs over mine, and then drawing them back; so entirely sociable and free and easy were we.'

Melville, unhappily married and prone to fixations on men like Hawthorne, was possibly gay himself, and certainly took pleasure in exploring male friendships at some length. Those insouciant 'brown tattooed legs over mine' form a lovely, lingering image. Queequeg and Ishmael share a relationship that veers charmingly between bromance and romance: 'Queequeg figured in the Highland costume – a shirt and socks – in which to my eyes, at least, he appeared to uncommon advantage.'

7 April

It is hard to escape nature this month: the insistent murmuring of spring breezes, the weather that shifts restlessly between heat and sodden downpours. Chaucer told us that this was a good month for 'folk to goon on pilgrimages'; and I try to think about that on my daily, effortful pilgrimage to work. Dawn is soft in the skies, coats are discarded. Life has potential.

---

* Ishmael notes an important fact of life here: 'everyone knows that in most people's estimation, to do anything coolly is to do it genteelly'; Queequeg is simply cooler than everybody else in the room.

The beginning of *The Canterbury Tales* (1387) is one of the great paeans to spring:[*]

> Whan that Aprille with his shoures soote,
> The droghte of March hath perced to the roote,
> And bathed every veyne in swich licóur
> Of which vertú engendred is the flour;
> Whan Zephirus eek with his swete breeth
> Inspired hath in every holt and heeth
> The tendre croppes, and the yonge sonne
> Hath in the Ram his halfe cours y-ronne,
> And smale foweles maken melodye,
> That slepen al the nyght with open ye,
> So priketh hem Natúre in hir corages,

At first glance, this may seem a bit forbidding, but if you allow yourself to follow the rhythm, the meaning starts to reveal itself, like the bud of a flower: we can feel life-giving fluidity in that swimmy collection of showers, bathing, liquid, pulsing veins and swelling roots; we are comforted by the quietude of the wind's breath, the tenderness of the crops, the youth of the sun, the melody of small birds. If nature is beginning to 'prick' or encourage people, it is only a beginning, the start of something that might be wonderful, and remains cautious and gentle.

Today I interview David Attenborough, the great natural historian and broadcaster. He has seen more natural wonder than perhaps almost anybody on the planet, and he has mourned its loss to a concomitant extent. He seems tired by it all: the weary insistence of someone who refuses to accept

---

[*] You might unhappily contrast this with Eliot's *The Waste Land*, which takes the Chaucerian imagery and knowingly perverts it: April to him being 'the cruellest month, breeding / Lilacs out of the dead land'.

defeat, but must sense the futility that strives every day to defeat him.

Talking to him, reading *Moby Dick*, I think a lot about our relationship with the natural world. In the evenings, Nadine and I watch* a show called *The Island*, in which folk are stranded on a deserted patch in the middle of the Pacific. And yet mankind's grubby impact is visible in every shot: the beaches of these pristine locations are like rubbish dumps, the murky sea washing up plastic tat at every moment.

So is *Moby Dick* a conservationist work? Typically, yes and no. Ishmael is vividly heartless in his revelling in the description of a slain whale: 'The red tide now poured from all sides of the monster like brooks down a hill. His tormented body rolled not in brine but in blood, which bubbled and seethed for furlongs behind in their wake. The slanting sun playing upon this crimson pond in the sea, sent back its reflection into every face, so that they all glowed to each other like red men.'

And the novel thrills to the chase of Moby Dick, and the captain's mania for slaughter. But it does pause to note the hypocrisy of hunting, that a whale 'must die the death and be murdered, in order to light the gay bridals and other merrymakings of men, and also to illuminate the solemn churches that preach unconditional inoffensiveness by all to all'. The tragedy of the novel is its basic belief that nature is boundless in its bounty, that mankind – with its limited technology, a creaking boat on a violent sea – could never entirely impose itself on the environment. 'We account the whale immortal in his species,

---

* We have a nine-month-old baby, so we can only watch one show at night, and it needs to be mindless. Since having children, Nadine has become constitutionally opposed to films, as they are too long. She also has this restrictive covenant on what we watch: nothing set in the past, the future or an alternate reality. That is rather limiting when you think about it.

however perishable in his individuality,' says Ishmael at one point. Wrongly, as it turns out. Reading *Moby Dick* is to be reminded of our collective hubris, our arrogant belief that the 'eternal whale will survive' whatever we do.

'Do you think you've got the work–life balance right, really?' asks Nadine, as I slope in after 9 p.m., having left before 7 a.m. The answer cannot be yes. I have to concede that my work is not arduous or laborious in any sense: reading, writing, broadcasting and editing. It is the very epitome of soft-handed sodding about. I think of that *Monty Python* sketch, in which the young man – who has rebelled and gone off to join a coal mine – has to return to his family of literary north Londoners, and his irascible playwright father:

> What do you know about getting up at five o'clock in t'morning to fly to Paris, back at the Old Vic for drinks at twelve, sweating the day through press interviews, television interviews and getting back here at ten to wrestle with the problem of a homosexual nymphomaniac drug-addict involved in the ritual murder of a well-known Scottish footballer. That's a full working day, lad, and don't you forget it!

The dad is livid with his son for 'poncing off to Barnsley, you and your coal-mining friends'; and his wife is the hand-wringing peacekeeper: 'You know what he's like after a few novels.'

So nobody is, rightly, going to feel sorry for me. I do regret working so much, missing my family. But every day I have that fear of failure, of fall, of not being able to provide. I am also, and always have been, a slave to the comforting rigour of routine: I like being on the same train in the morning, the first into the office, even as I resent the only fleeting glimpse of my new baby in my wake. I am conflicted; I wonder with Larkin why I let 'the toad work / Squat on my life'. At the same time, I am, as we all are, defined by my job, wondering whether I really want to drive work off from my life, to be 'courageous enough / To shout, Stuff your pension!'

Melville wrote a short story about office life, called 'Bartleby, the Scrivener' (1853), published shortly after *Moby Dick*. It has the immortal phrase, uttered by Bartleby when asked to perform some unpalatably dreary task when he would rather be staring at a brick wall: 'I would prefer not to.' My favourite office novel is *Something Happened* (1974), by Joseph Heller (the book he wrote after *Catch-22*, 1961). This is also good on the absurdity, the ordered insanity, the existential terror, of life at work. Kurt Vonnegut said of the two books that 'taken together, they tell a tale of pain and disappointments experienced by mediocre men of good will'. He saw Heller as 'the first major American writer to deal with unrelieved misery at novel length'. *Something Happened* is funny, but it is mean and relentless; it is the perfect book to read while you should be working.

9 April

Ishmael is a progressive figure, tolerant of others' beliefs and ideas: 'It's only his outside; a man can be honest in any sort of skin.' Remember, these are the words of a character written in 1851, when the US was hurtling towards a civil war about slavery. Melville gives Ishmael lines full of wisdom and charm that sparkle in the text: 'I cherish the greatest respect towards everybody's religious obligations, never mind how comical, and could not find it in my heart to undervalue even a congregation of ants worshipping a toad-stool.' Or: 'Old age is always wakeful; as if, the longer linked with life, the less man has to do with aught that looks like death.'

For the first hundred pages of the book especially, there is cleverness, humour,* action and memorable set-pieces like Father Mapple's sermon from a pulpit shaped like a prow. Ishmael finds himself, with his bosom pal Queequeg, aboard the *Pequod*, a ship ready to go whale hunting: 'Her ancient decks were worn and wrinkled, like the pilgrim-worshipped flagstone in Canterbury Cathedral where Becket bled.' And here the portentousness starts, here the sense of epic is formed that continues for the rest of the book. Central to that is the mesmerising figure of Ahab, that 'grand, ungodly, god-like man', gripped by his obsession to kill Moby Dick, a doomed desire that still shudders off the page: 'He tasks me; he heaps me; I see in him outrageous strength, with an inscrutable malice sinewing it. That inscrutable thing is chiefly what I hate; and be the white whale agent, or be the white whale principal, I will wreak that hate upon him. Talk not to me of blasphemy, man; I'd strike the sun if it insulted me.'

At points the novel breaks into a play script, with Ahab allowed to stump centre-stage to give soliloquies. And this tragic quality, this sense of destiny made flesh in the characters, is what has made the novel resonate. Ahab is unforgettable; his futile quest both a fine piece of novelistic plotting and a metaphor for the inadequacy of vengeance and the frailty of mortal planning. I come to realise that *Moby Dick* is a book that has fallen out of the wrong century: it does look back to the excitable breadth, that impossible farrago, of *Tristram Shandy*; and forward to the modernist, format-destroying monolith that is *Ulysses*. It has no place in the nineteenth century and its rational, well-structured mega novels (which is perhaps why nobody read it then).

---

* I like the landlady (one of the three women in the whole book) who asks for a sign to be made saying: 'No suicides permitted here, and no smoking in the parlour'.

11 April

On Radio 4, we are debating the effect on creativity of the deadline:* is it a spur to excellence, or a cramp on creativity? I have, I think, never missed a deadline in my life: I have a pathological determination to deliver something when I said I would.

But maybe that means my artistic side has simply shrivelled; if I were more creative, perhaps I would be more focused on means, rather than ends. Douglas Adams had the great response to this issue: 'I love deadlines. I like the whooshing sound they make as they fly by.' His editor had to physically stay in the same flat as him, stopping him going out, to make sure he got the job done.

There is an app called 'Write or Die', which acts as a demonic prompt to stop procrastination; it actually starts deleting random letters from the text if you tarry too long. David Nicholls tried it when sweating over the sequel to *One Day* (2009): he ended up with 35,000 words that he had to chuck away as useless. 'It was as if I was writing with a gun to my head,' he said.

But history records greatness produced to time. Evelyn Waugh wrote *Brideshead Revisited* in his only three-month leave during the Second World War. Orwell produced *1984* (1949) with a more literal sense of a deadline: he knew he was terminally ill and had to write quickly. And Dickens was writing many of his novels as serial instalments for magazines, which meant he could never dwell on matters of plot indefinitely. It is an impossible question as to whether these writers could have done more with longer, or if more scratching and revision and procrastination would only have marred their inspired musings.

---

* The term probably comes from the boundary mark outside a prison camp, by the way: if you breached that deadline, you were shot. Fair to say its meaning has become a little more elastic in the creative sector.

We come back to Shakespeare, that combination of hack and genius, battling the unforgiving deadlines of the theatre. It was thanks to commercial requirements that he produced *Lear*, *Macbeth* and *Antony and Cleopatra* more or less in a year. A ticking clock, or a frowning creditor, might be the friend of artistry after all.

12 April

Melville was not, it seems, governed much by deadlines or structure. And that eccentricity, that refusal to be bound by convention, does bring with it some problems. The scale of *Moby Dick* is so overwhelming that Ishmael more or less needs to keep apologising for it: 'God keep me from ever completing anything. This whole book is but a draught – nay, but the draught of a draught. Oh, Time, Strength, Cash, and Patience!'*

And he is not wrong: the book does indeed have such 'a large and liberal theme' that it can do no more than 'expand to its bulk'. It proceeds for the most part by digressions: 'gams' or conferences with other ships producing other stories; and endless attempts to categorise every minute detail of such a large subject. There is a chapter with the title 'Of Whales in Paint; in Teeth; in Wood; in Sheet-Iron; in Stone; in Mountains; in Stars'; there's a recipe for breaded whale brain; there's a chapter called 'The Crotch', giving specifications for the 'notched stick' used 'for the purpose of furnishing a rest for the wooden extremity of the harpoon'. Some pages reel with their very tedium.

Elsewhere, Melville – who has clearly lost control of his subject – loses control of his prose too.† We get moments of

---

* The clarion call of the author still to the present day.
† The book has more needless exclamations per paragraph than one of my emails.

helpless, endless alliteration: 'all the waves rolled by like scrolls of silver; and, by their soft, suffusing seethings, made what seemed a silvery silence, not a solitude; on such a silent night a silvery jet was seen far in advance of the white bubbles at the bow.' Melville is fond of coining adverbs that have no claim to legitimate existence, as with the sharks who 'smackingly feasted on its fatness'. Once you spot this, you see it everywhere, nestling in the writing, unaware of its own awkwardness: 'cannibally carving'; 'postponedly encountered'; 'hoveringly halting . . . the white sea-fowls longingly lingered over the agitated pool that he left'; 'sidelingly transplanted'; 'ripplingly withdrawing'. It can be ball-clenchingly bad.

And yet to appreciate *Moby Dick*, you have to embrace its very eccentricity, its refusal to conform or be tidied up. It is both silly and profound, moving and bewildering. Where else would you get a chapter ('The Cassock'), which is about the willy of a whale, described only as 'a very strange, enigmatical object'? At one point, someone takes the foreskin, cuts some arm-holes in it, and dresses up like a priest 'in the full canonicals of his calling'.

Or where you might get bewildered by a paragraph like this:

> Squeeze! squeeze! squeeze! all the morning long; I squeezed that sperm till I myself almost melted into it; I squeezed that sperm till a strange sort of insanity came over me; and I found myself unwittingly squeezing my co-labourers' hands in it, mistaking their hands for the gentle globules . . . Come; let us squeeze hands all round; nay, let us all squeeze ourselves into each other; let us squeeze ourselves universally into the very milk and sperm of kindness.*

---

* And yes, I realise that 'sperm' in this context means whale oil. But still.

I'll have what he's having, as that old lady almost says in *When Harry Met Sally*. No, *Moby Dick*[*] is worth an hour of my time (and your time) every day; it is unlike anything else we will ever read again. The literary critic Frank Kermode once offered an alternative definition of a classic, that it was 'patient of interpretation': you can endlessly return to find more to think about. *Moby Dick*, fittingly, almost meets this idea, even as it denies it: it is entirely impatient of interpretation, with its hectoring lists and infuriating digressions; but it rewards your patience with something arresting or new or unconsidered all the time. And not many books do that.

14 April

I have mentioned Elmore Leonard's rules for writing, and those strange guidelines for detective fiction. Well, today I am trying to come up with some of my own for the *TLS*, which we are in the process of redesigning.

Despite being 119 years old, the paper has no style guide at all, something I am trying to remedy. At the moment, rules are scowlingly enforced by senior members of staff, based on custom and precedent, and occasional whim. There are some happy little quirks as a result. Take this rule about apostrophes, which is workable in the absence of any other, and I have now made formal:

> With proper names/nouns ending in *s* that are singular, use an *s* after the apostrophe if the proper name/noun dates from a time

---

[*] One final fact: the bald-headed, electronic music star Moby (real name, Richard Melville Hall) is Herman Melville's great-great-great-nephew. So when you hear about him as a bit of creep (as when he was inappropriate with a sixteen-year-old Natalie Portman) you are quite within your rights to call him Moby Dick.

after Jesus (e.g. Rabelais's); do **not** if it dates from a time before Jesus (e.g. Aristophanes' plays). NB: Jesus is the first to take an *s* after the apostrophe: Jesus's.

No, there is no reason for it.

15 April

Zora Neale Hurston shares something with Herman Melville: they both died in obscurity, their novels out of print. Hurston was interred in an unmarked pauper's grave, the author of four novels, two musicals, several anthropological essays, two books of mythology and an autobiography. At the time of her death, in 1960, she was fourteen years into a mad, Melvillean project of writing a biography of Herod the Great, for which she had no publishing contract. Her autobiography was called, appropriately, *Dust Tracks in a Road* (1942), and it must have felt that her reputation was similarly transient, easily scrubbed away by the passage of time.

As with Melville, changing tastes resurrected her. In 1973 the novelist Alice Walker wrote an essay about her disappearance, which ultimately sparked her rediscovery by a new generation of black authors and opinion formers. Toni Morrison loves her. Oprah loves her. And her masterpiece is *Their Eyes Were Watching God*, an account of the troubled life and marriages of a woman called Janie, who refuses quite to be beaten down by the fate allotted to her. It was written in just seven weeks on a field trip to Haiti; 'a beautiful book about soulfulness', according to Zadie Smith.

I had not, to my shame, known very much about Hurston, which was one of the reasons I wanted to read her this month. In August 2018 the *TLS* ran a cover piece by Kristen Roupenian about 'sharp women' of the mid-twentieth century, which bemoaned the fact that, while attention was paid to figures like Dorothy Parker and Susan Sontag, Hurston was neglected. In the same issue, we ran a review of a Hurston book that had only just been published, *Barracoon* (2018), a work of anthropology based on her 1927 conversations with Kossola O-Lo-Loo-Ay, the last known survivor of the Atlantic slave trade. It was written in order to place on record aspects of the black American experience that had been neglected: 'All these words from the seller,' noted Hurston, 'but not one word from the sold.'

Hurston became modestly famous as part of the Harlem Renaissance, an intellectual movement in the 1920s and 1930s of black artists and writers. Hurston had been raised in Eatonville (the setting for much of *Their Eyes Were Watching God*), an all-black town in Florida. After a precarious existence in her twenties, working as a maid and manicurist, she ended up as the only black student at Barnard College, studying under Professor Franz Boas, known as 'Papa Franz'. One of her roles there was to measure the skulls of black people in Harlem to prove they were different to those of orang-utans.

While Hurston was not very conscious of race as a child,* she became so, especially as a black writer patronised by the white intellectual set in New York. But her reflections are never bitter

---

* She didn't think of herself as black until she visited a big town: 'I remember the very day that I became colored. Up to my thirteenth year I lived in the little Negro town of Eatonville, Florida. It is exclusively a colored town.' Janie is the opposite, as she lives with a white family for whom her grandmother works: 'Ah was wid dem white chillum so much till Ah didn't know Ah wuzn't white till Ah was round six years old.'

or filled with rancour. This is her recalling a night out with a white man at a bar playing jazz: 'Music. The great blobs of purple and red emotion have not touched him. He has only heard what I felt. He is far away and I see him but dimly across the ocean and the continent that have fallen between us. He is so pale with his whiteness then and I am so colored.'

The notion that difference can be an aesthetic experience, not a political one, is rather bracing. And throughout her life Hurston refused to follow simple views of the race divide, refused to show self-pity, believed that she was not 'tragically colored' or part of the 'sobbing school of Negrohood'. Hurston's non-fiction rings out across the ages as a clarion call of beauty and self-confidence: 'At certain times I have no race, I am me. When I set my hat at a certain angle and saunter down Seventh Avenue, Harlem City, feeling as snooty as the lions in front of the Forty-second Street Library . . . the cosmic Zora emerges. I belong to no race or time. I am the eternal feminine with its string of beads.'

This seems a prerogative of the structurally abused: to rise above prejudice, to deny its existence as an act of proud resistance. It is easy, and misleading, for a white man like me to say race does not exist, because it has not existed as an issue in my life. 'Colour blindness' then becomes either a naïve abrogation of responsibility, or a wilful refusal to recognise structural inequality. But when Hurston avers a denial of race, it feels like a statement of intent, an aspiration towards universality that her novels achieve, even if the world does not. *Their Eyes Were Watching God* may speak more loudly to a black woman, but its voice can be heard by all.

Travelling to work after an Easter spent at home amid sunshine and chaos. I may be getting sentimental as I get older (I was thirty-nine last week), but I feel the separation from my wife and children more keenly as time passes. Phoebe is now murmuring and reaching and amused by almost everything.

The love of family, especially of children, is missing in many of the books I read. Janie never has any children in *Their Eyes Were Watching God*, for example, and never even raises the issue. Children so often seem to get in the way of adults in fiction. I think of Updike: Rabbit always running away from his family; or those brittle, awful couples of *Couples* (1968), whose offspring are an inconvenience, a frustrating distraction from the next icy martini or furtive feel-up in the lounge room. That same surly rejection is there in *Revolutionary Road* (1961) by Richard Yates (which I read, unwisely, on my honeymoon).* Family life is stultifying, as is work life; children a burden and a shame. The novel is mesmeric, but its emptiness is ever-present. Contrast it, say, with George Eliot's *The Mill on the Floss* (1860), which takes us into the mind of a child, and its comprehensible desires and feelings: 'If we could recall that early bitterness, and the dim guesses, the strangely perspectiveless conception of life, that gave the bitterness its intensity, we should not pooh-pooh the griefs of our children.'

Many novelists forget that too easily. Perhaps love is seen as boring unless frustrated, diminished or denied. There's that line in *Anna Karenina* (1877), 'All happy families are alike; each unhappy family is unhappy in its own way', suggesting that while happiness might be the end of a story, it can never be the beginning. Proust observes, near the end of *À La Recherche*, that 'artists need pain and plenty of it in order to be artists at all;

---

* If you take only one lesson from this book, do NOT read *Revolutionary Road* on your honeymoon, or any romantic getaway.

happiness is a fine thing but largely without intellectual content.' Anguish is ever the driver of plot. And that is fine, but it doesn't help when the train is taking you away from home, and you are searching for consolation.

26 April

Should I confess to crassness by saying that I have to *like* a fictional character somewhere in a work of narrative to care about that narrative? I got to the TV show *Mad Men* very late – feeling it was like a sexier, more glib version of *Revolutionary Road* – and was unable to love it, because all the characters were impossible to love. I know we're all supposed to roll over for Don Draper, and rejoice in the cigarettes and hard liquor, but the show to me was no more than that: mannequins in beautiful clothes, beautifully shot, smoking raffishly. They didn't care for each other, or the children, and so I didn't care what happened to them.

It seems to me the engine of genre fiction is the bond you feel with the lead character – Jack Reacher, Harry Bosch, Travis McGee, Temperance Brennan, et al. – whose quest narrative you must support. But I think it goes further than that to all novels, however artistically rendered. We must fall in love a little with someone, or why would we bother? I care about Janie and her unflagging spirit despite her environment; I'm fond of Ishmael and Queequeg tucked up in bed together, as I was of the second Mrs de Winter back in January, or Arabella a month later. I risk being over-reductive, but to me the successful encouragement of an attachment to a character is one definition of successful writing.*

---

* The great Kurt Vonnegut had this as one of his rules of fiction: 'Give the reader at least one character he or she can root for.' Amen to that. He also said this, which I like: 'Write to please just one person. If you open a window and make love to the world, so to speak, your story will get pneumonia.'

I was reading at work about 'Team Scott vs Team Zelda': the Fitzgeralds, their fraught relationship and the consequences for their legacy. I did not realise quite how much Scott had taken from Zelda without attribution: lifting whole passages of her diary for *The Beautiful and the Damned* (1922); publishing under his own name stories and articles that she had written. When, in *The Great Gatsby*, Daisy says she hopes her baby daughter will be 'a beautiful little fool', she is quoting directly from what Zelda said after the birth of their child. The latter example seems to be the inevitable consequence of two people's lives and thoughts intermingling, what the author Joanna Scutts called 'the messy intertextuality of marriage'. But the rest feels like a fraud: his literary reputation – which no doubt paid the bills – was more important than hers.

As a literary couple, it is hard to think of a more fascinatingly intertextual pairing. T.S. Eliot and Vivienne Haigh-Wood may share some similarities: his pressing need for success; her continual illness. Eliot once wrote: 'To her, the marriage brought no happiness . . . To me, it brought the state of mind out of which came *The Waste Land*.' And unhappiness seems to be the lot of the woman in what often seem to be unequal literary partnerships: think of Ted Hughes and Sylvia Plath, too. When I recall the Brownings, though, who forged their relationship in letters, using the common currency of shared vocabulary, I feel more positive: their child was called Pen after all, a symbol of their collaboration at the level of both body and mind.

In all this, it would be wrong to forget James Joyce's marriage to Nora Barnacle, not least because of their filthy sex correspondence. His effusions have been preserved for posterity, and they are not for the faint-hearted: 'The smallest things give me a great cockstand – a whorish movement of your mouth, a little brown stain on the seat of your white drawers, a sudden dirty word spluttered out by your wet lips, a sudden immodest noise* made by you behind and then a bad smell slowly curling up out of your backside.' Nora's own letters, which presumably encouraged – and apparently even initiated – this sort of lustiness, have so far gone undiscovered, although Joyce mentions that they may be dirtier than his (which is pretty hard to imagine).

28 April

Their Eyes Were Watching God turns more on the axis of male–female relationships than black–white. Hurston didn't want to limit her sympathies: 'I have ceased to think in terms of race; I think only in terms of individuals. I am interested in you now, not as a Negro man but as a man. I am not interested in the race problem, but I am interested in the problems of individuals, white ones and black ones.'

The individual at the novel's centre is Janie, a much-married figure of mystery returning to her home: 'So the beginning of this was a woman and she had come back from burying the dead.' The novel is framed by Janie talking to her friend Phoeby on the porch about her life, her three relationships and her aspirations for the future. Janie, we learn, is 'full of that oldest human longing: self revelation'; Phoeby is full of 'hungry listening'.

Women's spoken voices were critical for Hurston. They shaped her experience of storytelling from a young age: 'The

---

* Joyce was evidently rather taken by this particular bodily function. He also said this: 'You had an arse full of farts that night, darling, and I fucked them out of you, big fat fellows, long windy ones, quick little merry cracks and a lot of tiny little naughty farties ending in a long gush from your hole.'

front porch might seem a daring place for the rest of the town, but it was a gallery seat for me. My favorite place was atop the gatepost. Proscenium box for a born first-nighter.'

We see this theatrical power of the spoken word in the novel, and get cameos of women talking, figures who 'became lords of sounds and lesser things', who 'passed nations through their mouths' or 'passed around the pictures of their thoughts'. Janie's story is not much of a happy one: her mother was born after her grandmother was raped by a slave-owner; Janie born after her mother was raped by a schoolteacher. The fear of men drives Janie's grandmother to marry her off after she is caught canoodling with a man at the gate: 'Ah can't die easy thinkin' maybe de menfolks white or black is makin' a spit cup outa you.'

The first marriage is to an old, wealthy miser, who mistreats her; the second to a go-getting entrepreneur called Joe, with 'bow-down command in his face', who refuses to recognise Janie as a sensual human being; the third to a great sensualist, nicknamed Tea Cake, who takes Janie to the Everglades and a life filled with colour and strife, 'dancing, fighting, singing, crying, laughing, winning and losing love every hour'.

The idea of wedded love, indeed, in the book is a travesty; marriage is little more than a painful rite of passage: 'She knew now that marriage did not make love. Janie's first dream was dead, so she became a woman.' What Janie is seeking is a life of natural vigour, of the sort of freedom embodied in the efflorescence of springtime. What she has to endure is the purgatory of the human condition. But the pulsing power of the natural world emerges most strongly in the book: 'Every morning the world flung itself over and exposed the town to the sun.' As I sit in my train each morning, rumbling through the over-built city, swathed in fumes and clad in unremitting concrete, then the invocation of a long-dead American woman still has the power to move me.

Like all of us, Janie is searching for 'flower dust and spring-time sprinkled over everything'; she is a figure who tries to make 'summertime out of lonesomeness'. Janie's ideal state is Eden, with 'kissing bees singing of the beginning of the world', or the 'kissing darkness' of peaceful repose. Contrast that with the human touch that hurts even as it seeks to caress: Nanny sees a man 'lacerating her Janie with a kiss'; a man caring for his wife is dismissed as 'kissin' yo' foot and 'taint in uh man tuh kiss foot long'.

29 April

I am coming to the end of *Their Eyes Were Watching God* and trying to work out why it seems to work so well as a piece of storytelling. It comes largely from Hurston looking at things from Janie's vantage point: her desire to escape two restrictive marriages; her third, hopeless love for Tea Cake, a gambler and a dreamer, who gives her a glimpse of that Edenic ideal ('he could be a bee to a blossom – a pear tree blossom in the spring'), but ultimately only grants her 'self-crushing love'.

The novel departs briefly and tellingly from Janie's perspective when Tea Cake beats her. The prose loses its lyricism, and we get the view – for a terrifying second – of the entitled male: 'he just slapped her around a bit to show he was boss.' Hurston knows what she is doing here; it is a part of a refusal to be idealistic, to pretend that life has inevitable solutions, that romance can triumph. At the end, the natural world, celebrated throughout so much, turns violent in the form of a hurricane that destroys Janie's home: 'Havoc was there with her mouth open'; and destruction comes in 'the meanest moment of eternity'.

So there is hard-earned wisdom in Janie's words to Phoeby, on the porch in the gathering gloom; something that feels like sentimentality, but is not quite: 'Love ain't somethin' lak uh grindstone dat's de same thing everywhere and do de same thing tuh everything it touch. Love is lak de sea. It's uh movin' thing, but still and all, it takes its shape from de shore it meets, and it's different with every shore.' Love is like the sea: moving and still, shaped and shapeless. It is a wonderful image, is it not?

30 April

I realise that I have been entranced by the American voice – if there is such a thing – for as long as I have been reading seriously. The course of American literature is varied and uncharitable, but there is something there both exotic and familiar, bewitching to an Englishman. Americans and their writings share certain points of reference, but remain proudly and excitingly *other* at the same time. Whether it is Ishmael filled with philosophy, or Janie in tune with the natural world around her, or Hemingway's silent moochers near Lake Michigan, or Fitzgerald's brittle, glittery gatherings, or Garrison Keillor's homespun tales of Lake Wobegon (in which 'all the women are strong, all the men are good-looking and all the children are above average').

There's a moment in David Lodge's *Changing Places**(1975), where an English professor is contemplating life in Plotinus (a thinly disguised version of Berkeley in California), and he has a moment of pro-American enlightenment. I find it later at work:

---

* A book full of sex and other books and silly academics. I like it very much. It gave the world the parlour game Humiliation: each person has to name a book they haven't read, and get points for everyone who *has* read it. One professor wins with *Hamlet*, and is promptly fired for negligence. I imagine playing this at the *TLS* would be similarly fraught. My Humiliation book would be – until this year – Hardy's *Tess of the d'Urbervilles* (1891), by the way.

He thought of Henry Miller sitting over a beer in some scruffy Parisian café with his notebook on his knee and the smell of cunt still lingering on his fingers and he felt some distant kinship with that coarse, uneven priapic imagination. He understood American Literature for the first time in his life that afternoon, sitting in Pierre's on Cable Street as the river of Plotinus life flowed past, understood its prodigality and indecorum, its yea-saying heterogeneity, understood Walt Whitman who laid end to end words never seen in each other's company before outside of a dictionary, and Herman Melville who split the atom of a traditional novel in the effort to make whaling a universal meta-phor and smuggled into a book addressed to the most puritanical reading public the world has ever known a chapter on the whale's foreskin and got away with it; understood why Mark Twain nearly wrote a sequel to *Huckleberry Finn* in which Tom Sawyer was to sell Huck into slavery, and why Stephen Crane wrote his great war-novel first and experienced war afterwards, and what Gertrude Stein meant when she said that 'anything one is remembering is a repetition, but existing as a human being, that is being, listening and hearing is never repetition'; understood all that, though he couldn't have explained it.

I think of the prodigality of Annie Proulx too, one of the great chroniclers of the middle wild states of America. To read her writing is to get a sense of the place, the feel of the very dirt beneath the feet. Proulx is a realist – despite the occasional eccentricities she celebrates – a writer who shows, as Steinbeck put it, that American philosophy 'is thinking': descriptions immersed in the real.* But she is a poet all the same, filling her

* Steinbeck wanted to call *Of Mice and Men* (1937), that slender tale of lost opportunity and friendship, *Something That Happened*, which reflects the real-ist American tradition in fiction. His eventual title was better, though, and I

book with unforgettable, tactile images: the 'days of clutching love' in a young marriage; 'dippers of goose-bump water' from a stream; 'strong clouds rubbing against the sky like a finger drawn over skin'.

As the month draws to an end, I feel almost euphoric at the thought of this type of fiction, which transports me from a grubby train, and workaday thoughts, and all those diurnal stresses and pressures, to another landscape entirely.

~

Further Reading

The Scarlet Letter (1850) by Nathaniel Hawthorne
Uncle Tom's Cabin (1852) by Harriet Beecher Stowe
Little Women (1869) by Louisa May Alcott
The Portrait of a Lady (1881) by Henry James
Adventures of Huckleberry Finn (1884) by Mark Twain
The Red Badge of Courage (1895) by Stephen Crane
The Jungle (1906) by Upton Sinclair
My Antonia (1918) by Willa Cather
Main Street (1920) by Sinclair Lewis
The Age of Innocence (1920) by Edith Wharton
The Great Gatsby (1925) by F. Scott Fitzgerald
The Sun Also Rises (1926) by Ernest Hemingway
The Sound and the Fury (1929) by William Faulkner
Cannery Row (1945) by John Steinbeck
The Catcher in the Rye (1951) by J.D. Salinger
Invisible Man (1952) by Ralph Ellison
Lolita (1955) by Vladimir Nabokov

---

see that it inspired this month the name of a *Wu-Tang Clan* documentary series: *Of Mics and Men*. That's a great title too.

On the Road (1957) by Jack Kerouac
To Kill a Mockingbird (1960) by Harper Lee
The Color Purple (1982) by Alice Walker
Blood Meridian (1985) by Cormac McCarthy
Beloved (1987) by Toni Morrison

May

Historical Novels

Romola (1863) by George Eliot
The King Must Die (1958) by Mary Renault

George Eliot is one of those writers who is clearly magnificent, whom I have read quite a bit, but hasn't really entered my personal pantheon in the way that, say, Austen, James or Dickens have. *Middlemarch* (1871) is one of the great Victorian novels, but I was pleased to try a less well-known book this month. Even at the *TLS*, when I mentioned *Romola*, I was greeted with a frown of mild incomprehension. The one person who confessed to having read it came back ten minutes later, sighed and said, 'No, I was confusing it with *Daniel Deronda*.' *TLS* staff *never* admit literary ignorance if they can help it. Clearly this was a book worth looking at.

The American actress and writer Lena Dunham once tweeted a link to George Eliot's *Wikipedia* page, with this comment: 'The soapiest most scandalous thing you'll read this month. Thesis: she was ugly AND horny!' It is not perhaps the most evocative thesis ever to be written about one of the nineteenth century's greatest novelists, but it does reflect a certain way others have approached her. Henry James, who admired her greatly and whose sinuous prose style had something in common with Eliot's, said she was 'magnificently ugly, deliciously hideous'. He once blurted: 'Behold me literally in love with this great horse-faced bluestocking.'

The alleged horniness comes from the fact that Eliot had certain 'attachments' as a young woman,* before heading off on a European tour with the already married George Henry Lewes. He was estranged from his wife, who had gone on to have several children with his friend Thornton Leigh Hunt, and stayed with Eliot for years, but – despite Eliot being widely known as Mrs Lewes – the couple never wed. After Lewes's death, Eliot did get married, to Johnny Cross, a financial adviser twenty years her junior. On their honeymoon in Venice, he was seen to leap out of their hotel bedroom into the Grand Canal and swim away. Eliot's biographer Frederick Karl offered this speculation: 'What we have, in any event, is a response to some-thing in his relationship to Eliot, to Venice, to his honeymoon and to marriage, possibly to his dead mother, possibly to his cohabitation with a woman of maternal age, possibly to demands made on him he could not fulfil, possibly to his recognition of impotence or even disgust.'

Spot the trademark, feverish equivocation of the biographer lacking information: the event could 'possibly' be linked to almost anything. But it all adds to that Dunhamish view of Eliot, highly sexed even in her later years, enough to send a young man into the murky water. She even had a stalker, a man called Alexander Main, who liked to cut up her books for quotes, saying creepy things like, 'Here I am clipping and slashing great gashes out of writings every line of which I hold sacred, and

---

* Including with the philosopher Herbert Spencer and her then boss, John Chapman of the *Westminster Review*. She stayed briefly in Chapman's home, apparently much to the disquiet of his wife and live-in mistress.

finding a delight almost fiendish in the work of destruction."* He sounds nice.

Alexander Main would have an answer, but is reading actually a productive use of time? This morning, I drag myself to the station after a broken night's sleep. Phoebe woke at 1 a.m. and took an hour to settle. I am now at the age where recovery from sleeplessness is getting harder. My body certainly feels old each dawn, when consciousness seeps in and sensation emerges.

It is hard to concentrate on *Romola*, my eyes flickering, my head nodding. It reminds me of the long hours I used to spend in libraries at university: those moments when my mind started to drift towards somnolence, and only a conversation could spark me back to any sort of wakefulness. There are no conversations on a commuter train (thank God) to jolt me, so my journey today is a fuzzy, blurry one. Not much spark emerges from Eliot's leisurely, stately stroll around fifteenth-century Florence either.

My life is fixated on productivity and use of time. I juggle various jobs with various responsibilities; I don't feel I can afford to let half-hours slip by without something being achieved. I have a theory (I always have a theory) that there are three main things in life: family; work; friends. And it is possible to do only two of them well. So I am friendless, in that I spend no time

---

* Main produced a book called *Wise, Witty, and Tender Sayings, in Prose and Verse, Selected from the Works of George Eliot*. As Rebecca Mead has pointed out, it even contains a saying from Eliot about the futility of collecting sayings: 'Such people early discern that the mysterious complexity of our life is not to be embraced by maxims, and that to lace ourselves up in formulas of that sort is to repress all the divine promptings and inspirations that spring from growing insight and sympathy.'

socialising with people outside work or family. My colleagues and my family have become my friends in a sense, and I am fine with that. I don't think my dad had friends when he worked either. If I have a problem, there is nobody other than my wife I would speak to; if I have an evening free, there is nobody I would go out with other than her.

This daily hour I spend reading is a relief and a joy and a break from myself. Perhaps I could use the time better: learn a language; or work more. But reading is both pleasure and productivity: it makes us feel stronger, more empathetic, more settled into repose or startled into thought. At least I want to think so. Kafka had a line that 'a book must be the axe for the frozen sea within us', which is lovely, the sense of using someone else's words to liberate our self.

Do we buy that? 'None are so old as those who have outlived enthusiasm,' said old Henry David Thoreau. I wonder what he would have made of South Western Trains at six forty-five on a blustery May morning.

5 May

George Eliot was herself a fictional creation of the author. She was born Mary Ann Evans in a rural, religious household in Warwickshire. She went on to live in Nuneaton (not far from where I grew up), before moving to Geneva and then London. She was brilliantly intelligent, could read Latin, Greek, French, German and Italian, and managed to make a respectable living as a literary journalist. Then in 1859, at the age of forty, she became George Eliot, novelist, almost instantly feted as a major literary figure in her own right.

Romola was her fourth book, a painstaking labour of historical detailing. Eliot said she could 'swear by every sentence as having been written with my best blood, such as it is, and with the most ardent care for veracity of which my nature is capable'. She liked the novel more than everybody else has done since. It is a sweeping tale of the fate of the Florentine Republic from the death of its ruler Lorenzo de' Medici on 9 April 1492 to the execution of firebrand, ascetic preacher Girolamo Savonarola on 23 May 1498. Eliot was forensic in her research – to a fault, indisputably – into the facts of the period. In her diary, she noted her efforts to define 'particulars, first, about Lorenzo de' Medici's death; secondly, about the possible retardation of Easter; third, about Corpus Christi Day; fourthly, about Savonarola's preaching in the Quaresima of 1492'. Anthony Trollope thought such attention was liable to 'fire too much over the heads of her readers'.

It does a little over mine, I must confess. But one of the pleasures of historical fiction is the sense of being connected to a foreign place, and immersed in its environment, the sniffs and squelches of a life lived before us. Eliot offers a prologue that covers the theme of what the historian G.M. Trevelyan called 'the broad sameness of the human lot', the sense that we are all treading the same spot of earth as those who have long since passed:

> And as the faint light of his course pierced into the dwellings of men, it fell, as now, on the rosy warmth of nestling children; on the haggard waking of sorrow and sickness; on the hasty uprising of the hard-handed labourer; and on the late sleep of the night-student, who had been questioning the stars or the sages, or his own soul, for that hidden knowledge which would break through the barrier of man's brief life, and show its dark path, that seemed to bend no whither, to be an arc in an immeasurable circle of light and glory.

The pace of the novel is reflected here: the winding sentences, dense with clarity and sure-handed beauty, but also the visible marks of effortful labour. *Romola* is not a fast read, nor does it move forward with frenetic action. It tells the tale of a young woman, the daughter of a dying scholar, who falls in love with Tito Melema, a Greek intellectual adventurer freshly arrived in Florence. Tito – unbeknown to his new acquaintances – has left his adopted father, Baldassarre, behind in slavery, using the family jewels not to obtain his ransom, but to build a new life for himself in a city teeming with opportunities for a clever young man. Tito marries Romola, but betrays her not only by selling her father's library for his own gain, but also by having a secret relationship with Tessa, a 'sweet, pouting, innocent round thing' he meets in a crowd.

9 May

There's a new survey out today, suggesting that performing creative acts for at least fifteen minutes a day is good for you, mentally. Interestingly, it includes reading as a creative act, but not – say – watching TV or going to the cinema.

That feels right to me. Reading is not passive; it is a communing of a remote mind with your own, what our friend George Eliot called 'an extension of sympathy', a mingling to which you must bring something of yourself (experiences that chime or clash, your individual understanding of words and phrases, the echoes of other books, and so on). More so than watching a film, I reckon, in which the images come unbidden through our eyes. Reading is distraction and action at once. John Ruskin would agree with the action part. This is from one of his lectures in 1863: 'When you come to a good book, you must ask yourself, "Am I inclined to work as an Australian miner would? Are my pickaxes and shovels in good order, and am I in good trim myself, my sleeves well up to the elbow, and my breath good, and my temper?"'

Now there is a solid metaphor, and the typically Victorian view that hard work and domination are the true keys to any enterprise. I like something from Zora Neale Hurston as a counterpoint. This is when we are told that Janie struggles to sense her own worth, because she never finds a good example to inspire her: 'She didn't read books so she didn't know that she was the world and the heavens boiled down to a drop.'

10 May

It is clear that Eliot is a little in love with Romola herself: 'her hair* was of a reddish gold colour, enriched by an unbroken small ripple, such as may be seen in the sunset clouds on grandest autumnal evenings'; 'her radiant beauty, made so loveably mortal by her soft hazel eyes'. But this ethereal beauty is also, to an extent, a religious zealot: she supports the rise of Savonarola, the preacher who burns books and has bands of people marching the streets, like ISIS thugs, 'wearing a garb which concealed the whole head and face except the eyes', demanding that women remove jewellery and cosmetics. Romola does not exactly approve of this, but her 'life had given her an affinity for sadness which inevitably made her unjust towards merriment'. This child of a scholar and book collector sees no evil in a conflagration of paper in the streets of Florence.

Historical fiction is, inevitably, always about the present. And Eliot – unmarried at the time, surrounded by examples of the unhappily wed – is especially acute about the imbalance in

---

* The novel goes on, at almost perverse length, about the 'rippling gold' of her hair. Which makes the choice of a dark-haired woman for the cover of my Penguin Classic especially infuriating. Read the fucking book you are publishing!

power between men and women,* and the colourless sadness of an unhappy marriage. Romola ends up nursing 'her bruised, despairing love' for Tito, from whom she cannot publicly break: 'She was thrown back again on the conflict between the demands of an outward law, which she recognised as a widely-ramifying obligation, and the demands of inner moral facts which were becoming more and more peremptory.' That is a Victorian preoccupation as much as a Renaissance one.

12 May

A friend† of mine is struggling to finish a book, *The Grapes of Wrath* (1939) by Steinbeck: 'It's so long; it just feels like an effort to get through it.' As I have been struggling with the small-print heft of *Romola*, I do feel a pang of empathy. It is a legitimate question: should you persist with books you've stopped enjoying?

The answer must be no, mustn't it? Life is not preparation for a test, reading is not a chore or a series of repetitions at a gym. And yet I reckon many of you – as has happened to me, although less so these days – have doughtily ploughed on with a demoralising novel simply in order to finish it. The case for such self-evident futility is, I suppose, that you may find some local joy in a later sentence, page or character that makes the prior effort worthwhile.

In a world of fleeting concentration, the bleeps and blurts of ubiquitous technology, I wonder if there is merit in the sort of mental conditioning that unrewarding reading can bring. Perhaps there is. I failed to finish *Moby Dick* when I was younger,

---

* Eliot was not exactly a proto-feminist throughout her life. 'Woman,' she once wrote, 'does not yet deserve a better lot than man gives her.'
† All right, colleague.

but happily returned to it (almost exactly) twenty years later: the book hadn't changed; I had. I try this morning to recall books that defeated me, or which I had failed, or which were just not working at that time in my life: *The Golden Bowl* (1904) by Henry James; *Gravity's Rainbow* (1973) by Thomas Pynchon; *The Island of the Day Before* (1994) by Umberto Eco; *Atlas Shrugged* (1957) by Ayn Rand. There will be many more.

So if you are flagging with this book now, do not worry. Put it aside for a while, you may come back to it, or not. Duty is the enemy of pleasure, I reckon.* And if you don't want to take my word for it, think of that great reader, Samuel Johnson, who had this exchange with his friend James Elphinston:

> ELPHINSTON: What, have you not read it through?
> JOHNSON: No, Sir, do *you* read books *through*?

13 May

Tito's status as a villain in *Romola* is a modest one: his behaviour is too comprehensible, and he is prey to larger forces beyond his control. Eliot is good at insinuating his creepy softness, but – as things go – a hangdog and handsome desire to be liked is not the worst trait ever committed to paper. Eliot is acute on how such a man might be drawn into bad behaviour, insidiously, almost blamelessly: 'His dread generated no active malignity, and he would still have been glad not to give pain to any mortal. He had simply chosen to make life easy to himself – to carry his human lot, if possible, in such a way that it should pinch him nowhere; and the choice had, at various times, landed him in unexpected positions.'

---

* As it happens, there's some really good stuff to come, so you might want to hold on for a bit longer.

Tito manages both to commit his father to a life of brutal slavery, while maintaining a 'native repugnance to sights of death and pain'. He is a hypocrite, but one whose actions are understandable, even when they cause distress to others. When we learn 'at that moment he would have been capable of treading the breath from a smiling child for the sake of his own safety' we realise that this attractive intellectual is capable of real evil, even if the novel does not show him committing it. I like that ambivalence, that refusal to be cartoonishly extravagant in the moulding of a villain. It all contributes to the quietness of the novel as a whole.

But who *is* the worst villain in literature? As I am reading Victorian fiction, I think instantly of Gilbert Osmond, the creepy husband of Isabel Archer in *The Portrait of a Lady*. He is wilfully cruel, and also splendidly camp in that spindly cruelty: he collects tiny, pristine pots and *bibelots*, can circle his entire ankle between forefinger and thumb, like a grinning, art-loving skeleton.

Mrs Danvers from *Rebecca*, we know, brings a certain camp to her meanness as well, which I think helps in any memorable villain. Uriah Heep from *David Copperfield* (1850) is physically repellent, as if his moral malaise has stripped away his comforting flesh: he 'had hardly any eyebrows, and no eyelashes, and eyes of a red-brown, so unsheltered and unshaded, that I remember wondering how he went to sleep. He was high-shouldered and bony; dressed in decent black, with a white wisp of a neckcloth; buttoned up to the throat; and had a long, lank, skeleton hand.'

We've seen Aaron and his wilful, gratuitous cruelty in *Titus Andronicus*, a tendency shared by Lady Macbeth. Who could forget this moment, when she is urging her husband to murder?

> I have given suck, and know
> How tender 'tis to love the babe that milks me:
> I would, while it was smiling in my face,
> Have plucked my nipple from his boneless gums,
> And dashed the brains out, had I so sworn as you
> Have done to this.

I quickly realise that this is an impossible game to play: names crowd into my mind effortlessly. Patrick Bateman, the amoral American Psycho of Bret Easton Ellis's novel, so convincing in the banality of his evil that many dim-witted male readers regard him as an anti-hero. Or Humbert Humbert, literature's most notorious paedophile and narrator of *Lolita* (1955), who says things like this, eyes glinting: 'I have all the characteristics which, according to writers on the sex interests of children, start the responses stirring in a little girl: clean-cut jaw, muscular hand, deep sonorous voice, broad shoulder.'

Great villains have to have charm to make them plausible, perhaps: Satan in Milton's *Paradise Lost* (1667), or his distant cousin, the devilish Woland in Bulgakov's *The Master and Margarita* (1967). We have to be tempted by the devil's party, at least, to understand the peril they pose. Tito is charming, but ultimately not devilish enough: stealing a library – even to someone like me, who is on his thirty-something thousandth word on the subject of books – doesn't sneak him into the pantheon of evil.

15 May

The Arts Council has said that funding should go to projects that can demonstrate 'relevance' as a virtue, and ahead of, say, excellence, as a trumping priority. It is a watchword of the age, and comes – I think – from a legitimate train of thought. To be 'relevant' is, at its most generous interpretation, to be worth experiencing, to make sense in a modern age, to speak loudly and concordantly with the time.

Plus, a salutary further question is always required: relevant to whom? So much art has been the preserve of cultural elites, those with the education or encouragement to take part in certain types of artistic endeavour. If art is to be relevant, it should be relevant for everybody, and should not exclude people either tacitly or openly.

But we can see the danger here: much unsubtlety can be achieved in the service of relevance. The other day, I saw a novelist go on a morning TV show to argue that Shakespeare wasn't relevant, because he wrote in difficult language and not about things that matter to young people today. To which the obvious point is this: excellence is always relevant, beauty is always relevant. And some things are universal: love, hate, revenge, death, jealousy, anxiety. They never fade from our collective being.

There is a point about difficulty, though. I don't find Shakespeare difficult because I have read him for a long time, and was taught – at least in a rudimentary fashion – how to read him at school. But I now spend a chunk of existence attending cultural events that would otherwise intimidate me, especially opera and ballet. I feel I don't know how to appreciate them properly because I have never been given the tools to do so. I am learning now, because I have to. How much more could I have enjoyed, how much more could have felt relevant to me, if I had known more?

16 May

Where *Romola* flags is in its relentless fixation upon Florentine politics (what we might call Eliot's 'most ardent care for veracity' problem). This is a chronicle not of passionate people, but of 'certain grand political and social conditions which made an epoch in the history of Italy'. The pace does quicken in the second half* as tensions within the city come to a head, and the arrival of Baldassarre brings with it a satisfying blast of melodrama. He is a revenger in the mould of a Dumas novel ('I am not alone in the world; I shall never be alone, for my revenge is with me'), and becomes something of a tragic figure: dementia is striking him and he struggles to articulate his case against Tito or persist in a city that no longer understands him:

> He was a shattered, bewildered, lonely old man; yet he desired to live: he waited for something of which he had no distinct vision – something dim, formless – that startled him, and made strong pulsations within him, like that unknown thing which we look for when we start from sleep, though no voice or touch has waked us. Baldassarre desired to live; and therefore he crept out in the grey light, and seated himself in the long grass, and watched the waters that had a faint promise in them.

This is moving, and beautiful. At its best, *Romola* captures those twilit moments of the human soul, the grey light of our uncertainty. Indeed it is a novel set in a sort of constant dusk: its heroine 'soothed by the gloom which seemed to cover her like a mourning garment and shut out the discord of joy'. Sadly, Romola disappears from the novel for about a hundred pages, while Eliot focuses on the politics of Florence and the travails of Savonarola. Her account of his character is deft and complex, but perhaps explains the novel's overall lack of forcefulness:

> A consciousness in which irrevocable errors and lapses from veracity were so entwined with noble purposes and sincere

---

* A marginal note on my book reads: 'finally some fucking plot!' about 200 pages in.

beliefs, in which self-justifying expediency was so inwoven with the tissue of a great work which the whole being seemed as unable to abandon as the body was unable to abandon glowing and trembling before the objects of hope and fear, that it was perhaps impossible, whatever course might be adopted, for the conscience to find perfect repose.

You probably have to read that sentence twice, if you ever manage to read it once. Did the world need this conscientious account of a fifteenth-century consciousness? Perhaps not. But I am glad still to have read it.

18 May

Historical fiction feeds our desire to experience otherness, the L.P. Hartley view that 'The past is a foreign country: they do things differently there.' Fredric Jameson called it a 'craving for historicity', and I certainly feel it. I want the novel to make me feel part of another landscape for a while, to transport me.

The publishing industry that has grown up to service these needs can often do it very badly. Elmore Leonard has a character that refers to historical fiction as 'full of rapes and adverbs', and we have all read books that flounce along with too much colourful description, the plot given cheap energy by the threat of bloody or sexual violence.

Bad historical fiction also often sniffs the rank air of the period too deeply. There is an oversimplified equation in an author's mind: the past did cleanliness and sewerage differently, so I better reflect that constantly; history equals stench. An over-reliance on the contingent look and feel of a period is normally a sign of an imagination struggling to inhabit it in other respects. Weather often helps too. Historical novels – as with actual history books – set in the Middle Ages tend to begin with a rainy or windswept scene. Novels set in the classical world give you an early blast of arid heat. I pick up a book on the *TLS* table this morning, Conn Iggulden's latest, *The Falcon of Sparta* (which is a perfectly enjoyable novel, by the way; I end up reading it all later), and sure enough this is the first line: 'In Babylon, starlings gaped in the heat, showing dark tongues.* Beyond vast city walls, the sun leaned on those who laboured in the fields, pressing them down.'

But even this gives me the tingle of being transported, I think. Mary Renault is considered as *elevated* historical fiction, if that means anything, the sort of genre writing that people who like proper literature also like. She joins the ranks of Robert Graves, Patrick O'Brian and Gore Vidal in that respect: who produce books you can both savour and consume in a greedy gulp.

19 May

I have just been writing about smells, and then pick up a historical novel in a charity shop† that reeks for good reason. Its title is *Retribution Road* by a French novelist called Antonin Varenne (translated by Sam Taylor), and is set partially in the London of the Great Stink of 1858. That was a summer of horrific heat that made life in the capital unbearable, such was the stench of human waste sitting untreated in the streets and pouring into the Thames.

---

* This prompted a very specific Google search from me: 'Do birds have tongues?' And, yes, they do. You can see a starling's tongue when it opens its mouth. Don't say you never learned anything from this book.

† One of the great pleasures in life – and I am being serious here – is discovering previously unknown books in charity shops. It is allowing serendipity into your reading, grabbing something by chance and being surprised. I owe my fondness for Gore Vidal to Oxfam: I bought *Lincoln* (1984) randomly in my early twenties, and went on to read almost everything he ever wrote.

This was one of the lines in a local paper: 'We can colonise the remotest ends of the earth; we can conquer India; we can pay the interest of the most enormous debt ever contracted; we can spread our name, and our fame, and our fructifying wealth to every part of the world; but we cannot clean the River Thames.'

Varenne uses this roiling, rancid city as the backdrop to a sergeant returned from Burma, where he has been horribly tortured as a prisoner of war. The filth of London continually reminds him of the disgusting conditions in which he had been kept, and prevents him from recovering.

In real life, it took the actions of an engineer, Joseph Bazalgette, supported by the legislation of Benjamin Disraeli (then Chancellor), to begin a process of sewerage and environmental improvements. Thus, when politicians cannot leave their houses without gagging, things eventually do change. As things currently stand, London is a vast cauldron of polluted air once more: is there a catalyst coming?

We ran a review of Rosemary Ashton's book on the Stink in the *TLS*, which features figures like Dickens and, happily, Darwin: thus giving me the irresistible headline, 'On the origin of faeces'. I'm here all week.

22 May

Mary Renault's *The King Must Die* is a fine imaginative achievement. It takes us to the heat of the Greek plains 'among thyme and heath and smoothed gray boulders, rain-scoured and hot with sun, where lizards basked and darted' and its tumultuous coast, 'the very stones, which twinkle with sparks like silver, seem to flash and glitter under the kiss of the god. Water and air are clear as crystal.' In 1950s Britain, a land of recent rationing and damp, narrowness and exhaustion, this must have been an intravenous hit of summer.

Renault had already escaped the post-war drear of her home country. In 1947 she won the startling prize of $150,000 from the movie studio MGM for her novel *Return to the Night*, and moved to South Africa almost on a whim 'in a burst of released claustrophobia after that dreadful winter when it froze for three months and there was no heating and we couldn't find anywhere to live'. Renault was already a novelist, writing contemporary fiction that was light and artful, but it took her move to another country to send her imagination racing back to the past.

The classical world also offered a place in which homosexuality could be described without apologetic glossing or self-conscious wriggling.* Renault – like Daphne du Maurier – wished she could have been a boy; she once said, 'I think a lot of people are intermediately sexed.' And, like du Maurier, 'boyishness' in her fiction is often synonymous with attractiveness, especially when used to describe a woman. Unlike du Maurier, Renault was out, living with her partner Julie Mullard, a young nurse she had met in the war. But she was not a campaigner for gay rights in any sense: 'defensive stridency is not, on the whole, much more attractive than self-pity,' she once noted, terming gay rights a lot of 'needless bellyaching and fuss' about something that was merely a 'slight deviation of the sexual urge'.

The King Must Die has gay characters, but the issue is dealt with briskly and without extraneous dwelling: 'As for the girls, they made do with one another, so old a custom that no one questioned it.' Or: 'Everyone knows there is a good deal of this among the Minyans; and one cannot wonder . . . I see no sense in looking down on this; most customs have a reason; even among Hellenes, in a long war where girls are scarce and the leaders are

---

* It is striking that Renault's exact contemporary, Marguerite Yourcenar, was another lesbian novelist who became known, with *Memoirs of Hadrian* (1951), for her classical settings.

first served, the young men's friendships grow tenderer than they were.'

This is perhaps why Renault's books became so inspirational to gay people: they were matter-of-fact about an issue that was treated so often with either coded periphrasis or moralistic hysteria. And this approach points to another strength in *The King Must Die*: it is a text of demythologisation, an essay in bringing the weight of lived experience to something often treated as exceptional. It tells the tale of Theseus, a young man in search of his destiny, who believed he was the son of Poseidon, but was in fact the illegitimate child of the King of Athens. This is Renault talking about him: 'A well-defined personality emerges. It is that of a light-weight; brave and aggressive, physically tough and quick; highly sexed and rather promiscuous; touchily proud, but with a feeling for the underdog; resembling Alexander in his precocious competence, gift of leadership, and romantic sense of destiny.'

She also made him short, which she felt was key to his 'touchy' ambitions, and kept him from straying into the boringly heroic. The book gives us the Theseus tale, but in a plausible, naturalistic setting. So the Minotaur is not a savage monster, but the mean-spirited son of King Minos; the Athenian youths are made to become 'bull-dancers' or fighters at the Cretan court, not simple sacrifices to a fantastic creature; the Labyrinth is the winding centre of the city of Knossos, which Ariadne helps Theseus navigate by the use of a thread. This is myth based on archaeology,* not epic.

And yet your tolerance for the novel will depend on how much you like writing that does drift towards the poetic, and the

---

* Renault visited the excavations of Sir Arthur Evans in Crete in 1964 and said: 'The sight winded me like a blow in the belly . . . I feel like a goatherd who comes in from the back hills and sees his first city.'

Attic. There are references to 'Herakles, Zeus-begot in a three-fold night', and people say things like 'Greeting, Lady, in the name of whatever god or goddess is honoured here above the rest. For I think you serve a powerful deity, to whom a traveller ought to pay some homage or other, before he passes by.' I occasionally wince at a bit of over-ripe, choric prose ('the black oak soil, rich with the scents of spring, drank down my tears into the fallen leaves of ages'), but this approach does allow Renault to be unashamedly poetic too.

She is deft in her metaphorical description: 'Moonlight lay on the strait, and a night bird called, soft and bubbling, like water from a narrow jar.' That 'narrow' is a nice touch, responding to how sound is changed by the size of the vessel. Renault is sensitive to small tremblings: 'A secret so long kept is like a lyre-string stretched near breaking, which a feather will sound, or a breath of air.' That image gets picked up later, the note returning anew: 'Always drawn between us was a tight-wound lute string that never snapped, yet never slackened; and, brushed or breathed upon, filled the air between with its secret sound.'

When you are reading on a train, as part of your daily routine, something that is evocative like this is especially effective. There is sensuality throughout, especially towards female characters. Ariadne is minutely examined, as she might well be by a 'lusty' figure like Theseus: 'her hair was fine and dark, with a soft burnish on it; a curling lock had fallen down over her breast; I could see tiny creases in the gilded nipple.' There is that sense of boyishness again: 'like a field lily, upright and small, round breast and thighs, a waist to snap in your fingers'.

25 May

I have enjoyed writing a diary of reading, and today something made me think about the reading of diaries. Elton John revealed in a newspaper that he once wrote this as a journal entry: 'Woke up, watched *Grandstand*. Wrote "Candle in the Wind". Went to London, bought Rolls-Royce. Ringo Starr came for dinner.'

It reminds me of this one from Tolstoy on 25 January 1851: 'I've fallen in love or imagine that I have; went to a party and lost my head. Bought a horse which I don't need at all.' What a line that is. This was Kafka on 2 August 1914: 'Germany has declared war on Russia. Went swimming in the afternoon.' Diaries, after all, record both the banal and the earth-shattering, the sublime and the ridiculous. As Richard Burton noted in November 1969: 'Prince Rainer and Grace are coming to lunch today and Rainer is bringing either a tiger or a panther as a present for E.* What the hell are we going to do with a PANTHER or a TIGER?' Good question. Here is the racing driver Stirling Moss after a colossal car crash: 'Shunt. Back. Legs. Nose. Bruises. Bugger.'

Hemingway started a diary at the age of nine, and his style was already becoming fixed into place: 'My name is Ernest Miller Hemingway I was born on July 21 1899. My favourite authors are Kipling, O. Henry and Stuart Edward White. My favourite flower is Lady Slipper and Tiger Lily. My favourite sports are Trout fishing, Hiking, shooting, football and boxing. My favourite studies are English, Zoology and Chemistry. I intend to travel and write.'

I love that self-assured final sentence. My mind also flits to Pepys (his burying of Parmesan cheese to escape the Great Fire of London; his flirtations and abusive relationships;† his feeling-up of a 'monstrous fat' woman), and the other great diarist of world literature, Adrian Mole. I was a child in 1980s Leicestershire,

---

* That's the actress Elizabeth Taylor for those under forty.
† We had a piece in the *TLS*, with the headline 'Samuel creeps', which began: 'Samuel Pepys was a serial sexual assaulter.'

fond of books, riddled with self-doubt, and Sue Townsend's creation was like a malign alter ego, both funny and sad.

28 May

The much-criticised Edward Bulwer-Lytton argued for the relevance of historical fiction by noting that 'the affections are immortal'. Human beings love, hate, fight, fuck, fear, betray, live and die in the same way, whatever their setting. And there is something in that. But there is a layer of estrangement in a text set in the ancient world that is both limiting and enlivening: a chance to embrace both sameness and difference. *The King Must Die* is a museum piece, an elaborately wrought tribute to the past; but there is just enough throbbing of life to make it matter today.

29 May

The rest of the month is a holiday by the sea in Sussex. I take *Jaws* to reread for a marine flavour,* along with an early copy of Lee Child's new Reacher novel, some John Buchan, and a book about nineteenth-century pragmatist philosophers. We read as a family while Phoebe naps, four of us sprawled in ungainly positions, preoccupied. Family reading is a lovely thing to do, I think.

~

* I do love contextual reading, where my location matches that of the book. I used to live by the Thames in London, and read *Our Mutual Friend* (1865), the last (and greatest) full novel by Dickens, one wet, cold winter. The rain pummelling the choppy waters outside my bedroom was a happy companion to my imagination, as I followed Dickens into the murky waterways of the capital.

Further Reading

Ivanhoe (1819) by Walter Scott
A Tale of Two Cities (1859) by Charles Dickens
Les Misérables (1862) by Victor Hugo
War and Peace (1869) by Leo Tolstoy
I Claudius (1934) by Robert Graves
The Launching of Roger Brook (1947) by Dennis Wheatley
The Corner That Held Them (1948) by Sylvia Townsend Warner
The Man on a Donkey (1952) by H.F.M. Prescott
The Cornerstone (1953) by Zoé Oldenbourg
The Iron King (1955) by Maurice Druon
The Game of Kings (1961) by Dorothy Dunnett
Master and Commander (1969) by Patrick O'Brian
Earthly Powers (1980) by Anthony Burgess
The Name of the Rose (1980) by Umberto Eco
Sharpe's Eagle (1981) by Bernard Cornwell
Lincoln (1984) by Gore Vidal
The Pillars of the Earth (1989) by Ken Follett
The Silver Pigs (1989) by Lindsey Davis
The Alienist (1994) by Caleb Carr
The March (2005) by E.L. Doctorow
Wolf Hall (2009) by Hilary Mantel
The Underground Railroad (2016) by Colson Whitehead

SUMMER

June

Plays That Aren't by Shakespeare

Iphigenia in Aulis (*c*.407 BC) by Euripides
The Rover (1677) by Aphra Benn
The Importance of Being Earnest (1895) by Oscar Wilde
Waiting for Godot (1953) by Samuel Beckett
Top Girls (1982) by Caryl Churchill

2 June

In my third year at university, I had to take a three-hour exam on the subject of tragedy, the form of drama established by the Greeks and then shaped, transformed and translated ever since. One of the questions was this: 'Tragedy: when you lose control and you got no soul, it's tragedy – discuss how this applies to the theory of the form as a whole', referencing a song by the Bee Gees (and then the Abba-lite band Steps). I didn't write an essay on it, and moved on to another question. But some enterprising soul taking the exam did the correct thing: put their pen down, left the examination room, and telephoned the *Daily Mail*, which duly ran a 'Cambridge dumbing down' screech of an article, saddened by yet another example of civilisation collapsing around us. The *Guardian* retorted with a po-faced intellectual symposium from literary types discussing the quotation seriously. I was oblivious to all of it.

All this goes to show, though, that our concept of the tragic is all-pervasive, and this theatrical form – invented in the fifth century BC as a religious rite of sorts – still speaks directly to all of us, including the Bee Gees.

We talked about this a bit in the Shakespeare chapter, but the simple idea of a tragedy, from whatever age, is to give some structure to the mindless shriek of grief held within, and to do so without that shriek being muted to the point of incomprehension or magnified to the point of madness. My theory is that all tragedy is effectively a gloss on that one line near the end of *King Lear*: 'The worst is not / So long as we can say "This is the worst."' If we can speak it, frame it, comprehend it, it is within the bounds of human experience, and so something more destructive is always possible. That is what a tragic drama is both exploring and achieving: our ability to take the shapeless bellow of despair and give it some shape that makes it comprehensible. 'To find a form that accommodates the mess,' said Samuel Beckett, 'that is the task of the artist.'

The term 'tragedy' has more earthy origins: '*tragoida*' in Greek meant 'goat-song'. It is disputed, but the etymology is probably connected to the fact that tragedies were performed in Greece in competitions for which the prize was a goat.* We do know that they began as ritualised, religious experiences: chants and tales performed for the benefit of the community. There are three of these early Greek tragedians whose work has survived: the grandfather of the medium, Aeschylus; his successor, and elaborator, Sophocles, who probably added the idea of having three actors; and the firebrand who followed them both, Euripides.

---

* Alternatively, there may have been a sacrifice of a goat as part of the ritual. Or maybe it has nothing to do with goats at all. This all happened a long time ago.

Euripides, by unwitting chance, has left us the most plays out of all the Greeks: nineteen of them. He is the most modern of ancient playwrights, but perhaps the least popular in his day. Some of this is down to his risk-taking: he was an associate of Socrates, the philosopher who was executed for his intellectual decadence. Euripides probably accepted exile instead, but he seems to have ruffled the same feathers through his refusal to crook the knee to religious orthodoxy. He is one of the most notable literary atheists, an exposer of the snake-oil of soothsayers, and a doubter of the practical existence of the deities he is writing about.

We can talk about the popularity of each man with some confidence because play writing was one of the competitive sports of the ancient world: every year at the City Dionysia festival, each man would stage four plays (three tragedies and a strange comic thing called a satyr play) and be judged. Aeschylus won thirteen times, Sophocles twenty times and Euripides just five.

It was Aeschylus who really began, most likely, the shift from drama as religious rite to drama as source of exciting plot. He was a war hero,[*] who fought the Persians at Salamis and Marathon, and even wrote a play about the contemporary conflict. He also wrote the first narrative trilogy, the *Oresteia*, telling the murderous tale of the Trojan War and its impact on the family of Agamemnon and Clytemnestra.

That story is the context for my first play this month, *Iphigenia in Aulis*, which was performed just after Euripides' death in 407 BC, and posthumously won him his fifth prize. Everybody

---

[*] His grave does not even mention his writing, just his fighting. The legend that he died when an eagle dropped a tortoise on his bald head, thinking it was a rock, seems inevitably to be untrue.

watching this back then knew the story, already a common tale that had been dramatised by Aeschylus within living memory. So no spoiler alerts are necessary: King Agamemnon, leading the Greek army to snatch back Helen from Troy on behalf of his brother Menelaus (her angry husband), is advised to sacrifice his daughter, Iphigenia, in order to propitiate the gods and enable the fleet to sail. In doing so, he will set in train a whole series of bloody events: Clytemnestra, his wife, will take a lover in his absence and then murder her husband on his return; his son Orestes will then murder his own mother in revenge, and be pursued by madness (embodied by creatures called the Furies) until a jury trial in Athens finds his actions justified. You are supposed to know this before you start, because it allows Euripides to play with the dramatic ironies and also examine some of the received pieces of wisdom.

At one level, the tale of the *Oresteia* is one of women being violently silenced, endangered by a patriarchal world that – in the form of Athenian courts – then is allowed to forgive itself. Euripides is more nuanced than that. *Iphigenia in Aulis* is a play about power politics, its inescapable corruption; a play about unjust wars that sacrifice the innocent to no purpose. We know at the beginning that the Trojan War will be bloody and long; we know that families will be destroyed by it; we know it was brought about by a combination of hubris, pride, manly swaggering and contempt for human life. The modern parallels are obvious.

7 June

I regard *Iphigenia in Aulis* as Sorkinesque political drama. Euripides was master of a technique (which you see all the time in slick American shows) called stichomythia: single lines each spoken by different people at machine-gun speed. He was also fascinated by the grubby reality of leadership, where grasping desires meet inadequate performance. This is Menelaus describing how Agamemnon lobbied for command of the army:

> Do you remember how humble
> You were to all the people, grasping the hand
> Keeping open the doors of your house, yes,
> Open to all, granting to every man, even the lowly
> The right to address and hail you by name.

The Greek army is a grand coalition; it is filled with male egos like Agamemnon and Menelaus, Odysseus and Achilles, all of whom are seeking reputation and success at any cost. And the cost to Agamemnon may be his daughter, Iphigenia. Having been told by a soothsayer he must sacrifice her, he summons her to the camp with a fake promise of marriage to Achilles, and then he is caught in the bind: if he refuses to kill her, the army will turn on him; he has made a public promise he is compelled to keep, 'a compulsion absolute / now works the slaughter of the child'.

This is acute political commentary. Euripides notes that 'decorum rules our lives and we, by service / To the mob, become its slaves': leaders in thrall to powerful backers are not in a position of authority at all.* Much of the play is an examination of arguments about ethical action or moral absolutes. Propositions are tested all the time: military action is a reasonable response to a question of honour; it is wrong for a personal quarrel to shed the blood of others; a child should be protected by her father at all costs; sacrifice is at the heart of all war; it is always wrong to kill your children.

Amid all this is the tragic figure of Iphigenia, at once loving to her dad ('Oh turn away from all of them, / My father – be

---

* Compare, in happier circumstances, the hapless Jim Hacker in *Yes, Prime Minister*: 'It's the people's will. I am their leader; I must follow them.'

here and mine only, now'), noble in her thoughts about sacrifice, and crushingly realistic too:

> Men are mad, I say, who pray for death;
> It is better that we live ever so
> Miserably than die in glory.

It is impossible not to feel the dry-throat choke of sorrow when she clings to her mother, briefly, before facing her death, the shortening of her years, the removal of possibilities:

> These things coming to pass, Mother, will be
> A remembrance for you. They will be
> My children, my marriage; through the years
> My good name and my glory.

I feel the gooseflesh shudder of sympathy today, and am filled with admiration for words, translated in slightly effortful poetry, that can move me like this from across two millennia.

10 June

The ending of *Iphigenia* has been the subject of much tinkering and dispute. The original version is brutal; we hear of her summary dispatch, after all those fine words of dispute finally come to bloody quietus:

> Where she shall drip
> With streams of flowing blood
> And die,
> Her body's lovely neck
> Slashed with sword and to death.

But another version exists, probably written years after Euripides' death. In it, a messenger arrives to report 'a thing of awe and wonder', that the goddess Artemis switched Iphigenia for a deer at the last minute and so saved her life. Although Euripides did not write this version, he had actually conceived of it in an earlier play, *Iphigenia Among the Taurians* (*c*.414 BC), in which this very plot-line played out. There, she is living on the shores of the Black Sea, being compelled to perform human sacrifice as press-ganged priestess, before being rescued by her brother, Orestes.*

I think about endings this month, because there are lots of moans about the conclusion of *Game of Thrones* on television. I don't watch it, because of my wife's restrictive rules for what we can watch together, but cannot escape the cultural moment. Hundreds of thousands of contumacious fans have registered their disapproval of the scripting of the whole final series too, which – in their view – has mishandled some of the character arcs.

Excessive fan engagement with artistic creation is nothing new. When Samuel Richardson's Pamela – in a moment of frankly unsettling sexual politics – finally married the employer who had been continually attempting to assault her, bells were rung in villages across the country. And we all know of the collective grief when Dickens killed Little Nell† in *The Old Curiosity Shop* (1840). Successful characters enter our lives, and we feel we have some sort of proprietary relationship to them.

---

* A good example of a 'tragedy' with a happy ending: Aristotle thought it still achieved the catharsis, the emotional release integral to the drama, because its resolution was so neat.
† Not for Oscar Wilde, who said: 'One must have a heart of stone to read the death of Little Nell without laughing.'

In such circumstances, finding an ending that is meaningful and satisfying can be very difficult. Henry James once said that 'the whole of anything is never told. You can only take what groups together.' Many of his books end in moments of irresolution as a result. Dickens had written *Great Expectations* without a happy ending – 'The winding up will be away from all such things as they conventionally go,' he said – leaving Pip and Estella apart, her in another marriage. But Edward Bulwer-Lytton convinced him to change it to allow the spectre of reconciliation. It ends with Pip saying, 'I saw no shadow of another parting from her', prompting much disagreement and dispute ever since.

Happy endings are one of the joys of fiction to a rank sentimentalist like me: I read often in pursuit of a satisfying resolution, to see – as Austen put it – 'in the tell-tale compression of the pages before them, that we are all hastening together to perfect felicity'. But such contrived felicity can frustrate a sense of realism or artistic coherence. *King Lear* was ruined for centuries by those desperate to have him survive in his dotage, reconciled to Cordelia.

Maybe a book that simply stops is preferable, and more honest. Look at *The Canterbury Tales*: it is supposed to contain two stories from each pilgrim on the way there, and two more on the way back. Some do not even manage one. This was a book designed never to be finished, and the fate of its characters remains ever suspended in our collective imaginations as a result. You think I am going to keep writing until December; you will just have to see if I do.

11 June

The act of *reading* plays on a commute may be heresy to some. Drama, the argument goes, does not exist on the page, but on the stage: plays are written down to be used for performance, not consumed for pleasure like a pared-back novel of well-timed dialogue.

I come from a background of reading voraciously, and attending the theatre only sporadically. I went with my school to a touring performance of *Macbeth* in Nottingham, starring Shakespeare-denier Mark Rylance and Jane Horrocks (who was then especially famous for playing a vacuous PA called Bubbles in *Absolutely Fabulous*). It was atrocious. The setting had been transported to a modern Hare Krishna sect, the witches were three teenage girls dropping Ecstasy, and Lady Macbeth – played by Horrocks more or less as a character from a sitcom – wet herself during the sleepwalking scene.

At the end, the cast came forward for a subdued curtain call, and someone at the back of the theatre shouted with stentorian relish, 'Rubbish! Rip off!' to which Rylance screamed back, without missing a beat, 'Fuck off!' It was so well-timed, I thought (and still think) it was choreographed as a retort to bad reviews. Either way, it was a fitting summary, and more or less a representative description, of my early theatre experience as a whole: overworked Shakespeare; or classical plays, neutered by translation and performed with breast-baring, ululating weirdness.

Since then, especially in the last few years, I have seen some wonderful plays, and quite a lot of clunkers. Last night, I saw *A Midsummer Night's Dream* at the Bridge Theatre next to my office; and the force of the argument for watching Shakespeare in performance was renewed. The play was in the round, and I was one of the groundlings allowed to promenade near the stage, being shoved by actor-security types, manoeuvred around the wood outside Athens. The version was by turns irreverent, silly, arresting, funny, visually astonishing, intensely musical. Even I – for whom karaoke or middle-aged drunken dance-floor thrustings form a version of a personal hell

– looked indulgently upon the final scenes in which the stage disappears and the actors and the audience join together in an impromptu disco.

And yet it was Shakespearean: the carnivalesque chaos, the jokes, the same-sex horseplay. I saw one distinguished critic standing aloof, harrumphing over his paunch and his warm Chablis, but it was impossible for me to be cynical. Plays should be played, of course. But I still took quiet pleasure in the text before and afterwards; I like to think of the words rebounding inside my own head too.

12 June

I move on a few decades from Shakespeare today, and a playwright from the next century. In many ways, the most interesting story from Aphra Behn is the story of Aphra Behn. And yet we do not know confidently that much about her: we do not know who the 'Behn' was whose name she took, only that the marriage does not appear to have been successful; we know she wrote a book about Surinam, *Oroonoko* (1688), but not whether she ever visited it; we do not know where she lived or died, as she appears in no tax records or church records at all. Germaine Greer was surely right to call her 'a palimpsest; she has scratched herself out'.

We do know that she was a spy for Charles II, code-named Astraea, unsuccessful and impoverished. Indeed, government papers are our best record for her existence outside her literary works: she went to Antwerp to convince a man called William Scot to become a double agent for the crown. Her letters to her handlers show that she had no money, and was moving in a world where almost everybody seemed to be spying on everybody else. Her mission ended in failure, and penury may have propelled her to a writerly life. That she succeeded in this is a triumph of talent: she ended her career in the company of the great literary figures of her age (such as Dryden), even if she was never truly able to make ends meet.

To Virginia Woolf she was a heroine, a critical figure in the rise of women's literature. This is from *A Room of One's Own* (1929): 'All women together ought to let flowers fall upon the tomb of Aphra Behn which is, most scandalously but rather appropriately, in Westminster Abbey, for it was she who earned them the right to speak their minds.'

That tomb has this rather fun epitaph:* 'Here lies a Proof that Wit can never be Defence enough against Mortality'. Her wit, though, was best displayed in *The Rover*, her most successful play. Behn was writing in the time of the Restoration, in which the Puritan suppression of theatricals had been reversed and licence once more granted to playwrights. In this world, comedies could become more raunchy, more risqué, and female parts were played, for the first time, by female actors. Such riot did not last long: the Glorious Revolution of 1688 brought in two humourless Protestants to the throne, and a new moralism reigned in the theatre.

13 June

Today, *The Rover* could be happily recast in a place like Ibiza or on the set of *Love Island*: young men and women, intoxicated by their own sense of sexual promise, running amok around a town in which rules no longer apply. For Ibiza, though, read seventeenth-century Naples during a festival of masked revelry, in which people can get up to no good with anonymity. The plot revolves around the serious courtship of Florinda by Belvile, an

---

* Up there with Spike Milligan's 'I told you I was sick', perhaps. Or Rodney Dangerfield's 'There goes the neighbourhood'.

English colonel, in the teeth of her presumed marriage to Antonio, the viceroy's son. Belvile's companions, in this 'lads on tour' scenario, are very much seeking their own pleasure, especially Willmore, the eponymous 'rover'.

For rover, read 'shagger', or – in the words of the play – 'a shameroon, a very beggar; nay, a pirate-beggar, whose business is to rifle and be gone, a no-purchase, no-pay tatterdemalion, an English picaroon; a rogue that fights for daily drink, and takes a pride in being loyally lousy.'* He is a 'mad fellow for a wench', someone who wants 'all the honey of matrimony, but none of the sting', quite the nicest metaphor for adultery I have ever read.

Among his many attempted exploits, Willmore falls for the true star of the show: Hellena. She is very much Behn's innovation, a sassy and witty figure in control of her own sexual destiny. In fact, she may be one of the earliest characters in theatre truly to give voice to a woman's desire, and to be allowed a recognisably female gaze. She is cynical about marriage imposed upon her: 'What shall I get? A cradle full of noise and mischief, with a pack of repentance at my back?' And sardonic about her alternative future as a member of a religious community, which she refuses to accept: 'I should have stayed in the nunnery still, if I had liked my Lady Abbess as well as she liked me.' We cannot help but feel, like Willmore, that she 'hast one virtue I adore: good nature'. She, on the other hand, knows she has fallen for someone rather inappropriate: 'how his unconstant humour makes me love him'. Behn seemed to have a soft spot for a bad boy, too.

* And yes, I am getting this put on a business card.

16 June

The Rover shows the sexual politics of the age with unflinching clarity. Rape is a legitimate tool of the powerful, a daily threat to women. The blustering, buffoonish Blunt is robbed by a sex worker, and falls into a 'common-shore' or sewer, leading him to threaten to rape any woman in revenge. His only concern is the propriety of status, and fear of arrest: 'It would anger us vilely to be trussed up for a rape upon a maid of quality, when we only believe we ruffle a harlot.'

What all this reveals is a play that speaks to our age, but is not representative of our thinking. Behn is deft, and funny, in conveying the struggles between men and women to find mutually acceptable fates; and she is determined also to dramatise the sort of unequal power dynamic that can still be allowed to persist. The play gets its happy ending, but with Willmore and Hellena entering into a marriage that neither can entirely guarantee will be always content:

> Lead on, no other dangers they can dread,
> Who venture in the storms o'th' marriage bed.

Throughout, there is a spirit of cynicism, and I feel enlivened by it each morning. Indeed, Behn looks ahead to someone like Oscar Wilde and his comedies of sparring couples, which is a happy coincidence, because that is where my next journey will take me.

18 June

I am experiencing Oscar Wilde on the way to preparing a bit of the paper that commemorates fifty years since the Stonewall riots in New York. I didn't know anything about them, or the fact that they gave the name to the charity Stonewall. The

Stonewall Inn was a place, owned by the Mafia, in the Greenwich Village area of New York, a hang-out for the especially indigent and marginalised members of the nascent gay community. It was semi-tolerated by police, who were well bribed, and conducted raids almost by appointment and early enough in the evening not to ruin business. But late one night in June 1969 they burst in unannounced, turning the lights on and exposing everyone to what might be a lifetime of notoriety. The response, unplanned, was to fight back, which led to the police being barricaded inside the inn, nights of rioting, and a general sense that gay rights could now join civil rights as a touchstone of the age.

When I was growing up in the 1980s in a provincial town in England, there was little discussion of homosexuality. My parents had probably never met an out gay person in their lives. The sight of men kissing on television, a rarity in itself, would lead to channels being flipped in embarrassment. The lesson was that people somewhere (not here) might be gay, but it was not to be talked about.

There was not much homosexuality in the books I read either. I remember it in *Brideshead Revisited*, and when I read Edmund White's *A Boy's Own Story* (1982), squirming in unfamiliar discomfort at his frank account of 'cornholing' with his friend. Now I feel more aware of a gay pantheon of books: *Orlando* (1928) by Virginia Woolf, with its trans hero(ine) based on her lover Vita Sackville-West; *Giovanni's Room* (1956) by James Baldwin; *Rubyfruit Jungle** (1973) by Rita Mae Brown; *The Well of Loneliness* (1928) by Radclyffe Hall; and so on, and on.

That last book was banned on the basis that it 'would induce thoughts of a most impure character and would glorify the

---

* Perhaps the most prominent novel to be named after a metaphor for female genitalia.

horrible tendency of lesbianism'. When the ban was appealed against, the jury were not allowed even to read the novel, so perilous was it to their souls. It all seems so pathetically laughable now.

At the moment on Netflix there is a new series of *Tales of the City* by Armistead Maupin. This began as a serialised novel in the *San Francisco Chronicle* in the 1970s. Maupin has told how the paper's beleaguered managing editor kept a wall chart with two columns, one headed 'heterosexual', the other 'homosexual'. The rule was that at no time should the gay characters number more than a third of the total population of the fiction. Maupin responded by writing a section in which a male Great Dane humped one of his female character's legs, and insisted that it be counted in the hetero column. When the show became a TV series on Channel 4 in 1993 (I was thirteen: it passed my insulated world by completely), it was considered racy and daring. The new version is gentle in its queer storytelling, unopposed by any angst.

It really is striking how the discourse around gay life has changed.* I spend quite a bit of time with my children watching films from my own childhood I fondly like to imagine they will enjoy.† And I am endlessly struck by the references to, the hateful asides about, 'fags' and 'faggots', the assumption of their basic shamefulness. My children don't even notice it; the words and

---

* Another interesting fact here, according to the comedy show *QI*: until 1979 in Sweden, homosexuality was classified as a mental illness, and so campaigners used to call in and say they were 'too gay to work'.

† I'm talking classics like *Crocodile Dundee*, *Teen Wolf*, *Bill and Ted's Excellent Adventure*, *Back to the Future* and the like. My favourite line in all of them comes from the coach in *Teen Wolf*, who offers this piece of life advice: 'Never get less than twelve hours' sleep. Never play cards with a guy who's got the same first name as a city. And never go near a lady who's got a tattoo of a dagger on her body. Stick with that, everything else is cream cheese.'

the politics pass them by because they are so foreign, and illogical, to them. They know other pupils with two mums or two dads, and it is a mild difference soon forgotten amid the tumult of life.

19 June

It is a cliché to note the sheer modernity of Oscar Wilde, and has been for many years. This is Richard Ellman, his biographer in 1987, setting the tone for much of the ready appreciation towards him: 'He belongs to our world more than Victoria's now. Beyond the reach of a scandal, his best writings validated by time, he comes before us still, a towering figure, laughing and weeping, with parables and paradoxes, so generous, so amusing, and so right.'

It is easy to wonder whether Wilde has been over-promoted by posterity thanks to his martyrdom, his queerness, the unfairness of his fate. He is indeed, almost to a fault, a figure for the modern world: ambiguous, provocative, narcissistic; one can readily imagine him tweeting away his wry paradoxes, the subject of much fulmination and adoration. He seemed to have known this himself, saying once: 'Fifty years . . . or a hundred years hence . . . my comedies and my stories . . . will be known and read by millions, and even my unhappy fate will call forth worldwide sympathy.'

He was proved right. Wilde's death at the age of forty-four in 1900 meant no senescent folly could corrupt the reputation he had accrued: for being witty, for being decadent, for being wronged. His contemporary Frank Harris said that 'Oscar Wilde's greatest play was his own life. It was a five act tragedy with Greek implications and he was its most ardent spectator', which fits his own sense that he 'put his genius into his living and his talent into his writing'.

In such circumstances, it is perhaps hard purely to judge the writing, but we must try. In *The Picture of Dorian Gray* (1890), Wilde left a short novel of imaginative delight; in *The Ballad of Reading Gaol* (1898), he dramatised the brutal inadequacies of the prison system; and in his prison letters, collected as *De Profundis* (1905), we got an immersive sense of a self searching for explanations* that is strikingly beautiful to read now. There were also children's stories, short stories, bits of poetry and prose here and there.

What about the plays upon which much of his reputation rests? I find an old BBC recording of *The Importance of Being Earnest*, and listen to it each day. It is very traditionally rendered, to a fault, filled with clinking teacups and clipped RP. The plot is – almost parodically – formulaic: Jack Worthing has created an alter ego for himself in the city, called Ernest, so he can have a bit of licentious fun, and is pursuing Gwendoline, his friend Algernon's cousin; Algernon has created the character of an invalid friend called Bunbury, to enable him to get away from social engagements. Algy is in love with Cecily, Jack's ward. Jack's own birth is suspect, as he was found as a baby in a hand-bag in Victoria Station, a failure of etiquette which means that Gwendoline's mother, Lady Bracknell, forbids his marriage. Gwendoline loves Jack but thinks he is called Ernest; Algy pretends to be Ernest when he visits Jack in the country, and Cecily falls in love with him on that basis ('it had always been a girlish dream of mine to love someone whose name was Ernest'). It all ends as we might imagine: wrongs righted, heritage established, and the prospect of the Shakespearean resolution of marriage for all.

---

* Noël Coward would not agree; he called it 'one long wail of self-pity' written by 'a posing, artificial old queen'.

But is *The Importance of Being Earnest* really that good? Wilde's wit is revealed in his aphorisms of inversion, which play with expectation and then – sometimes predictably – disappoint it. There is little drama here; instead it reads like a carefully constructed compilation of quotations:

- The amount of women in London who flirt with their own husbands is perfectly scandalous. It looks so bad. It is simply washing one's clean linen in public.
- To lose one parent, Mr Worthing, may be regarded as a misfortune; to lose both looks like carelessness.
- Few parents nowadays pay any regard to what their children say to them. The old-fashioned respect for the young is fast dying out.
- It is always painful to part from people whom one has known for a very brief space of time. The absence of old friends one can endure with equanimity. But even a momentary separation from anyone to whom one has just been introduced is almost unbearable.
- Indeed, no woman should ever be quite accurate about her age. It looks so calculating.

And so on and on. These are nice moments, certainly, and the icy comedy between Gwendoline and Cecily, when they both believe themselves to be rivals for a man called Ernest, is expertly done:

CECILY: When I see a spade I call it a spade.
GWENDOLEN: I am glad to say that I have never seen a spade.

But there is little counterbalance to the archness of the wit. Wilde knows this, of course, and nods to it in the dialogue:

ALGERNON: All women become like their mothers. That is
    their tragedy. No man does. That's his.
JACK: Is that clever?
ALGERNON: It is perfectly phrased! and quite as true as any
    observation in civilised life should be.

If Wilde had never been arrested, had never become a symbol of
a degrading, barbaric attitude to homosexuality, he might have
come to be regarded as a maker of perfect phrases, slight and
satisfying, but nothing more. As I sit here listening to the blithe,
glib jousting of the aristocratic characters, it is impossible to avoid
musing on the fate of their creator. Even this play, at one level,
reads like a coded dramatisation of queer London: 'earnest' was
slang for gay; 'Cecily' for rent boy; and the notion of double lives
away from the restrictive rules of codified existence is easily seen
as an appropriate metaphor for those with concealed desires.

Last year, I went to an exhibition of queer art in a London
gallery, and stood transfixed by the card the Marquess of
Queensberry left at Wilde's club: 'For Oscar Wilde, posing as a
somdomite [sic]'. This led to Wilde's – in retrospect – insane
decision to sue the marquess for libel, which in turn led to his
own prosecution for committing indecent acts. I am struck by
the fact that, like an irascible tweeter, the marquess cannot even
spell his insult correctly, and that such a small, small-minded
piece of meanness had such consequences. The imprisonment
of Oscar Wilde has helped shape the British relationship with
homosexuality, and indeed prison; it was a seismic event born
from the petty mind of one man.

Wilde was destroyed by his confinement, and could never get
the joy or the light back in his writing: 'I suppose it's all in me
somewhere,' he said once in Paris, 'but I don't seem to feel it.
My sense of humour is now concentrated on the grotesqueness
of tragedy.'

But his humour has survived. Someone once said that, when it comes to Wilde's plays, you might as well analyse a soufflé. Nothing in the arts is so formidably underrated as comedy, dismissed as eggy froth in comparison to the depths of serious ideas. And yet nothing gives more pleasure. Wilde has given me diversion and enjoyment over the last few days, and the contained thrill of listening to perfectly rounded sentences. *The Importance of Being Earnest* is Wodehousian, all those aunts and confusions, and there is very little wrong with that.

23 June

Samuel Beckett went to the same grammar school in Enniskillen as Oscar Wilde, but the similarities do not extend a great deal further. I start *Waiting for Godot* today, knowing that I will finish it this week, leaving me room to squeeze in one more play this month.

Godot is a play famously inscrutable in its definitive meaning. And reading it, rather than watching it, does not aid comprehension greatly. It is a play that contains its own criticism ('Nothing happens.* Nobody comes, nobody goes, it's awful!'), but there is enjoyment in the shambling, rambling, absurdist way in which inaction is portrayed. The plot boils down to two tramp-like men, Vladimir and Estragon, waiting by a tree for a man called Godot. At the end of each act, a boy arrives, promising Godot will come the next day. On the two days covered by the play, the only other visitors are Pozzo, a figure of anxious rage, and his slave Lucky, who bandy around some philosophy and leave. And that, more or less, is that.

Beckett was impatient with people who sought to find greater import in 'this fucking play' that helped to make his name: 'It

---

* Someone once observed that, given its two-act structure, it is a play where nothing happens, twice.

means what you want it to mean,' he told the director Peter Hall. And he apparently once informed the actor Ralph Richardson, 'if by Godot I had meant God I would have said God, not Godot. This seemed to disappoint him greatly.' It has been well observed that, in any event, it is a play not about Godot,[*] but about waiting; it is a comment on the static status of human existence. 'Everything oozes,' says Estragon (travestying Heraclitus); and Pozzo screams at one point, 'Have you not done tormenting me with your accursed time!' In Beckett, time is a constant preoccupation. Here is our philosophical duo:

VLADIMIR: That passed the time.
ESTRAGON: It would have passed in any case.
VLADIMIR: Yes, but not so rapidly.

25 June

In some ways, reading not watching Beckett adds another layer of alienating flatness to the play, and that makes it rather thrilling: this is desperately bleak stuff to be consuming on the way to work. On stage there is necessarily more colour, more room for farcical business. How is one to react to stage directions on the page like this, one wonders:

Estragon takes his hat. Vladimir adjusts his hat on his head. Estragon puts on his hat in place of Lucky's which he hands to Vladimir. Vladimir takes Lucky's hat. Estragon adjusts his hat on his head. Vladimir puts on Lucky's hat in place of his own which he hands

---

[*] There was a French cyclist called Godeau, who Beckett once had to wait to see. The source of the name may be as prosaic as that. The 'Godot-God' argument is weakened slightly by the fact that the play was originally written in French, *En Attendant Godot*, where the pun does not exist.

> to Estragon. Estragon takes Vladimir's hat. Vladimir adjusts Lucky's
> hat on his head. Estragon hands Vladimir's hat back to Vladimir
> who takes it and hands it back to Estragon who takes it and hands
> it back to Vladimir who takes it and throws it down.

Everything oozes when you read this, certainly, and that contributes to the overall feeling of sterility that Beckett intended in performance: 'precision, clarity, hardness. No sentimentality, no indulgence.' When first produced,* the play bewildered many, but was rescued by Harold Hobson writing in the *Sunday Times*, who said: 'Go and see *Waiting for Godot*. At the worst you will discover a curiosity, a four-leaved clover, a black tulip; at the best, something that will securely lodge in a corner of your mind for as long as you live.'

Beckett was no fan of the industry surrounding his work generally. I am pleased to say that the *TLS* pops up in his novel *Molloy*, but only as a means of insulating a homeless person: 'admirably suited,' apparently, 'with a never-failing toughness and impermeability'. And in *Godot* look what the culminating insult, the worst possible jibe, is:

VLADIMIR: Moron!
ESTRAGON: Vermin!
VLADIMIR: Abortion!
ESTRAGON: Morpion!
VLADIMIR: Sewer-rat!
ESTRAGON: Curate!
VLADIMIR: Cretin!
ESTRAGON: (with finality) Crritic!

* In the UK that is. The American production bombed entirely, not least because it was misleadingly advertised as the 'laugh sensation of two continents'.

My favourite piece of criticism about the play came in a 2009 review by Eric Griffiths of a production involving the 'national treasures' Patrick Stewart and Ian McKellen, about which most of London at the time was rolling over in orgiastic approval. Griffiths, a Beckett scholar,* was withering in his judgement of how it had blithely treated the play and its author, failing to engage with what Beckett had actually said he intended to do: 'Both audience and cast are feigning interest, like minor royalty asking the staff of a municipal swimming pool they have just opened but will never use, "Do you get through a lot of chlorine?"'

I think Beckett would have enjoyed that. He was a mordant man, conscious of his own status as a bitter fool of the age. When *The Times* asked him for his hopes for 1984, he gave them exactly what they would have wanted: 'resolutions colon zero stop period hopes colon zero stop Beckett.'

Beckett's absurdist legacy is not really his fault. He has left a damaging stain on modern fiction, for example, along with Camus and Kafka: all those dry, brittle novels with nameless characters wandering through a recognisable but anonymous landscape confronting their own insubstantiality. On a hot train, with a buzzing brain, a bit of the real thing is fine with me. And what is more relevant to modern commuter travel than the ending of the play?

VLADIMIR: Well? Shall we go?
ESTRAGON: Yes, let's go.
[They do not move.]

---

* I once toyed with doing a dissertation on Beckett at university, and was sent to Eric Griffiths as a possible supervisor for it. Within five minutes he suggested that – to do it properly – I would have to read all of Beckett in English and French, all of Proust in French, and most of St Augustine in Latin. I decided to do a paper on Victorian literature instead.

The most memorable scene I have encountered this month is the first one of Caryl Churchill's *Top Girls*. I came to it completely cold, without having read any synopsis, and was confronted by a dinner party involving a strange group of women. It is hosted by Marlene, who runs an employment agency in the 1980s, and – eventually, as the meal approaches dessert – she explains who her guests are:

> This is Joan who was Pope in the ninth century, and Isabella Bird, the Victorian traveller, and Lady Nijo from Japan, Emperor's concubine and Buddhist nun, thirteenth century, nearer your own time, and Gret who was painted by Bruegel. Griselda's in Boccaccio and Petrarch and Chaucer because of her extraordinary marriage. I'd like profiteroles because they're disgusting.

So this is a dinner party of the semi-afterlife, a dazzling concept. Not all the figures are recognisable, and need a bit of research. Last year on holiday, as it happens, I had read a novel called *Pope Joan* (1996) by Donna Woolfolk Cross, which told the apocryphal tale of a woman whose dazzling intellect led to her eventually becoming Pope before her identity was discovered when she gave birth. It is all probably untrue, alas.

I use my phone to look at *Dulle Griet* (1563), the painting by Bruegel, which is one of those mad hellscape visions that haunt the imagination: in it, an armour-clad crone leads women – who swarm all over the canvas – on the rampage into a satanic, giant mouth. One woman is lustily disembowelling a corpse, and others are waving spears, but the incidental details are even more striking: a monkey holding a turkey; a fish with legs; a figure bending over with a key protruding from an orifice that might be a mouth, might be an anus.

These remind me of Hieronymus Bosch, born a century earlier, and his own hellish visions.

The feat of imagination that brings these characters together is striking. They all have their tales of woe and abuse and loss: 'Patient Griselda', who had to give up her children to apparent death at the order of her husband; and Lady Nijo, whose child was also taken:

> NIJO: He cut the cord with a short sword, wrapped the baby in
>   white and took it away. It was only a girl but I was sorry to
>   lose it.
> GRISELDA: I asked him to give her back so I could kiss her. And
>   I asked him to bury her where no animals could dig her up.
>   / It
> ISABELLA: Oh my dear.
> GRISELDA: was Walter's child to do what he liked with.

This dialogue – unlike the stichomythia of Greek tragedy, and of Beckett – is deliberately overlapping and confused. The '/' punctuation shows when the next actor is supposed to interrupt, and the whole play is woven together tightly with contrapuntal female voices. We are at once asked to celebrate this chorus of women, but also to question how much they are really in harmony with one another. Marlene proposes a toast to the table ('We've all come a long way. To our courage and the way we changed our lives and our extraordinary achievements'), but it is striking how little they actually listen to or empathise with one another. The evening disintegrates into shouts and protests. Joan vomits in the corner. A silent, nameless woman serves the food unheeded.

The rest of the play moves to the present day (the early 1980s) and features Marlene's business and her family life: her sister Joyce, stuck in neglected poverty, and her niece, Angie, a lost teenage soul desperate for recognition. This is all well done, and there are shocking moments. Here is Angie talking to her young friend:

ANGIE: Mind my hair / you silly cunt
KIT: Stupid fucking cow, I hate you.

At one point, Kit brings out her finger covered in period blood, and Angie licks it, while declaring her desire to kill her mother. Not much has really changed since the *Oresteia*. There is little consolation in this world for women: they battle competing desires for family and professional success, and seem resigned that one will come at the expense of the other.

The structure of the play (that shift in perspective after the first act) feels rather uneven, though, and Churchill has said it is in response to 'the "maleness" of the traditional structure of plays, with conflict and building in a certain way to a climax'. Perhaps it is my maleness that does not find it wholly satisfying, but I can still testify to the imaginative force of the story. It's a happy non-climax to end the month.

~

Further Reading

The Oresteia (458 BC) by Aeschylus
Oedipus Rex (*c.*429 BC) by Sophocles
The Frogs (405 BC) by Aristophanes
Doctor Faustus (1592) by Christopher Marlowe
Volpone (1606) by Ben Jonson
Tartuffe (1664) by Molière
Phèdre (1677) by Jean Racine
A Doll's House (1879) by Henrik Ibsen

The Cherry Orchard (1904) by Anton Chekhov
Pygmalion (1913) by George Bernard Shaw
Six Characters in Search of an Author (1921) by Luigi Pirandello
The Children's Hour (1934) by Lillian Hellman
Our Town (1938) by Thornton Wilder
Mother Courage and Her Children (1939) by Bertolt Brecht
No Exit (1944) by Jean-Paul Sartre
A Streetcar Named Desire (1947) by Tennessee Williams
Death of a Salesman (1949) by Arthur Miller
The Chairs (1952) by Eugène Ionesco
Look Back in Anger (1956) by John Osborne
Long Day's Journey into Night (1956) by Eugene O'Neill
The Birthday Party (1957) by Harold Pinter
A Taste of Honey (1958) by Shelagh Delaney
A Raisin in the Sun (1959) by Lorraine Hansberry
Who's Afraid of Virginia Woolf (1962) by Edward Albee
Rosencrantz and Guildenstern Are Dead (1966) by Tom Stoppard
Death and the King's Horseman (1975) by Wole Soyinka
Translations (1980) by Brian Friel
Noises Off (1982) by Michael Frayn
Glengarry Glenn Ross (1983) by David Mamet
Fences (1985) by August Wilson
Angels in America (1991) by Tony Kushner
The Vagina Monologues (1996) by Eve Ensler
War Horse (2007) by Michael Morpurgo
Jerusalem (2009) by Jez Butterworth
Enron (2009) by Lucy Prebble

July

Comic Fiction

Love in a Cold Climate (1949) by Nancy Mitford
A Confederacy of Dunces (1980) by John Kennedy Toole

I have reached the age of thirty-nine fairly ignorant – as we know – about many things, and that includes the Mitford sisters. Trawling around the cavities of my brain, I can pretty much only come up with vague outlines: of poshness, Fascism and brittle literariness.

It is unfair to be so reductive, though the poshness is indisputable. Nancy Mitford famously wrote the essay 'The English Aristocracy', in which she dwelled on the distinctions between 'U' (upper-class people) and 'non-U' (everybody else). It said things like: 'U-speakers eat luncheon in the middle of the day and dinner in the evening. Non-U-speakers (also U-children and U-dogs) have their dinner in the middle of the day.' She made a list of words that are recognisably the idiolect of the elite, and I remember realising that, growing up, I failed her linguistic test at every turn: I said serviette, not napkin; settee not sofa; toilet not lavatory; and so on.

A modern version of this type of exclusive cataloguing popped up on social media this year, and it still makes me laugh.

The interior designer Nicky Haslam (who, let us be clear, is no Mitford) came up with a list of 'things he found common'. They are, one hopes, tongue-in-cheek, and are very funny: breakfast meetings; being on time; tours of the house; conservatories; self-pity; swans; mindfulness; Bono; rinsing fruit; loving your parents; not eating carbs; organic food; being ill; using dog walkers. That is not even all of them. I love the fact that loving your parents is common.

The Mitfords are often considered in terms of their own family relationships, all those sisters born to Lord and Lady Redesdale. Nancy was the cleverest, and joined by: Jessica, known as Decca, a communist; Pamela, of lesser fame, called the 'rural Mitford' by John Betjeman; Debo, who became the Duchess of Devonshire, and chatelaine of Chatsworth House; Diana, the Fascist wife of Oswald Mosley; and Unity,* who idolised Hitler and Goebbels, and unsuccessfully tried to kill herself with a bullet to the head when the Second World War was declared.

Nancy and Decca (the two most interesting Mitfords) distanced themselves from all that Fascism. At nineteen, Decca eloped with her second cousin Esmond Romilly† to fight in the Spanish Civil War on the side of the Republicans. She ended up as a rather brilliant journalist in America, writing the muck-raking classic *The American Way of Death* (1963), in which she exposed the fraudulent world of the funeral business as a 'huge, macabre and expensive practical joke on the American public'. Her own funeral cost $475, by the way.

Nancy herself went into print against the rising tide of Fascism with *Wigs on the Green* (1935), a parody of the excesses of the movement. At the time, Diana was in the process of leaving her

---

* Her middle name was Valkyrie, which seems appropriate enough.
† Who was Churchill's nephew. The world of the posh is very small.

husband for Mosley and had attended the first Nuremberg rally with Unity. Coldness, to say the least, arose between Nancy and Diana that was to persist for a decade, with the former telling the Home Office that the latter was 'an extremely dangerous person' at the outbreak of war. MI5 indeed thought Diana was a 'public danger', who was 'far cleverer and more dangerous than her husband'. She was imprisoned for three years in 1940, and not allowed a passport until 1949.

Coldness is in the title – and in the very ether – of Nancy's most famous novel: *Love in a Cold Climate*. It is one of those books often dubbed a classic by those who can recall reading it in their youth (I am clutching this morning my wife's battered copy from her teenage years). We will see how well it has aged.

3 July

Summer descends upon London like a hot fog, a time of parched throats and itchy eyes, of concrete heating up ominously on all sides. Henry James once said: 'Summer afternoon – summer afternoon; to me those have always been the two most beautiful words in the English language.' But that is for someone lounging in a garden, head in the cool shadows of a resplendent tree, not superglued to the tacky skin of the fat person next to them on a commuter train. A Victorian city, actually, would have been even more unbearable than our own: no air conditioning, no respite, fouled streets, air pollution even worse than today. Conan Doyle's Watson recalls: 'Baker Street was like an oven, and the glare of the sunlight upon the yellow brickwork of the house across the road was painful to the eye. It was hard to believe that these were the same walls which loomed so gloomily through the fogs of winter.'

The place to be in the hot weather is the countryside not the city. Wodehouse's Blandings Castle always embraces summer;

indeed Wodehouse is perhaps the laureate of idle days, for those pleasantly stupefied by heat, lulled in a hammock away from the fraught toil of everyday life.* Summers in fiction seem to be a combination of such moments of breeze-tickled repose, and torrid glimpses of something more dangerous and unstable. I think of the tales from the Riviera, as by F. Scott Fitzgerald or in *The Talented Mr Ripley* (1955) by Patricia Highsmith, where murder and impersonation swelter in the sun. Or Ian McEwan's *Atonement* (2001), where the consequential moments that govern an entire lifetime all take place in one summer, and are looked back upon endlessly, the way we all do with summers of the past.

I hate the heat, the discomfort of it; the squinting harshness makes me irrational. Remember Meursault, the figure in *The Stranger* (1942) by Camus, who murders someone in the sun on the wretched day his mother is buried: 'The heat was beginning to scorch my cheeks; beads of sweat were gathering in my eyebrows. It was just the same sort of heat as at my mother's funeral, and I had the same disagreeable sensations – especially in my forehead, where all the veins seemed to be bursting through the skin. I couldn't stand it any longer, and took another step forward.'

You wouldn't read that novel on a beach, but who really enjoys reading on a beach anyway? Clammy skin scoured with sand, as you restlessly alter between impossible positions to hold a book with comfort. The *TLS* – in common with the rest of the civilised world, it seems – does a 'summer reads' section once a year, contributing to the fiction that hot days suit some sort of mental exertion. The opposite is true: give me a cold

---

* I'm not rereading Wodehouse this month, even though he is – to my mind – the greatest writer of comic fiction in the language. He is now too familiar to me, I think, to write too much about. Plus, I read him in the bath, not on the train.

afternoon and a quiet room, or even a quiet train, and that is the place. Keep the summer for sweating and griping.

4 July
Love in a Cold Climate is a follow-up to *The Pursuit of Love* (1945), both narrated by Frances 'Fanny' Logan. This time Fanny is focusing on the 'very grand and very rich' Hampton family, in particular Polly, the daughter of Lord and Lady Montdore. We are warned at the beginning that 'the beauty of Polly and the importance of her family are essential elements of this story'. It is set between the wars, when 'the age of luxury was ended and that of comfort had begun'. But this is hardly a comfortable novel; instead it is unapologetically aware of the superficiality of its subject matter, its essential heartlessness. Very little of note happens in the pages, other than the unsatisfactory affairs of its principals. The 'love' in the title is ironic; the coldness very much is not.

Marriage does not fare well. Fanny falls in pallid love with Arthur Wincham, and commits herself to what that entails with brisk cynicism: 'I had already dived over that verge and was swimming away in a blue sea of illusion towards, I supposed, the islands of the blest, but really towards domesticity, maternity and the usual lot of womankind.'

Mitford is unremitting on the institution of marriage itself:* a bad option, but – as Lady Mountford puts it – 'by far the best career open to any woman'. Fanny's own mother is regularly calumniated as 'the Bolter', someone who failed to take the

---

* Her own personal life was not exactly charmed. She was married to a gay man, Peter Rodd, and in love with an unattainable one, Colonel Gaston Palewski, a dashing member of de Gaulle's cabinet. He was no looker (apparently he had a face 'like an unpeeled King Edward'), and appears in the novels as the 'short, stocky, very dark' Fabrice de Sauveterre. Nancy moved to Paris to be near him, apparently in hope of a formal union that never transpired.

institution seriously. She sounds like a lot of fun, and we could have done with more of her: 'Ghastly scandal after ghastly scandal, elopements, horse-whippings, puts herself up as a prize in a lottery, cannibal kings – I don't know what all – headlines in the papers, libel actions, and yet she only has to appear in London, and her friends queue up to give parties for her.'

Polly throws herself away on Boy Dougdale, the former lover of her mother, known to everyone as the Lecherous Lecturer, and the subject of protracted gossip among the children: 'He took Linda up on to the roof and did all sorts of blissful things to her; at least, she could easily see how they would be blissful with anybody except the Lecturer. And I got some great sexy pinches as he passed the nursery landing.'

This jars with modern sensibilities; and it is immediately clear that Mitford is not exactly a #MeToo author. In fact, *Love in a Cold Climate* feels like a museum piece to me, an exotic and extinct world preserved as if beneath sterile glass, to be nodded and tutted over. This is a place of formal dinners and debutantes and 'eggy-peggy', a made-up language designed to prevent children from eavesdropping: 'Egg-is shegg-ee reggealleggy, pweggoor swegg-eet?' Indeed, the book is, among other things, a faithful transcript of the customs and conversations of a different species. It is U; and so it feels perhaps not for me.

8 July

Today I'm set to interview the director Ivo van Hove about his theatrical version of *The Fountainhead* (1943), one of those interminable, glassily dull novels by Ayn Rand. I have read it, the story of the ropey, rapey architect Howard Roark, but can remember almost nothing about it.

I see it has become the proud example of books enjoyed by right-wing politicians. Donald Trump, no great reader, claimed that the novel 'relates to business, beauty, life and inner emotions. That book relates to . . . everything.' Sajid Javid, the current Home Secretary, implausibly claims to read *The Fountainhead* every year, something that surely should disqualify him from high office. I can see the attraction at one level: this is fiction as political wet dream, all strength and individualism and power at the expense of the unlettered herd.

I remember watching the film *Dirty Dancing* – that tale of 1950s summer campery starring Patrick Swayze – which had a horrible character called Robbie Gould, a waiter (while he was awaiting enrolment in Yale Medical School), a seducer of young women, and procurer of their abortions. At one point, he thrusts a novel into the hands of Baby, saying charmingly that 'some people count and some people don't'. The novel is *The Fountainhead* and he wants her to take its lessons to heart: 'I think you'll enjoy it, but return it; I have notes in there.'

It is a good joke about a writer who would readily appear on a list of most humourless in fiction. That is quite a fun list to consider, actually; let me think of a few candidates whose work – whatever else its qualities – never seems to provoke the merest hint of a smile: Paulo Coelho, J.R.R. Tolkien, Alice Walker, John Grisham. There will be others.

9 July

So where do the humorous pleasures come in Nancy Mitford? Well, almost entirely in the colourfully monstrous cast of truly English eccentrics that populate the pages. Like Davey, the family invalid – 'it was his all-absorbing occupation, and one which he enjoyed beyond all words' – who is on a diet that includes a designated day 'for getting drunk'. Or Aunt Sadie, 'who believed in no illness except appendicitis', married to the magnificent Uncle Matthew, a grotesque old gargoyle, a bore and a bloviator, with a glint in his eye. This is the best passage of the whole book, about Matthew's superstitious habit of writing someone's name on a piece of paper in the hope that they would die within a year:

> The drawers at Alconleigh were full of little slips bearing the names of those whom my uncle wanted out of the way, private hates of his and various public figures such as Bernard Shaw, de Valera, Gandhi, Lloyd George, and the Kaiser, while every single drawer in the whole house contained the name Labby, Linda's old dog. The spell hardly ever seemed to work, even Labby having lived far beyond the age usual in Labradors, but he went hopefully on, and if one of the characters did happen to be carried off in the course of nature he would look pleased but guilty for a day or two.

We are beginning to get a sense of Mitfordian brilliance, the waspish celebration of eccentricity. This is encapsulated in Lady Montdore, one of the towering ogres of British fiction, a woman with 'the charm of a purring puma'. I perhaps can do no more than offer, helplessly, a series of quotations from her, the product of my snortings and underlinings this week.

- On needing the toilet:* 'I go in the morning, and that is that. I don't have to be let out like a dog at intervals, thank goodness – there's nothing so common, to my mind.'
- On empathy: 'I love being so dry in here and seeing all those poor people so wet.'
- On wedding nights: 'Above all, don't go wasting money on underclothes, there is nothing stupider – I always borrow Montdore's myself.'

* Sorry, lavatory.

I start to realise that the best way to appreciate *Love in a Cold Climate* is to give myself up to the detailed, pitch-perfect sense of its characters and their habitat, and not expect very much more.

10 July

I constantly – much to their eye-rolling consternation – tell my children about the etymology of words. They normally interrupt with things like, 'Yes, yes, I'm sure it's from the Greek for something.' Which is probably the fate of parents the world over* when they try to impress their kids.

But understanding why a word became a word is one of the great puzzle solutions of life. There is often a story to enjoy, or a fact to assimilate. Just today I heard the theory that the word 'job' comes from a mis-transcription of a numbered list in Latin: '*i. opus*', which is to say 'work that is first to do', and became 'i.ob' or 'job'. Is it not magnificent that someone's mistake became a term that has had a universal use in the English language? I see from my phone that this may be untrue, but nobody actually knows: Samuel Johnson in his *Dictionary* said with customary asperity that it was simply 'a low word now much in use of which I cannot tell the etymology'. One other theory is that it comes from a verb 'job' meaning 'peck'. 'Negotiate' I know from Latin comes from '*necotium*' or 'business', but '*necotium*' literally means 'not idleness': so the sense of work as simply the opposite of having a relaxing time. Is that not interesting?

* My dad, I recall, took our family regularly to see Neolithic stone formations in the British countryside: quoits, I think they were called. He did this in spite of the rather lukewarm support from my mum, and outright hostility from my brother. 'Yes, yes, another medium-sized stone in the middle of an otherwise empty field, Dad.'

Knowing a piece of etymology is like knowing a secret. Like when you read the word 'dunce', meaning a stupid person, and recognise it comes from the thirteenth-century philosopher Duns Scotus, who was actually very clever, but whose theories were discredited by the humanists a couple of centuries later. So his adherents or 'duns' were known as dunces.

I think life is fractionally better for knowing that the word 'clue' comes from the Greek for a ball of thread, thus linking back to our tale of Theseus and the Minotaur; or that a palace is named after one big building on the Palatine Hill in Rome where emperors lived. That's a genuine etymology, I promise, and 'genuine' is interesting because it comes from the Latin for knee, because Roman fathers acknowledged their legitimate offspring by placing them on their knees. Barbarians became known as such because to Roman ears they seemed to make unintelligible noises, 'bar bar bar', and the word followed the sound.

I'll stop now, I promise. But did you know that the word 'apron' was originally 'napron' (cognate with 'napkin'),* but when people said 'a napron' it eventually was understood as 'an apron'? The reverse is true for 'newt', which was originally 'an ewt'.

12 July

Mitford is evocative on food, as one would expect from someone writing in the comparative privation of the post-war period. My mouth waters at the thought of 'a huge breakfast of porridge and cream, kedgeree, eggs, cold ham, and slice upon slice of toast covered with Cooper's Oxford' or 'enough sugary food to

---

* Let's not get into the whole 'serviette' thing.

stock a pastrycook's shop'. Look how Fanny links consumption to identity:

> Soup, fish, pheasant, beefsteak, asparagus, pudding, savoury, fruit. Hampton food, Aunt Sadie used to call it, and indeed it had a character of its own which can best be described by saying that it was like mountains of the very most delicious imaginable nursery food, plain and wholesome, made of first-class materials, each thing tasting strongly of itself.

This is indeed a novel that tastes strongly of itself, is unashamedly definitive. And that provides some comfort, I think, to readers: it is a novel of the nursery, of straightforwardness, of nostalgia. I can imagine teenage girls, like my wife, reading it and admiring the cynicism: something written by a woman that does not romanticise or compromise. It is good on girlish desire, for example:

> From a tiny child, ever since I could remember, in fact, some delicious image had been enshrined in my heart, last thought at night, first thought in the morning. Fred Terry as Sir Percy Blakeney, Lord Byron, Rudolph Valentino, Henry V, Gerald du Maurier, blissful Mrs Ashton at my school, Steerforth, Napoleon, the guard on the 4.45: image had succeeded image.

But if there is comfort about 'dear old sex', there is also realism about lovelessness. Nobody finds either happiness, or even the comfort of legitimate sorrow. After a stillbirth, Lady Montdore is expectedly horrendous ('I expect it was just as well, children are such an awful expense, nowadays'), but Fanny – our guide, our friendly narrator – is no better: 'she seemed to me rather like a cow whose calf has been taken away from it at birth, unconscious of her loss.' Reading this dried my throat; I thought of my baby, and marvelled in horror at such a reaction.

And that, perhaps, is the most visceral response that *Love in a Cold Climate* can provoke. It can be filed with early Evelyn Waugh,* as brilliant, but rather slight. It is a chronicle of the rich, frozen in their cold climate, not doing very much: 'So here we all are, my darling; having our lovely cake and eating it too, one's great aim in life.' As I sigh and look around me, interested in but never fascinated by this novel, I think of this line by Raymond Chandler: 'They say the rich can always protect themselves and that in their world it is always summer. I've lived with them and they are bored and lonely people.'

This is right, but does a book about them become a bit boring too? For a short work, I did not wish *Love in a Cold Climate* much longer. It has given me Lady Montdore and Uncle Matthew, and it has made me crave carbohydrates, but not much *happens* in it. I think of Chandler again: 'When in doubt, have a man come through a door with a gun in his hand.' Mitford, perhaps, fails to give us something quite like that.

14 July

The circumstances surrounding the publication of *A Confederacy of Dunces* are more famous than the book itself, and far from funny. John Kennedy Toole was a wise-cracking teacher and former soldier – known to his friends as Ken – whose life spiralled into decay, depression and boozy obesity. He was a literary failure. His first novel, *The Neon Bible*, written when he was sixteen, had gone unpublished. He described it as a 'grim, adolescent, sociological attack upon the hatreds caused by the various

---

* He was a great friend of Nancy, though did not like *Love in a Cold Climate* very much in first draft. 'It isn't a book yet,' he said, and told her to start again.

Calvinist religions in the South'. His new work, about a fat, irascible New Orleans native, was going nowhere. Publishers showed interest in it, then recoiled. Life was miserable. In March 1969 Ken went on a road trip, stopping at the home of the writer he most admired, Flannery O'Connor.* Then he ran a hose from his exhaust into his car, and ended it all. He was thirty-one.

The title of the book he had believed in, that he had feverishly worked on into the night on an army base in Puerto Rico in his twenties, was taken from Swift: 'When a true genius appears in the world, you may know him by this sign, that the dunces are all in confederacy against him.' It was an ironic reference to the preposterous self-belief of its anti-hero, Ignatius T. Reilly, in the face of all the evidence of the real world against him, but it can be read as an ironic commentary on the publishing industry too.

Ironies always abound in the presence of this author, this book. *A Confederacy of Dunces* is a novel about the turbulent, erratic and unhealthy relationship between a slob and his sottish, embattled mother.† This is not a hymn to maternal love. And yet it owes its publication to the indefatigable efforts of Thelma Toole, Ken's mum, who refused to accept the rejections that continued for more than a decade after his death.

It all could have been different, from a publishing perspective at least. For two years, Ken had been in correspondence with the great New York (and eventually *New Yorker*) editor, Robert Gottlieb, who had just published the irreverent, mould-breaking *Catch-22*. Gottlieb was tempted, but could not quite get past the eccentricity of it all: 'With all its wonderfulness,' he

---

* A fine exponent of Southern Gothic. She once said: 'Anything that comes out of the South is going to be called grotesque by the northern reader, unless it is grotesque, in which case it is going to be called realistic.'
† It even has a line in which Ignatius refuses to leave his writings behind: 'We must never let them fall into the hands of my mother. She may make a fortune from them. It would be too ironic.' Now that is ironic.

said, the book 'does not have a reason. It isn't really about anything. And that's something no one can do anything about.' His final letter still held out desperate, hopeless hope for Ken: a promise to 'read, reread, edit, perhaps publish, generally cope, until you are fed up with me. What more can I say?'

Gottlieb said no more. Ken eventually abandoned the manuscript, and tried to write another novel called – after a line by Poe on the subject of death – *The Conqueror Worm*. That never came to anything; his depression continued, worsened by surrounding politics, the notable deaths of the decade (the assassinations of Martin Luther King and the Kennedys). When he took his own life, Ken left only a copy of the *Confederacy* text and a suicide note, which Thelma quickly destroyed, calling it 'bizarre and preposterous. Violent. Ill-fated. Ill-fated. Nothing. Insane ravings.' We'll never know what he said at the last.

Thelma was undaunted at least about the future of the manuscript. For a decade she persisted, ending up at the door of Walker Percy, a writer based at Loyola University, refusing to leave until he read her dead son's words. Here is what happened when he decided reluctantly to read a few pages, according to Percy in a foreword to the book:

> My only fear was that this one might not be bad enough, or might be just good enough, so that I would have to keep reading.*
>
> In this case I read on. And on. First with the sinking feeling that it was not bad enough to quit, then with a prickle of interest, then a growing excitement, and finally an incredulity: surely it was not possible that it was so good.

Reading it now, on a train forty years later, I share that experience, that prickling sensation, what Nabokov called the 'tell-tale tingle

---

* 'The fear of every editor,' says my editor, somewhat passive-aggressively.

between the shoulderblades' we get when we experience great writing. Thanks to Percy, *Confederacy* was published by a small press with a print run of 2,500 copies. Since then it has sold more than 1.5 million copies. It was on the bestseller list as late as this January, after an endorsement from the comedian Billy Connolly, who called it – as I see from a jaunty sticker on my paperback – 'my favourite book of all time'. Bowie loved it. Anthony Burgess loved it, saying, 'This funny book is the kind one wants to keep quoting from.' We'll start doing that in a moment.

15 July

Thinking about other literary rejections, I read in the *TLS* that T.S. Eliot – in his role as Faber publisher – rejected the *Paddington Bear* books, with the unimprovably high-handed remark: 'As one's sympathies and affections are all with the bear it is difficult to laugh with the author. Moreover the Brown family are perfect fools.'

Eliot turned down Orwell twice, famously rejecting *Animal Farm* in 1944, essentially for political reasons: we were firm allies with Stalin's Russia at the time, and a book that aggressively satirised communism was likely to be unpopular with the establishment. Eliot dressed up his refusal more subtly than that, saying: 'And after all, your pigs are far more intelligent than the other animals, and therefore the best qualified to run the farm – in fact, there couldn't have been an Animal Farm at all without them: so that what was needed (someone might argue), was not more communism but more public-spirited pigs.'

'Public-spirited pigs' has not been judged favourably by posterity. My favourite ever rejection was for Nabokov's *Lolita*,[*]

---

[*] As you might imagine, this book was not easy to get published, except in France. One publisher helpfully recommended 'that it be buried under a stone for a thousand years'.

as he recalled in the book's Afterword: 'One reader suggested that his firm might consider publication if I turned my Lolita into a twelve-year-old lad and had him seduced by Humbert, a farmer, in a barn, amidst gaunt and arid surroundings, all this set forth in short, strong "realistic" sentences. ("He acts crazy. We all act crazy, I guess. I guess God acts crazy", etc.)'

This makes me laugh out loud, and as an act of missing the point of a book will for ever preside in the publishing pantheon. There are others, of course. *The Diary of Anne Frank* (1947) was rejected by Knopf with the scarcely conceivable line: 'a dreary record of typical family bickering, petty annoyances and adolescent emotions'. Or what about the publisher who wondered, having read *Moby Dick*, 'Does it have to be a whale?' They suggested Ahab might be rewritten so that he is 'struggling with a depravity towards young, perhaps voluptuous maidens'. I love the 'perhaps' there more than words can say. Something similar could have happened to Darwin and *On the Origin of Species* (1859): one of the publisher's readers suggested he took out everything except for the references to pigeons, because 'everybody is interested in pigeons'.

One of my favourite novels ever is *The Sun Also Rises* by Hemingway, which received this rejection letter: 'If I may be frank, Mr Hemingway – you certainly are in your prose – I found your efforts to be both tedious and offensive. You really are a man's man, aren't you? I wouldn't be surprised to hear that you had penned this entire story locked up at the club, ink in one hand, brandy in the other.'

I regularly reread the novel with great pleasure, but there will be many readers – possibly female readers – who are nodding their heads at this assessment.

17 July

I'm on holiday now, by a lake in the Cotswolds. I take *A Confederacy of Dunces*, but have time for some other books too. As this is a month for comic novels, I grab a *Flashman** novel as I leave, *Flashman and the Redskins* (1982), and coincidentally receive an email from a journalist asking about the series and the perhaps questionable nature of its politics.

It is a good question. Why do I love these books? The (anti-) hero is undeniably a racist misogynist, and the narrative is peppered with slurs that are far beyond the realms of acceptable speech. This is done ironically in the sense that Flashman is not supposed to be nice or reasonable, and the whole series is an overt testament to his folly, his moral cowardice and lack of judgement. But it is not clear that its author, George MacDonald Fraser, would have disagreed that much with his own creation. Fraser was an old soldier, an old colonialist, a reactionary.† His autobiography has twenty pages on the 'race relations industry', which makes him splutter with outrage.

If Fraser is Blimpish,‡ he evidently was aware of that fact himself, and at least partially playing with the role. And the *Flashman* novels themselves are not shy in exposing the

---

* The conceit behind the series is that it tells the story of Flashman, the bully from Thomas Hughes's *Tom Brown's School Days* (1857). He narrates a 'truthful' version of his life as a pathetic poltroon, bumbling through Victorian history mistakenly heralded as a brave hero, when in fact he is 'a scoundrel, a liar, a cheat, a thief, a coward – and, oh yes, a toady'. The history part is told via footnotes. I do, ahem, love a footnote.

† Fraser also co-wrote the Bond movie *Octopussy* (1983), which has a moment in which Bond gives his winnings to an Indian person, saying, 'That should keep you in curry for a while.'

‡ Colonel Blimp was drawn by David Low in the *Evening Standard* in the 1930s, a caricature of an old British soldier, issuing reactionary opinions from inside a Turkish bath. Orwell said he was representative of the 'half-pay colonel with his bull neck and diminutive brain'.

arrogance, the tragic hubris, of the British Empire. Ultimately, they make the case that humanity in all its guises is prey to the same unpleasant tendencies: to be sexually, politically, violently rapacious, provided people feel they can get away with it. They carry a certain amount of equal-opportunity cruelty.

I read the books for the history,* for the brio in the adventure, for the comedy. These are satirical novels, written as a pastiche of a certain type of person and thinking. But I still feel uncomfortable in parts. There is the sense that, to adopt the old saw about Brexit, not everyone who likes *Flashman* is racist, but every racist would like *Flashman*. And perhaps I forgive the fun I have reading them too readily; it may be a product of my own white privilege that I choose not to wince too much, or take too much offence. Yet the act of reading allows for ambivalence, for self-questioning, and it is possible to retain countervailing thoughts at the same time.

19 July

Pretty much as soon as *Confederacy* was published, people tried to film it, without success. Almost the entire pantheon of fat, white American actors have been lined up over the decades to play Ignatius: John Belushi, John Candy, Chris Farley, John Goodman, Zach Galifianakis. The British comic writer Stephen Fry moved to New York in the 1990s to pen a script, which was never made. The Oscar-winning director Steven Soderbergh got closest in recent years with a script, a cast (Will Ferrell as Ignatius) and a read-through, but never proceeded to actual

---

* I had literally never heard any detail of the Indian Mutiny or the Taiping Rebellion in China (the latter the bloodiest civil war in human history) until I read *Flashman*. There is not a series of books that has replaced my ignorance more.

filming. 'I think it's cursed,' said he. 'I'm not prone to superstition, but that project has got bad mojo on it.' It is both ironic and fitting that this cursed joy of a novel, this hymn to bad mojo, should struggle to become a movie. Ignatius himself only went to the cinema to be disgusted by it, 'so that his disbelieving eyes could drink in every blasphemous technicolored moment'.

So let's meet Ignatius T. Reilly where he belongs, on the page, as something instantly unforgettable:

> A green hunting cap* squeezed the top of the fleshy balloon of a head. The green earflaps, full of large ears and uncut hair and the fine bristles that grew in the ears themselves, stuck out on either side like turn signals indicating two directions at once.

This apparition is known all around New Orleans – 'that fat mother that got him the green cap' – as he calmly and heedlessly manoeuvres his way in and out of dramas, beginning with his near-arrest outside the D.H. Holmes department store. Ignatius is startlingly fat: sitting on a stool 'he looked like an eggplant balanced atop a thumb tack'; when he dons a smock to work on a hot-dog cart, it 'made him look like a giant dinosaur egg about to hatch'.

His vast obesity is accompanied by noxious parps and belches, due to confessed problems with his 'pyloric valve'. He also masturbates a lot, sometimes using 'a rubber glove, a piece of fabric from a silk umbrella, a jar of Noxema', but sometimes without such bits of abhorrent apparatus as 'putting them away

---

* Possibly the most recognisable piece of headwear in all fiction, alongside Holmes's deerstalker (although Conan Doyle never specified it as such, going no further than a 'close-fitting cloth cap' or an 'ear-flapped travelling cap'), Pratchett's Rincewind and his hat with the word 'Wizzard' on it, and Oddjob's black bowler.

again after it was all over had eventually grown too depressing'. This is a man too melancholic to clean up after his own emissions. In the first few pages, he is straining for a suitable mental image to prompt his manipulations, and settles on 'the familiar figure of the large and devoted collie that had been his pet when he was in high school'. Really.

So hang on: what stops this from becoming garish, gratuitous, disgusting?* It is a fair question. I think it is because Ken gives Ignatius dignified consistency, a ridiculousness that almost – but never quite – verges on the charming. He has an arresting mental life too: 'He often bloated while lying in bed in the morning contemplating the unfortunate turn that events had taken since the Reformation.' This is a figure born in the wrong era, surrounded by dunces who refuse to understand him, writing 'a lengthy indictment against our century' on his Red Chief tablets, his own consolation of philosophy in the model of his great hero Boethius.

This is eccentricity raised to the level of art. The character Ignatius most reminds me of is Wodehouse's Psmith, to whom he is a malevolent, obese transatlantic cousin. Like Psmith, he has a horror of what he perceives to be crass modernity, all that 'mascara and lipstick and other vulgarities'. Unlike Psmith, this has corroded his soul: 'Optimism nauseates me. It is perverse. Since man's fall, his proper position in the universe has been one of misery.' Psmith is lovable, his world full of idyllic charm, a sense of rightness; Ignatius carries with him none of that. At one point, Mrs Reilly says, 'You ain't only crazy, Ignatius. You mean, too,' and she is right. The genius of the author is to make us like him, to cheer him on nonetheless.

---

* You are starting, I would imagine, to recognise why this may have been a tricky book to get published.

There is genius too, I think, in the surrounding carnival of activity that animates the novel. Ignatius is surrounded by unforgettable satellites, drawn to him by his malign gravity. So there is the Night of Joy bar, home of Lana Lee's pornography distribution racket, and characters like Darlene (a stripper with a parrot in her act) and Burma Jones, the black sweeper who 'would get arrested for vagrancy if he didn't work'. Jones's words are rendered in patois ('Look at that. She think I got siphlus and TB and a hard on and I gonna cut her up with a razor and lif her purse. Ooo-wee') in an act of trans-racial ventriloquism that may be, wrongly, tutted over now. But his plight is acutely portrayed, both funny and sad.

Then there is the office of Levy Pants, 'a silent and smoky plea for urban renewal', one of literature's truly iconic places of work. Ignatius gets a clerical job there, and spends his time painting posters, sending abusive letters and adopting a filing system that strongly involves a bin. Here is his unimprovable tip for increased productivity: 'I have taken to arriving at the office one hour later than I am expected. Therefore, I am far more rested and refreshed when I do arrive, and I avoid that bleak first hour of the working day during which my still sluggish senses and body make every chore a penance. I find that in arriving later, the work which I do perform is of a much higher quality.'

Try that on your boss today. At Levy Pants, Ignatius works with the poor, misunderstood Mr Gonzalez and the frankly abused Miss Trixie, old and confused, desperate to retire: she 'drifted off toward the ladies' room as if she were tacking into a gale. Miss Trixie was never perfectly vertical; she and the floor always met at an angle of less than ninety degrees.' Here, as with Mitford, we get the comic strength of the whole novel: its cast of formidably funny characters. Levy Pants is owned by Mr and

Mrs Levy, a feuding couple, whose wealth is poisoned by their mutual dislike: 'For Christmas, Mrs Levy always compiled not a gift list but rather a list of the injustices and brutalities she had suffered since August. The girls got this list in their stockings. The only gift Mrs Levy asked of the girls was that they attack their father. Mrs Levy loved Christmas.'

Another deplorable mother figure, we notice.

28 July

In all this, who could forget Ignatius's girlfriend, of sorts, the magnificent Myrna Minkoff? She believes everything comes down to sex, and is campaigning vigorously for equality: she writes, for example, a 'Petition Which Aggressively Demands More and Better Sex for All and a Crash Program for Minorities!'. She and Ignatius, mad and blithe as they are, seem destined for one another. This is a comedy after all, and must end with couples coming together, wrongs being righted, all's well that ends well. I will leave it to you to imagine whether that can survive in the garish New Orleans of John Kennedy Toole.

I see that neither book this month is a comedy in a classical sense, really: for Mitford, marriage is not a happy ending, but a troubled beginning, and it is scarcely idealised in *Confederacy* either. There are whole books – whole careers – spent on musing on the various categories of comedy and its literary manifestations. I will not, you'll be pleased to hear, be reproducing them now. The experience is all; you know what you find amusing. As the comedian Ken Dodd* once astutely noted: 'Freud said that laughter is the outward expression of the psyche. But Freud never had to play the Glasgow Empire.'

---

* This is my favourite joke of his, by the way: 'I just read a book about Stockholm Syndrome, it started off badly but by the end I really liked it.'

I do not laugh when I read; I internalise the jokes, I inhale a sense of happy pleasure. Comedy to me is about structure: there is a neatness, an intricacy when a written joke works. I think of Wodehouse and his marginal annotations to his own drafts: 'Okay', 'good', 'very good', 'very good XX'. He knows when a trick comes off, when a piece of plotting makes sense, when a verbal sally succeeds.

I see I keep coming back to Wodehouse, even when I am not reading him. I am one of those Englishmen, as Martin Amis drily noted once, 'who, in the pantheon of world literature, would place Wodehouse somewhere between Homer and Dante'. And I see that my two choices this month have an infernal relationship with the great man: Mitford and her malevolent aunts and marital scrapes; Ignatius as a charmless Psmith.

If tragedy is about putting the wordless into words, comedy is also about finding a form to accommodate the mess. All those impulses, those extravagant human tendencies, those bodily temptations and fluids, need to be channelled into something. Thankfully, it is something you can be seen with on a train in the morning.

~

Further Reading

Three Men in a Boat (1889) by Jerome K. Jerome
The Diary of a Nobody (1892) by George and Weedon
    Grossmith
Psmith Journalist (1915) by P.G. Wodehouse
Decline and Fall (1928) by Evelyn Waugh
1066 and All That (1930) by W.C. Sellar and R.J. Yeatman
Cold Comfort Farm (1932) by Stella Gibbons
The Code of the Woosters (1938) by P.G. Wodehouse

The Portable Dorothy Parker (1944)

Lucky Jim (1954) by Kingsley Amis

The Compleet Molesworth (1958) by Geoffrey Willans and
 Ronald Searle

Catch-22 (1961) by Joseph Heller

A House for Mr Biswas (1961) by V.S. Naipaul

The Third Policeman (1967) by Flann O'Brien

Flashman (1969) by George MacDonald Fraser

Portnoy's Complaint (1969) by Philip Roth

The Bottle Factory Outing (1974) by Beryl Bainbridge

The Hitchhiker's Guide to the Galaxy (1979) by Douglas Adams

The Complete Yes Minister (1981) by Jonathan Lynn and Antony
 Jay

The Secret Diary of Adrian Mole, aged 13¾ (1982) by Sue
 Townsend

Guards! Guards! (1989) by Terry Pratchett

The Shipping News (1993) by Annie Proulx

Bridget Jones's Diary (1996) by Helen Fielding

August

Translated Classics

The Way by Swann's (1913) by Marcel Proust,
translated by Lydia Davis
The Radetzky March (1932) by Joseph Roth,
translated by Joachim Neugroschel

Today I watch the new Tarantino movie, *Once Upon a Time in Hollywood*, a self-indulgent, beautiful, sometimes silly exercise in showing off, set in 1969 around the murder of Sharon Tate by members of the Manson family. I also get to interview the two male stars of the film, Brad Pitt and Leonardo DiCaprio. At one level, that is enviable and exciting: sharing oxygen with two of the most famous, lusted-after men on the planet. At another, it is rather shrivelling to the soul: queuing up amid the flunkies and the fetchers in an anonymous luxury hotel, grateful for ten minutes of snatched time, ever conscious of your own inadequacy. As it happens, both were charming, which is not always the case with big names, and both could talk intelligently about the film. Where I saw self-indulgence, they saw the work of an auteur.

The film ends with some of the most graphic violence I have ever seen in a mainstream movie. Some of it directed at young, frail-looking women. I have thought a lot this year about violent writing, about its place in my own personal canon. And I have found beauty in descriptions of awfulness. Why should I be appalled by Tarantino? First, I think it is the sophomoric stupidity of it: it comes gratuitously at the movie's end, and you can almost see the director's preternaturally arched eyebrow, his smirk at the audience. It is done purely to shock, to revel in its own cartoon mayhem.

The moment that a woman's face is repeatedly smashed into a mantelpiece feels a relic of a bygone age, in which representations of violence were never challenged. There is now more recognition that, in almost all plot-driven art, the victims are disproportionally women; the battered female body is there, a grisly MacGuffin, in the majority of crime novels and thrillers. And Tarantino – and thriller writers – should have the freedom to make use of this imagery, but we too have the freedom to reflect on it. There is nothing artful, or innovative, about a large man caving in the face of a small woman.

3 August

Is there anything that connects Quentin Tarantino with Marcel Proust? Well, up to a point. Both are interested in the sensuous detail that sparks a memory: Tarantino's films are filled with little nods to his childhood past, the sound of a TV heedlessly babbling, say, or the crayon-like colour of food packaging; a nostalgia for lost time. The comparison probably better end there.

So here I am, now confronting the first book of what is, according to the critic Harold Bloom, 'widely recognised as the major novel of the twentieth century': Proust's *À La Recherche du Temps Perdu*, literally translated as *In Search of Lost Time*. It is intimidating. There is a *New Yorker* cartoon somewhere set in a bookshop, in which a Christmas shopper says dolefully: 'I want something to get even with him for that new translation of Proust he got me last year.' This is fiction as potential punishment, effort and work.

The whole novel consists of around 3,000 pages in seven volumes; I am, more modestly, tackling just the first book, *Du Côté de Chez Swann*, translated by Lydia Davis as *The Way by Swann's*. But that still looms large: over a quarter is written in sentences lasting more than ten lines; the prose is more meandering and attenuated even than late Henry James. The novel is in three parts: the narrator recalling his childhood in the village of Combray; the story of Swann – his parents' friend – and his frustrated love in Paris for the courtesan Odette in the years before the narrator was born; and the narrator's own childish friendship with their daughter Gilberte. There is a lot of musing about memory in between.

5 August

Translation is the least glamorous of all literary work: it is under-appreciated and under-paid. A translator has to attempt something that may be impossible in the first place: to render another person's voice – with all its context and textures – in another language, which may have little in the way of shared culture or idiom. '*Traduttore, traditore*', say the Italians, which I *think* means 'to translate is to betray'; there will always be failure, slippage, when one writer takes on another's words and tries to translate them without changing them. Slang is hard to translate, jokes too, because both carry the freight of a nation's linguistic and moral history.

Proust came to English first thanks to the translation by Charles Kenneth Scott Moncrieff, a rather florid figure, who was expelled from Winchester for publishing a story about a gay headmaster, and had an affair (of some sort) with Wilfred Owen. Moncrieff himself died before he completed all the volumes, and his work was finished off by others. My version comes from this century, though, part of a reissue of the whole book based on a newly researched text.

Incidentally, Joseph Conrad, who was Polish, but spoke French and English, preferred Moncrieff to the original: 'I was more interested and fascinated by your rendering than by Proust's creation,' he wrote to the presumably elated translator. 'One has revealed something to me and there is no revelation in the other.' This seems unfathomable.

And yet look at Moncrieff's version of the title: *Remembrance of Things Past*, far from the literal translation of *In Search of Lost Time*. The reference comes not from the dilettante world of early century Paris, but from Shakespeare and Sonnet 30:* 'When to the sessions of sweet silent thought / I summon up remembrance of things past'. Does that matter? Perhaps there is an added frisson here, a bonus texture: Shakespeare, like Proust, felt moved to some extent by homosexual love; his sonnets are a playful, painful exploration of his desire.

We always confront new authors with our brain saturated with older words and ideas: there is no direct, frictionless passage of one person's thoughts to our own. We will always be one move away from the author's vision. To read is to betray at one level; and yet also to have faith, to believe in the existence of a connection. This latter act of faith is at the centre of translation.

---

* Shakespeare is himself quoting the Geneva Bible and the Wisdom of Solomon: 'for a double grief came upon them, and a groaning for the remembrance of things past'. So the connotation reaches back to a Jewish book, written in Greek, probably in Egypt in the first century BC, via a group of Protestant exiles escaping Catholic tyranny in the reign of Queen Mary.

The title of Proust's first book is not straightforward in English. Moncrieff took *Du Côté de chez Swann* and made it *Swann's Way*. Lydia Davis preferred the more literal *The Way by Swann's*, as matching the French, and its suggestion of the physical journey rather than anything more metaphorical. It was nearly neither: Proust for a while considered *Gardens in a Cup of Tea*, in tribute to the dunked madeleine that is its most famous moment.*

This reminds me of other titles that never quite made it. Jane Austen thankfully shifted from the boring *First Impressions* to *Pride and Prejudice*; and Melville, we know, also finally dismissed the prosaic *The Whale* in favour of *Moby Dick* (hyphen or not). Do titles matter? It is impossible to test. Would *Catch-11*, as Heller once envisaged it, have entered the parlance as well as *Catch-22*? I am rather saddened that Fitzgerald preferred *The Great Gatsby* to the classically inflected, rather absurd *Trimalchio in West Egg*. And, for that matter, that Bram Stoker rejected his own working title of *The Dead Un-Dead* in favour of *Dracula* (1897). Tolstoy very nearly went for *All's Well That Ends Well* instead of *War and Peace* (1869), which sounds like an apocryphal claim but is not.

6 August

At the beginning of *The Way by Swann's* the narrator spends a lot of time musing about being in bed, those 'lovely cheeks of the pillow, which, full and fresh, are like the cheeks of our childhood', which is almost meaningful, but not quite. The book was

---

* Samuel Beckett, a true Proustian, once said that 'the whole of Proust's world comes out of a tea-cup': that sensuous sense of memory that is the novel's preoccupation.

initially rejected by publishers,* not least because of such gauzy, breathy meditations. This is the bedroom:

> Where in icy weather the pleasure you enjoy is the feeling that you are separated from the outdoors (like the sea swallow which makes its nest deep in an underground passage in the warmth of the earth) and where, since the fire is kept burning all night in the fireplace, you sleep in a great cloak of warm, smoky air, pierced by the glimmers from the logs breaking into flame again, a sort of immaterial alcove, a warm cave hollowed in the heart of the room itself, a zone of heat with moving thermal contours . . .

The sentence goes on further, but you get the point. The publisher Ollendorff refused to continue reading: 'I don't see why a man should take thirty pages to describe how he turns over in his bed before he goes to sleep.' But if we pause and take the time, there is real pleasure within the cushioning of all those clauses. And the recognition of reality too: we have all marvelled at the heat or cool of a bedroom, the sensation of snuggling down to reach the escape of sleep. *The Way by Swann's* is like this throughout, a combination of longueur and sensuous imagination, what James called 'an inconceivable boredom associated with the most extreme ecstasy which it is possible to imagine'.

The literary world has always, largely, loved Proust. Here is Virginia Woolf:

> Proust so titillates my own desire for expression that I can hardly set out the sentence. Oh if I could write like that! I cry. And at

---

* André Gide turned it down for the *Nouvelle Revue Française*, and then bitterly regretted it: 'the most serious mistake ever made by the *NRF* and, since I bear the shame of being very much responsible for it, one of the most stinging and remorseful regrets of my life'.

the moment such is the astonishing vibration and saturation and intensification that he procures – there's something sexual in it – that I feel I *can* write like that, and seize my pen and then I *can't* write like that. Scarcely anyone so stimulates the nerves of language in me: it becomes an obsession.

Proust is a writers' writer; and often makes writers write badly, so intoxicated are they about the gifts on display. John Updike once wrote this mangled metaphor, for example, noting that the book 'remains as light and inviting as a feather bed, a nearly infinite mass of prose gently sighing up and down, like a calm sea glinting with myriad coins of moonlight'. Beds, boats, coins and the moon.

One antiphonal voice of the period is worth mentioning. Evelyn Waugh in his delightfully bitchy letters to Nancy Mitford: 'I am reading Proust for the first time . . . and am surprised to find him a mental defective.' He went on to parody Proust in *A Handful of Dust* (1934), with the first chapter called 'Du Côté de Chez Beaver'. I am growing to enjoy Proust, but this also makes me like Waugh even more.

When Proust died in 1922, 'a few English lovers of literature and English men of letters', as they called themselves, including Woolf, Conrad, Huxley and Forster, wrote a letter to the *TLS* to 'express our share of sorrow in the loss which the world of the spirit has suffered in his death'. They went on: 'Proust seemed to have found not only his past, but our own past as well, to give us back ourselves, life as we too had known and felt it – our common and everyday experience, but enriched and made beautiful and important by the alchemy of art.'

The 'everyday experience' finally being given its artistic due was one of the foundations of modernism, and *À La Recherche* was completed in a decade that produced *Ulysses* too: another imposing attempt to include everything of the everyday within the confines of prose. Proust had done little before; he had written a book of stories and poems, and then tried to write a novel called *Jean Santeuil*, which petered into nothing. In December 1908 he decided to write a piece of prose about the literary critic Charles Augustin Sainte-Beuve, which he daringly framed as a story told by a young boy to his mother.

That essay, mauled and moulded by the author's incessant brain, became his masterpiece, all 10,000 pages of fragments and sketches, restlessly reshaped and amended from 1908 until 1922, with notes called *paperoles* stuck on higgledy-piggledy throughout. Proust died before the final three volumes were published, at fifty-one, having only been famous for the three years since he won the Prix Goncourt for the second book, *À l'Ombre des Jeunes Filles en Fleur.*

7 August

The death of Toni Morrison was announced last night. She is one of the great authors of the twentieth century, the first black woman to win the Nobel Prize in Literature, and someone who elevated the black experience into high art. I talked to some American writers, such as Walter Mosley, who said that Morrison made an international audience recognise and value a different voice of American history: Morrison was, ultimately, 'unafraid of being black'. But, like Zora Neale Hurston, an obvious precursor, she also wanted to see past colour differences; the only race that she cared about, she once said, was the human race.

And she made use of the white canon in her work too: there is Faulkner, Melville, Shakespeare, the Greek tragedians inside

---

* Again widely praised, but not universally loved: his contemporary Joachim Gasquet called it 'sentimental onanism' (which is the worst kind of onanism, if you ask me).

her writing. She was 'as influential as T.S. Eliot to American literature', said the poet Claudia Rankine to me. The novelist Ladee Hubbard, who writes for the *TLS*, had been taught by her as a graduate, and was audibly moved when she recalled their time together.

Beloved (1987) is Morrison's masterpiece, the first of a trilogy that cemented her place within the canon. Before she had completed it, she won the Nobel, and immediately moved into the rarefied company of writers who are seen as iconic in their own lifetimes. Which is an irony in that the success of her prose is to place us inside the bloody reality, the thrums and stings of precarious existence, as felt by those previously silenced by history. *Beloved* is, among other things, a ghost story from a country haunted by its tragic past. Its account of the death of a child is unforgettable; the novel – as it says in the first line – is 'full of baby's venom'.

As a woman of colour with such spectacular gifts and impact upon the world, Morrison's every word has been pored over in search of solace and significance. And that is a shame: she is not to be read only as sound bite, shorn of context. But she did say this once, which has lingered with me: 'We die. That may be the meaning of life. But we do language. That may be the measure of our lives.'

Language is indeed how we measure our lives, how we make sense of things, and what we leave behind us: the things we have said and written. When we read, we give value to words, we seek their precision, their definition. The verb 'sounding' contains within it one of the truest double-meanings in our language: 'to sound' is to go deep like a diving whale, but also to make something ring out like a bell. We sound words and with words, and few have done it better than Toni Morrison.

10 August

So what do I get from the first book of Proust's modernist monster? I think of Nabokov's injunction to 'caress the detail, the divine detail', and it is clear how much he took that very idea from Proust. This is a novel filled with sensations. Like smells 'of the tall chestnut tree, the baskets of raspberries and a sprig of tarragon' or the 'central, sticky, stale, indigestible and fruity smell of the flowered coverlet' or hawthorns with their 'bitter-sweet scent of almonds . . . like the murmuring of an intense life'.

Proust was a famous invalid, whose life was expressed with murmuring intensity in his mind and on the page: an asthmatic who wrote breathlessly long sentences; a man enlivened by the heady scent of nature, but allergic to plants. As he continued to write *À La Recherche*, he was home-bound, stuck in a corkboard-lined room, living on a diet of fruit, ice cream and cold beer brought from the Ritz,* which sounds fun, but is probably not conducive to happiness.

In the absence of his own lived sensations, he gives us imagined interactions. The book is – almost absurdly – sensitive to the minutiae of surroundings: like the raindrop that 'still lingered to play on the ribs of a leaf and, hanging from the tip, tranquil and sparkling in the sun, would suddenly let go'. Or this asparagus: 'steeped in ultramarine and pink, whose tips, delicately painted with little strokes of mauve and azure, shade off imperceptibly down to their feet – still soiled though they are from the dirt of their garden-bed – with an iridescence that is not of this earth'.

---

* He was independently rich: earning around £200k in today's money every year, and with a net worth of around £7 million. He covered the cost for the printing of *Du Côté de Chez Swann*, which was the only way of getting it into circulation.

At points, the narrator's sensations mingle in synaesthetic wonder, swirling together sights and sounds and smells: music like 'a perfume, like a caress, it encircled him, enveloped him'; the name Gilberte 'a little cloud of precious colour'. This is a storm overwhelming his senses: 'When on summer evenings the melodious sky growls like a wild animal . . . I am the only one in ecstasy inhaling, through the noise of the falling rain, the smell of invisible, enduring lilacs.'

At moments, I feel overwhelmed too. The narrator is too sensitive, his prose filled with the anaphylaxis of overreaction: he wallows in 'a sort of puberty of grief' or wails in an 'ecstasy of waiting'. Truth be told, he is not a particularly edifying companion: he's a snitch, a telltale, a mummy's boy* desperate 'to devote the whole of the minute Mama would grant me to feeling her cheek against my lips'. He feels too much, and talks too much.

That makes him very good at appreciating art and culture: he's a 'young bookworm', whose occupations are 'reading, reverie, tears and sensuous pleasure'. Like Anthony Powell's narrator, Proust's figure sees the real world often as a reflection of the art world: Odette is said to look like Zipporah in Botticelli's *Youth of Moses* (1481–2), all blonde tresses falling on pale skin, a long, languorous, sensual neck;† a servant 'mused motionless, statuesque, useless, like the purely decorative warrior one sees in the most tumultuous paintings by Mantegna'.

---

* The narrator is named only once, with postmodern flourish: 'my Christian name which, if we give the narrator the same name as the author of this book, would be "My Marcel" or "My Darling Marcel".' Proust moaned about people incontinently conflating life and art, but *À La Recherche* certainly is about a writer learning to use memory as inspiration. Proust was a mummy's boy himself: he may have died mouthing the word 'mama'.

† Googling artwork while reading is a real modern pleasure. Do it now with Zipporah and you will see Proust's vision of Odette.

Great art and writing fill what we think is empty, define what we think is shapeless. I feel today reading Proust a sense of wonder at his perceptions, his command. Those little moments of summative excellence: 'the insolent indifference of the clock'; the 'flaxen billow' of overgrown graves; the steeple of a church 'so thin, so pink, that it seemed merely scratched on the sky by a fingernail'. It is Nabokovian, for all that I am getting things the wrong way round.

11 August

The Way by Swann's has a totemic opening line, immediately recognisable: 'For a long time, I went to bed early.'

Many memorable openers have a robust aphoristic quality. Think of *Pride and Prejudice*: 'It is a truth universally acknowledged, that a single man in possession of a good fortune, must be in want of a wife.' Or *Anna Karenina*: 'All happy families are alike; each unhappy family is unhappy in its own way'; or *The Go-Between* (1953): 'The past is a foreign country; they do things differently there.' There is certainty here, verging on the glib; nothing beautiful or musical, but something that brooks little confusion.

The alternative approach – which you see in Nabokov's short stories, for example – is the tantalising plunge into the unsettling, the hint of strangeness to come. Kafka's *The Metamorphosis* (1915) is the model: 'As Gregor Samsa awoke one morning from uneasy dreams he found himself transformed in his bed into a gigantic insect.' There is confidence here too: the unstated belief that the reader will have to make good their curiosity and carry on. See also that wonderful beginning to *One Hundred Years of Solitude* (1967), the novel that introduced me as a teenager breathlessly to magical realism (which is the right age to find this genre and retain optimism about it): 'Many years later, as he faced the firing squad, Colonel Aureliano Buendía was to remember that distant afternoon when his father took him to discover ice.' Or, more Kafkaesque still, J.G. Ballard's *High-Rise* (1975): 'Later, as he sat on his balcony eating the dog, Dr Robert Laing reflected on the unusual events that had taken place within this huge apartment building during the previous three months.' Notice how they all look to amazing events that have already happened, plunging us *in medias res* as if to exhort us to catch up on what we have missed.

This is an unending challenge, trying to recall the most insidiously effective beginnings of everything we have read. How about insouciant Anthony Burgess in *Earthly Powers* (1980): 'It was the afternoon of my eighty-first birthday, and I was in bed with my catamite when Ali announced that the archbishop had come to see me.' Then there's Orwell, inevitably: 'It was a bright cold day in April, and the clocks were striking thirteen.'

Do great books demand great opening lines, or do we just retrofit significance to the beginnings of classics? Perhaps the latter in the case of Proust, and his bedtime thought. As a counterbalance to all these incisive entrances, here is the opening to a great novel, *The Portrait of a Lady* by Henry James, which is a model of whimsical uncertainty:

> Under certain circumstances there are few hours in life more agreeable than the hour dedicated to the ceremony known as afternoon tea. There are circumstances in which, whether you partake of the tea or not – some people of course never do – the situation is in itself delightful. Those that I have in mind in beginning to unfold this simple history offered an admirable setting to an innocent pastime.

That stuttering parenthesis seems to denote the author clearing his throat, unsure of himself, before he commits to the novel that will ultimately seal his reputation. And we can forgive him that: a novel is more than its first moment, but what joy when that moment catches the light of the imagination immediately.

12 August

I was at the Book Festival in Edinburgh at the end of last week to talk about 'novels that have shaped our world'. Audience members suggested their formative fictions, books that had the most impact on them. It was a broadly canonical list: *War and Peace*, *A Passage to India* (1924), *Jane Eyre* (1847) and so on. I happened to mention *Pride and Prejudice*, a book I reread every couple of years, and a young woman said it literally changed her life: she started reading it at eighteen, fell in love with it, changed her university degree and was now a writer.

One other woman suggested *The Weirdstone of Brisingamen* (1960) by Alan Garner, as a major influence upon her childhood. I remember it from mine with great pleasure,* including the BBC radio version, which my parents must have recorded. This, I think, is the sort of book that is more genuinely formative, in a way that Proust would understand: the writing we read when our minds are fresh, pliable and able to receive impression. When I look back at my childhood, my memories coalesce around certain vivid reading experiences. Like the summer I discovered Richmal Crompton's *Just William* series, and found a soulmate in a scruffy, self-reliant schoolboy. I used to read them sitting atop a shed at the corner of my garden, eating apples

---

* Unlike the author, it must be said, who once called it 'a very bad book'. It was published to great success in the immediate aftermath of *The Lord of the Rings*. The one ineluctable rule of publishing is that, if something is successful, flood the market with things that are similar until the market is destroyed. Then repeat with something else.

(including the cores, as directed by the text) as I peered over the hedge into next door. For those moments, I was a different person in a different age.

When I visited my grandparents, I found books by James Herriot, telling of his travails as a Yorkshire vet.* They had already been made into a TV series, called *All Creatures Great and Small*, which we all watched as a family. But the books were more memorable. At one point, James Herriot is on a boat in the Baltic (I say all this from unbidden recollection from more than thirty years, so it could be slightly wrong as to detail), and everybody else is seasick apart from him. He gorges on hors d'oeuvres like pickled herring, relishing the meal, as all around him quaver and spew. When my mum asked me what I wanted for my birthday meal that year, I said, 'Hors d'oeuvres', not really knowing what they were, and ended up with a piece of mackerel, some green pepper and a small bowl of sweetcorn. But I had inhabited the world of the book for the moment.

When I was ten, I became enthralled by spy thrillers (which were the main novels available in my house): books by people like Len Deighton, John le Carré and a dreadful hack called Colin Forbes. I effortfully developed a taste for black coffee, so I could be like the diffident, brainy, nighthawk heroes who spent their time worrying and plotting late into the night. Here, perhaps, my love of genre fiction began.

Interesting, I see, that the first three books conjured by child-hood memory all then connect to food and drink: the crisp

* Years later, I interviewed the Nigerian-American novelist Akwaeke Emezi, whose debut novel *Freshwater* came out in 2018. It is a very experimental, fluid piece of writing about Igbo myth and non-binary identity. Imagine my surprise that Akwaeke had read James Herriot religiously as a child, and its influence had even taken them to veterinary college! Amazing the reach of writing, when you think about it.

sourness of apples, the misleading hors d'oeuvres, bitter black coffee. My madeleine moments.

Reading *The Way by Swann's* has been infuriating, enervating, energising and often breathtaking. And troubling notes do surface too. Swann's affair with Odette is told in tiresome, relentless, whiny detail. He becomes the traditional lover of all literature: endlessly wondering what his mistress is doing, mooning outside her house, intercepting her correspondence, neglecting his friends. He is a cliché even in 1913. And a brutish one: 'He felt he hated Odette, he would have liked to cut out those eyes of hers that he had loved so much just a moment ago, crush those pallid cheeks.' This gives him continual and violent visions of her infidelity: 'His soul bore them along, cast them aside, cradled them, like dead bodies. And it was poisoned by them.'

Sex in Proust is seldom loving, seldom satisfying. There is a moment in *The Way by Swann's* when the narrator spots two lesbians in amorous clench, who then proceed to spit on a photograph of one of their fathers. This vignette of relished sadism came from his own life: Proust, it is alleged, used to make prostitutes do this on photographs of his own female companions. Proust was himself a troubled gay man who never admitted it to the world, and the novel is filled with glimpses of sad, gay relationships. The women with whom the narrator is involved – whose names make them all sound like men: Gilberte, Albertine, Andrée – all end up having same-sex affairs around which the story circles. It has been argued that they stand as hidden proxies for male gay relationships. And Proust's angry dissatisfaction seeps from the pages. By the end of his life, he could only achieve arousal by watching starving rats fight in a cage in a male brothel, of all things.

Nabokov thought that *À La Recherche* celebrated 'the transmutation of sensation into sentiment, the ebb and tide of memory, waves of emotions such as desire, jealousy, and artistic euphoria'. But the first two only ring true for me: this is a novel of sensuous detail, of an accurate and moving account of remembering,* but lacking in waves of any real emotion *other than* artistic euphoria. This is art for the artist, not for the heartfelt reader. I wonder whether the heartstrings might be tugged more by Joseph Roth.

18 August

I know: with the whole world of non-English fiction to choose from, I should have looked further afield than another early-century European. But this month has selfishly been about remedying books that have long recommended themselves, and long been recommended, to me. If Proust is at the centre of Western literary consciousness by osmosis (not really read that much, but often quoted as an act of intellectual virtue-signalling; an author who has reached the heights of becoming an adjective), the same cannot be said about Joseph Roth, who is not even the most famous author with his own surname.

In the first paragraph of *The Radetzky March*, we learn of the man who becomes the 'hero of Solferino', Joseph Trotta, a soldier who saves the life of the Kaiser, and is ennobled as a reward: 'Fate had elected him for a special deed. But he then made sure that later times lost all memory of him.' For Joseph Trotta, read Joseph Roth. When Roth died, in 1939, a disappointed drunk, the world

---

* According to Jonah Lehrer's entertaining book *Proust Was A Neuroscientist* (2007), Proust foreshadowed scientific understanding in his treatment of recalled sensations. Apparently, taste and smell are the only two senses that link directly to the hippocampus, the home of memory.

descending into chaos and murder around him, his literary merits were little advocated. As with so many authors I have read this year, the declaration of genius was a long time coming, and came too late to be of benefit. But it did come, and *The Radetzky March* is now known as the masterpiece of a master-craftsman.

Roth was born in 1894, of Jewish origin, in what is now Ukraine. His father went mad just before he was born, and disappeared from his life, creating a vacuum that Roth's fiction endlessly and restlessly tried to fill. He joined the Hapsburg army in 1916, saying in retrospect that his 'strongest experience was the War and the destruction of my fatherland, the only one I ever had'. It is not clear if he ever actually fought. He said he became a Russian prisoner, though that has never been confirmed. In the 1920s he was a brilliantly successful journalist, mainly for the *Frankfurter Zeitung*, and an immediate and sensitive chronicler of the rise of Nazism in Germany. He had Hitler's number as early as 1924, and was forced to leave Berlin in January 1933,* weeks after *The Radetzky March* was published. He said this to his close companion Stefan Zweig: 'I won't bet a penny on our lives. They have succeeded in establishing a reign of barbarity. Do not fool yourself. Hell reigns.'

The 1930s were hell for Roth: his drinking worsened, he lived in hotels, away from his wife, Friederike Reichler, who was hospitalised with schizophrenia in 1933. She was later to be euthanased by the Nazis, as part of their eugenicist terror. Roth died before the Nazis could get him, in 1939, at the age of just forty-five, collapsing in a hotel room in a corner of Europe about to be swamped by darkness.

---

* In 1934 he wrote that Goebbels 'has caused truth to walk with the limp he has himself. The officially sanctioned German truth has been given its own club foot . . . Germany has started using its loudspeakers to drown out the cries of blood.'

All this background offers some explanation for the tenor of Roth's fiction, which has a fierce and melancholy beauty about it. 'Roth, you must become much sadder,' an editor apparently once remarked. 'The sadder you are, the better you write.' *The Radetzky March* is sad, remorseless and wonderful. It is a tale of decline: after Joseph Trotta is ennobled, 'severed from the long procession of his Slavic peasant forebears', he begins the life of a lonely aristocrat. Within twenty pages, he has been a hero, loses a wife and brings up a miserable adult son. This latter Trotta becomes a bureaucrat, a 'district captain', respected and never loved, protected by a certain 'bony hardness'. His son, Carl Joseph, is the main character in the novel. He becomes a soldier and lives his life, frustrated, in the borderlands of the empire, where people live 'between East and West, squeezed in between night and day – virtually as living ghosts spawned by the night and haunting the day'. This is a land of mud and marshes, insidiously croaking frogs and dissolute inhabitants, rotting their guts with a drink called '180 Proof'.

For, as the Trotta family struggles, so does the Austro-Hungarian Empire itself. The Battle of Solferino of 1859 was itself the beginning of the end of an era. As we, ahem, all know, it was between Austro-Hungary on one side and Sardinia-France on the other, but it was also the last time reigning monarchs on both sides personally led troops into battle.* The next major conflict would be less flamboyantly helmed in the mud of the Western Front. And *The Radetzky March* is repeatedly full of the looming advent of the First World War, and the decline of old empire. This is a novel that

---

* This was also the battle that inspired Jean-Henri Dunant to write the book that would lead to the creation of the Geneva Convention and the International Red Cross.

gives shape to the 'dim nocturnal abysses where storms slumber', the forces of bitter destruction that were going to herald modernity with terror. And it is explicit in doing so: 'They had no idea that several years later every last one of them, with no exception, would encounter Death. Their ears were not sharp enough to catch the whirring gears of the great hidden mills that were already grinding out the Great War.' The Radetzky March itself, the martial strains of which echo through the novel, begins as the sound of order, 'the "Marseillaise" of conservatism', and ends as a bitter, ironic anthem of doomed youth.

Roth does not seem much interested in considering the ills of imperialism, so rapt is he in the horrors of nationalism: the rise of single states destined to war with one another, and in which Jewish people could be isolated more easily. The Kaiser is another failed father figure, like the various male Trottas: 'He was the oldest emperor in the world. All around him Death was circling, circling and mowing.'

24 August

A final holiday of the year to an old house in Oxfordshire. I immediately check out the bookshelves, and happily see things I could read in an emergency, if I finish all the books I have brought with me (which has never happened, even once, in thirty years of going on holiday): *The Portrait of a Lady*, *Catcher in the Rye* (1951), *Lamentation* (2014) by the very fine writer of historical fiction C.J. Sansom. I have read all of them before, but – as we know – that is no tremendous barrier for me.

I think of the books I have discovered in holiday homes over the years, and a couple stand out because they have led me to a series that has gone on to provide hours of pleasure. In a damp, tiny villa in blustery Kent one summer, in which it rained so much it felt like the clouds and the sea were fusing into one brusque sodden mass, I picked up an old 1970s paperback by Peter O'Donnell featuring the comic book superhero Modesty Blaise. I read it almost in one go, and came home to order all the others. They tell the tale of a sort of female James Bond, who drops her skirt at the first sign of danger so she can fight without encumbrance, and manages to be both faintly titillating and satisfactorily feminist: Modesty is the definition of a strong, powerful woman. They are almost perfect light, guilt-free holiday reading.

In another south coast haven amid another sodden summer, I idly began reading a book called *Early Autumn* (1980) by Robert B. Parker. I had heard the name, because he had written a sequel to Chandler's *The Big Sleep*, called, in a somewhat gauche inspiration, *Perchance to Dream* (1991). I knew he was a big American crime writer, but little else. The book was one of the series featuring a private detective called Spenser: a wisecracking, literate Bostonian ('it's Spenser with an "s" like the author of *The Faerie Queene*'), who saw himself in the romantic mould of Sir Gawain. Spenser is a kind of liberal macho ideal: he works out, boxes well, drinks craft beer, eats carbs, has a black best friend, a feminist psychoanalyst girlfriend, and never loses a fight. I have read more than twenty books about him, and take a couple with me on this holiday to enjoy bibulously in the evenings.*

---

* Spenser is such a likeable character, I even take book recommendations from him. Tonight, he talks about reading Barbara Tuchman's *A Distant Mirror* (1978), a history of 'crusades and chivalry, plunder and plagues' from the 'Calamitous 14th Century'. I buy a second-hand copy, and it is a very good piece of narrative history.

Joseph Brodsky once said that there was a poem on every page of Roth, so let's try to work out why the prose feels so affecting, so effective. Roth, at one level, is also like an abstract artist,* a Kandinsky of the page; he uses big swatches of colour to set scenes and moods. In one paragraph alone we get this: 'the sun emerged like a blood-red orange'; 'on the water meadow in the wide, greenish glade framed by the blackish firs, the silvery mists rose clumsily, torn apart by the vehement, regular motions of the dark-blue uniforms. Pale and dismal, the sun then rose. Its matte silver, cool and alien, broke through the black branches. Frosty shudders passed like a cruel comb over the russet skins of the horses'; 'dark-blue jingling shadows'; 'a yellowly blinking lantern'. This sets the palette for the whole novel, and the colours tend to repeat themselves throughout. Thus the 'blinding red and demented yellow' of a brothel; or the army seen in abstract terms: 'the bloody red of the cavalry trousers still blazed over the parched yellow of the stubble fields, erupting from the grey of the infantrists like fire from clouds.'

Grey is an evocative colour to Roth, symbolic of leached-out authority. This is an officer: 'His yellowish-grey face was smiling. He was dressed in grey. He wore grey canvas shoes. Their edges were coated with the grey, fresh, shiny springtime mire of his land. A few small grey locks curled distinctly on his tiny skull.' The dull word is given the heft of the poetic, the potency of importance, by its repetition. It also points to another Rothism: colours already on the fade, bleeding out as they dissipate and dissolve: he is fond of 'yellowish', 'blackish', 'paleish' and so on.

Then there is the whiteness of the flesh, which comes with pallor suggestive of death. This is a female lover, cherished for a

---

* His name, in German, sounds like '*rot*' or red.

moment then lost: 'her white face floated naked, exposed, on the dark surface of the evening' . . . 'like a huge white oval flower' . . . 'the white hands emerged'. I have never read a novel more sensitive to hands, those agents of fleeting and dissatisfied connection. Roth writes about them almost with a fetish. Carl Joseph's 'own warm hands still contained the memory of her cool breasts'; the 'damp, broad and slack' hand of a cuckold receiving consolation; a lover's 'brown, hairy hands on her white shoulders'. Hands act as miniature metonymies, symbolising a character or a fate. Here are the Jews, who scratch out a frightened living on the border: 'on the backs of their deft hands, hard, red bristles stood rigid like tiny spears.'

There is something bolder, more certain in this prose than we might find in Proust. Roth is remorselessly definitive in his approach. And this makes him rather bleak. When Carl Joseph loses a lover, he thinks that 'the fat curling worms were just starting to gnaw cosily on her round white breasts'. The adjectives are almost gratuitous: but the image lingers in our minds. *The Radetzky March* is a good novel to read if you are feeling apocalyptic; it is as cosy as a gnawing worm. Perhaps that is healthful: a world preoccupied with Brexit and Trump might do well to think of times of genuine catastrophe. This is a novel set at the beginning of the First World War, written as the Second World War's onset became inexorable. Each morning, I am moved, unconsoled, by the misery.

Roth is a wonderful writer of set-pieces, and he never does better than in the novel's eventual plummet into violence, as war finally comes:

Fires surrounded the corpses dangling from trees, and the leaves were already crackling, drizzle heralding the bloody autumn. The old bark of ancient trees slowly charred, tiny, silvery, swelling sparks crept up along the fissures like fiery worms, reaching

> the foliage, and the green leaves curled, turned red, then black, then grey; the ropes broke, and the corpses plunged to the ground, their faces black, their bodies unscathed.

Civilisation brutalised in savage technicolour. Roth was, in the end, a pessimist, a renderer of misery. He said his book 'demonstrates the old and eternal truth that the individual is always defeated in the end'. But his legacy is, in fact, a triumph of the individual: the persecuted, angry, maddened man, destroyed by a force far greater than his own, but bequeathing to the world something beautiful and enduring.

~

Further Reading

The Odyssey (*c.* eighth century BC) by Homer
Metamorphoses (AD 8) by Ovid
The Tale of Genji (*c.* early eleventh century) by Murasaki Shikibu
Inferno (*c.* early fourteenth century) by Dante Alighieri
Essays (1580) by Michel de Montaigne
Don Quixote (1605) by Miguel de Cervantes
Madame Bovary (1856) by Gustave Flaubert
Crime and Punishment (1866) by Fyodor Dostoevsky
Anna Karenina (1877) by Leo Tolstoy
The House of Ulloa (1886) by Emilia Pardo Bazán
I Am a Cat (1905) by Soseki
The Metamorphosis (1915) by Franz Kafka
Kristin Lavransdatter (1922) by Sigrid Undset
The Magic Mountain (1924) by Thomas Mann
All Quiet on the Western Front (1929) by Erich Maria Remarque
Independent People (1934) by Halldór Laxness

The Stranger (1942) by Albert Camus

Labyrinths (1962) by Jorge Luis Borges

A Day in the Life of Ivan Denisovich (1962) by Alexander
  Solzhenitsyn

The Master and Margarita (1967) by Mikhail Bulgakov

Papillon (1969) by Henri Charrière

War's Unwomanly Face (1985) by Svetlana Alexievich

September

Poetry

Rumi: Selected Poems (1995), translated by Coleman Barks
Songs of Innocence and of Experience (1794) by William Blake
Don Juan (1819–24) by Lord Byron
Three books (1890, 1891 and 1894) by Emily Dickinson

2 September

As my poetry month starts, I see a trailer for a new show on
Apple TV called *Dickinson*. It is, slightly unbelievably, a stormy
series about the poet Emily. The voice-over has corset-
clad Americans saying things like, 'I have one purpose: to be a
great writer', and 'She's wild!' while the actress playing young
Emily does high kicks in her room, or strums a lute like it's
an electric guitar. Dickinson is made to stand as a teen rebel,
proto-millennial feminist, fighting the patriarchy at every
unconventional turn. You can imagine how the producers got
here: 'something punky and young, but a bit clever too, so we
don't look too obvious about it'.

The mind boggles at other possible attempts to sex up poets:
Brad Pitt IS *Larkin*, underneath whose polyester duffle coat lies
the sinewy body of an epochal lover; Sean Penn IS *Milton*,
blinded by power in a country at war with itself; Cara
Delevingne IS *Plath*, the tortured soul never allowed to be

herself in a world gone mad; and so on. The latter one could actually happen, come to think of it.

So a question: how many people actually sit and read poetry for pleasure? In a world in which everything has a metric, there seems to be a cultural desperation to make poetry appear popular. Hence the National Poetry Month in the US, and an International Poetry Day everywhere else, in which poems are posted like distress flares, signalling the intellectual virtue of the poster.

For the second time this year (after my Shakespeare sonnet experience of April), I want to try to establish my own relationship with the poetic form, which has been largely conditioned by my undergraduate experience. Will I find something to cling to, or think with, this month?

3 September

A couple of people (including my wife) saw the Rumi book in my bag, and nodded: 'Oh, that poet; he's always on Instagram.' That has been both his triumph and his curse: Rumi is everywhere and – appropriately enough for a self-renouncing mystic – nowhere; widely known and widely misunderstood. He is now the bestselling poet in translation in America, and more than 2 million of his books have been sold in recent decades around the world, a simply staggering number. On Amazon, you can buy at least seven Rumi calendars, Rumi sportswear, Rumi armchairs and shower curtains, even a Rumi colouring book. Beyoncé and Jay-Z named their daughter after him because 'Rumi is our favourite poet'; Madonna and Tilda Swinton are fans; Chris Martin said that some of his poetry 'kind of changed my life', and has a recital on a Coldplay album.*

---

* 'This being human is a guest house. / Every morning a new arrival. / A joy, a depression, a meanness, / some momentary awareness comes / as an unexpected visitor.' Which is about as meaningful as any Coldplay lyric.

Before I start reading this morning, I Google 'Rumi inspirational quotes', and am overwhelmed by images of mountains and sunsets, with pieties scrawled across them: 'Wherever you are, and whatever you do, be in love'; or 'You show your worth by what you seek!' or 'Lovely days don't come to you, you should walk to them'. This is not poetry, or philosophy, or religion: this is greeting-card glibness. What the hell is going on here?

The story begins away from the crass commercialism of modernity in the strange world of early Islamic mysticism. Jalal al-Din Rumi lived from 1207 to 1273, born in Afghanistan and spending most of his days in Konya, Turkey. His name 'Rumi' simply means 'Roman' or 'Western', because Konya was part of the eastern Roman Empire. And it is more than fitting, given his elevated status now in Western sensibilities. Rumi's father, who called himself 'the Sultan of Scholars', was actually a rather mediocre lawyer, but also a Sufi, an Islamic mystic: Sufism is the branch of the faith that is intensely inward and spiritual, otherworldly, impassioned and elemental.

Rumi followed in his father's footsteps, but not much happened until he met an old man called Shams of Tabriz, around 1244, himself a mystic in search of 'someone who could endure my company'. Their intense relationship – they were said to be so close 'that nobody knew who was the lover and who the beloved' – sparked the poetic urge in Rumi, and almost all of his writing then followed. Shams eventually left, and may have been murdered by Rumi's son, but Rumi then transferred his affections to two other men, a goldsmith called Saladin Zarkub, and his own student Husam Chelebi. Out of such close male bonding, which may well have been erotic, came intensely spiritual poetry.

And a lot of it: Rumi's major work is called the *Mathnawi*, a big rambling collection of thoughts in some 27,000 couplets;

and it is only part of the creative output of a man who did not even get going until he was thirty-seven. In the West, it has been translated and worked upon by Arabists, especially since Georgian times, but was not widely famous until it was popularised by an American poet who spoke no Persian and could not read the original words at all. This was Coleman Barks, who takes other people's literal translations (sometimes from the nineteenth century) and turns them into free verse, having been told by another poet, Robert Bly, in 1976, that Rumi's poems needed to be 'released from their cages'.

6 September

The American idea of free verse is at the heart of a lot of modern poetry, and responsible largely for how bad much of it is. Poetry for me is about the channelling of an idea, directing it into the most beautiful and affecting shape; 'emotion put into measure', as Thomas Hardy said. Which is why it involves rhythm and rhyme so much: self-imposed, measured constraints that compel creative order. Free verse, as the name suggests, abandons all that, and you are left with what feels like often arbitrary, untethered musings. Robert Frost said it was 'like playing tennis with the net down'. Of course, free verse can be beautiful, can be artfully arranged, but it carries none of the discipline of shape that makes poetry so powerful. Barks's version of Rumi, at two removes from the original, seems on first glance to be shapeless, occasionally gormless; but let's see what happens when I read it every single day.

9 September

Barks calls Rumi's poems, in his typical grating manner, 'chew toys for the intellect', which seems to be code for 'don't blame me if they don't make much sense'. There can be no doubt that Rumi has been appropriated for New Age sensibilities. This has meant, among other things, playing down the Islamic aspect to his thinking. The *Mathnawi* can be seen as a Koranic text, an explainer – as Rumi puts it – of 'the roots of the roots of the roots of the religion', but Barks's version is much less specific, more open to general interpretation. Take this line, which is sold as a bumper sticker in the US: 'Out beyond ideas of wrong-doing and rightdoing there is a field. I'll meet you there'. A decent message in its way. But the original words Rumi wrote were '*kufr*' ('infidelity', not wrongdoing) and '*iman*' ('religion', not rightdoing). It is Islam being minimised in favour of non-denominational spirituality.

That is fine to a certain extent: Rumi was someone who preached wide-ranging tolerance. Christian and Jewish characters from the Bible appear (including an emphasis on Joseph and Jesus), as does teaching that follows something like a Buddhist tradition. He was a unifier, which is no bad thing. At his best, Barks gives us a Rumi suggestive to my mind of Emerson and transcendentalism: 'make yourself particles', he says, which reminds us of Emerson's thought that 'I am nothing; I see all; the currents of the Universal Being circulate through me; I am part or particle of God.'

Rumi has been so often appropriated in this way because he seems to speak against the 'world-tangle' of modern living, and in support of renunciation, the quest for simplicity where 'the soul lives in the silent breath'. On a busy commuter train, thoughts buzzing with work worries and other material contemplations, it is not hard to see the appeal of this sort of giving up, embracing 'acts of helplessness' or 'this emptiness, more beautiful than existence'. But the problem is that existence can never be empty, our acts – whether useful or successful or not – are always moments of agency, compelled on us by a life that will not simply wait for us to sigh in dreamlike oblivion. Rumi offers impractical consolation, which – after all – is one definition of religion.

11 September

It has been well observed that Sufi poetry relies heavily on cliché, on familiar imagery, that it is an act of ecstasy not inventiveness. So we get plenty of metaphors of heat: 'Fire is my child, / but I must be consumed / and become fire.' And lots of liquid:* 'Be melting snow. / Wash yourself of yourself.' This feels rather like wishy-washing, to be honest. Animals appear regularly as metaphors: we are asked to think of the 'health of your heart-donkey' or that 'you are the free-swimming fish'. Or even:

> The rooster of lust, the peacock of wanting
> to be famous, the crow of ownership, and the duck
> of urgency, kill them and revive them
> in another form, changed and harmless.

I think we all need to kill the duck of urgency at some point in the day.

If Rumi uses animals metaphorically, much of his poetry also testifies to physicality, to animal reality. I hesitate to mention this, but one poem is called 'The Innocence of Gourdcrafting' and tells the story of a maid who 'had carved a flanged device / to fit on a donkey's penis, / to keep him from going too far into her'. Her mistress spots her getting pleasure this way, and – 'dizzy / with anticipation, her vagina glowing / and singing like

---

* Sometimes heat and liquid together: 'If you are a friend of God, fire is your water.' Poetic paradox is often annoying, as we saw with Shakespeare. Rumi-Barks likes a paradox: 'The sunlight is totally empty / And totally full.' Totally.

a nightingale' – decides to try herself, without noticing the use of the gourd. As a result the donkey 'pushed through and into her intestines / and, without a word, she died'.

What to make of this? There is unquestionably a strain of misogyny in Rumi, whose fondness for male company within a patriarchal society is not irrelevant. But the translation is foolish and inane (that 'glowing and singing' vagina), and Barks's treatment does nothing to advance the cause of the poet who has ultimately made his fortune.

At his best Rumi does offer a certain bracing earthiness, he is a spiritual figure not only for the religious but for 'those who believe only in the reality / of the sexual organs and the digestive tract'.* And there are moments that give pause, and cause for reflection:

> What the sayer of praise is really praising is
> himself, by saying implicitly,
> 'My eyes are clear.'

As a comment on the mentality of Twitter, say, that is acutely observed. But we want a poet to be more than sporadically wise, trimmed and primped for social media, and Rumi has become little other than a figure ripped from his historical context and travestied for the faux-wisdom of our shallow age. Jay-Z might like it, but I don't.

---

* There is a cookbook called *Sufi Cuisine* (2005), which mingled recipes with aphorisms from Rumi, and Barks concludes his own selected poems with some recipes for curry. Rumi relished food as metaphor: a lover of God was like a kebab; men are like chickpeas bubbling in a cauldron. Like Proust, he associated sweetness with transported, elevated feeling: death 'tastes like sugar'. He hated turnips, though, which seems reasonable enough to me.

12 September

William Blake was a visionary, like Rumi.* He was also a man in whom religious visions competed with a refusal to follow religious orthodoxy. He was famous for seeing God, and 'a tree filled with angels, bright angelic wings bespangling every bough like stars'. Wordsworth once said that 'There was no doubt that this poor man was mad, but there is something in the madness of this man which interests me more than the sanity of Lord Byron and Walter Scott.'

Like Rumi, he has been adopted by people of a not especially religious disposition. He was much praised in the 1960s, when Allen Ginsberg set some of his songs to music, having had a personal encounter with Blake's ghostly voice. Jim Morrison, of the Doors, studied Blake at UCLA, and two of his songs, 'You're Lost Little Girl' and 'End of the Night', are direct lifts of Blake's words, while the name of his band comes from a Blake quote: 'If the doors of perception were cleansed, everything would appear to man as it is, infinite', a line popularised by the title of a novel by Aldous Huxley. The sentiment sounds like it could have been written by a Californian ur-hipster, high on peyote, but it came from a grubby, eighteenth-century engraver from London. Indeed, the very idea of lost innocence meeting bitter experience feels like something from 1960s counter-culture, but is a great universal. And Blake's sense of the collision of opposites, the disparity and inequality of different existences, has a resonance that seems to be timeless.†

---

* In *Europe: A Prophecy* he has a fairy 'shew you all alive / The world, where every particle of dust breathes forth its joy'; that idea of creative force being in every part of being is something shared by many mystical writers.

† He has heavily influenced the children's writer Philip Pullman, and not only in the concept of lively dust. The Lyca of 'The Little Girl Lost' poem, surrounded by vivid animals, may have been transmuted into the Lyra of *His*

But how much is Blake read today beyond the words to the song 'Jerusalem', which was written simply as part of a preface to his long poem, *Milton*, and has – thanks to the musical hymn to which it was set by Sir Hubert Parry in 1916 – entered British culture? The *Sun* website even has an SEO[*] article written to catch people Googling details about it: 'What are lyrics to Jerusalem, who wrote the hymn, is it England's national anthem and what does it mean?' Well, it tells the fairly trippy tale of Joseph of Arimathea and Jesus visiting Glastonbury (it is *their* feet in ancient times walking on England's mountains green), and is now sung lustily at sporting events, often preferred to the real national anthem. George V certainly liked it more.

If this gave Blake slightly misleading renown, does it mean he is safely ensconced in the poetic pantheon in the same way that, say, Byron or Keats is? That is less clear. The critic Northrop Frye once said that the works of Blake form 'what is in proportion to its merits the least read body of poetry in the English language'. And there is something in that: his fans are devoted, but his output is troubling, often confusing and incomplete.

16 September

I reach for *Songs of Innocence and of Experience*, a compilation put together in 1794, after *Innocence* had appeared five years before on its own. The first section contains short, simple poems that

---

Dark Materials. Pullman came to Blake via Ginsberg, and said his mind reacted 'with the joyful immediacy of a flame leaping to meet a gas jet'.

[*] Search engine optimisation: newspaper websites publish articles deliberately to catch search enquiries. It is why you get things like 'Who is Boris Johnson's girlfriend, what is her job and how much does she weigh?' Depressing stuff.

repay rereading. It is a relaxing way to spend a journey in the city that was Blake's physical and spiritual home.

This is from 'Introduction':

> And I made a rural pen,
> And I stained the water clear,
> And I wrote my happy songs
> Every child may joy to hear.

Blake is indeed giving us a collection of 'happy songs', full of 'joy' and children. But just what is the word 'stain' doing in this reverie? It is a warning that contrariness always lurks, even amid nursery rhyme sensibility. And, as with nursery rhymes and fairy tales, Blake is never afraid to introduce the note of sorrow or terror. This is from 'The Chimney Sweeper':

> When my mother died I was very young,
> And my father sold me while yet my tongue
> Could scarcely cry 'Weep! weep! weep! weep!'
> So your chimneys I sweep, and in soot I sleep.

Blake wishes to indict the reader, they are all 'our' chimneys after all, and the cry of injustice is hammered home in single syllables; we hear how 'weep' is always there in the word 'sweep'. That figure appears again in *Experience*, in a poem about London:

> In every cry of every man,
> In every infant's cry of fear,
> In every voice, in every ban,
> The mind-forged manacles I hear:
> How the chimney-sweeper's cry
> Every blackening church appals,

> And the hapless soldier's sigh
> Runs in blood down palace walls.

This is magnificently, bitterly angry. And notice how the physical blackness of the sweep has transferred metaphorically to the church, one of the institutions (like the palace) that is so heedless of the plight of ordinary people. Blake is a poet of naive sensation, of 'joy' and 'smiles', but also compelled to testify to what 'mind-forged' human agency serves only to complicate and devastate. He bears witness to how 'man' gets connected to 'manacle' with too great an ease.

Blake's vision is dialectical. He believed the marriage of thesis and antithesis to produce a synthesis was vital to poetry, and indeed to life: 'without Contraries there is no progression. Attraction and Repulsion, Reason and Energy, Love and Hate, are necessary to Human existence.' The very structure of *Songs of Innocence and of Experience* testify to the power of contrariness: the one section contrasts with the other; poems interrelate, attract and repel. There are two songs called 'Holy Thursday', for example: the first speaks with 'harmonious thunderings', a very Blakean compromise in itself, but which then attenuates into the 'trembling cry' of the second poem. We are not in the 'green and pleasant land' of ancient times, but a place that is 'rich and fruitful' only to the wealthy few, of 'babes reduced to misery, fed with a cold and usurious hand'.

The established Church is often Blake's unwithering target, as in 'The Garden of Love':

> And the gates of this Chapel were shut,
> And 'Thou shalt not' writ over the door;
> So I turned to the Garden of Love
> That so many sweet flowers bore.
> And I saw it was filled with graves,

And tombstones where flowers should be;
And priests in black gowns were walking their rounds,
And binding with briars my joys and desires.

The contrasts are simple and arresting: where there should be 'sweet flowers', there intrudes instead the artificial structures of the church. Look at the last two lines: the internal rhymes ('gowns' and 'rounds', 'briars' and 'desires') enact the very process of restriction it describes, binding in the verse upon itself, in tribute to the behaviour of the priests.

I am each day unsettled by Blake: that contrast of his ingenuousness – he is as nakedly, naively political as a placard-holding protester – and his lurking complexity. Today, I spend almost an hour staring at one poem, and one of his most famous:

O rose, thou art sick!
The invisible worm,
That flies in the night,
In the howling storm,
Has found out thy bed
Of crimson joy,
And his dark secret love
Does thy life destroy.

In eight lines there is both clarity and confusion. Blake is fond of rhyming words that seem, by some secret force of historical felicity, to draw towards each other: 'joy' and 'destroy' here; elsewhere 'breath' and 'death', 'sleep' and 'weep'. They seem to speak to the unconscious life of the language, a naturalness of certain ideas attracting one another. But notice also how 'worm' and 'storm' stubbornly refuse to sound alike too: this whole poem is resisting glibness. What precisely is this invisible, flying creature with its destructive love? How is it possible to imagine that? The first five words are monosyllables, the simple idea of a flower riddled with some sort of canker, but the poem does not remain simple. 'Joy', another monosyllable, appears a lot in this collection, but is never straightforward: here it is crimson, sanguine, vulnerable to destruction. It is seldom simply joyful.

What Blake does time and time again is insert a little quiver of consternation into his verse, the testament to his sense of human corruption. This is from 'Infant Sorrow':

> Struggling in my father's hands,
> Striving against my swaddling bands,
> Bound and weary, I thought best
> To sulk upon my mother's breast.

Here the comfort of swaddling has become constriction, and the baby can only 'sulk', not 'suck' upon his mother's breast. That decisive tilt from 'suck' to 'sulk' is, I think, very representative of Blake: the little twist, the shudder, the move towards disquiet instead of comfort. I put the book in my bag, unsettled, and go on with my day.

18 September

Two days later, and I have fallen immediately, belatedly, predictably, somewhat boringly in love with Byron. He was an archetype of his age – the dark and handsome man of action and intelligence – but curiously ahead of it too. Facts about his life endlessly fascinate me. He fled England in 1816 (never to return) when his wife Annabella Milbanke filed for divorce accusing him of three things: incest,* homosexuality and heterosexual

---

* This was technically true: Byron was having an affair with Augusta Leigh, his half-sister.

sodomy. Only the latter two were actual crimes. He was anorexic and had a club foot. He lost his virginity at nine. As a student at Cambridge he had a pet bear. He was the father of Ada Lovelace, now known as the world's first computer programmer. He was an open-water swimmer, and a vegetarian (but not all the time). He was the inspiration behind Dracula.* He was not welcome in Poets' Corner in Westminster Abbey on his death due to his 'questionable morality', an omission unbelievably not rectified until 1969.

Byron supported the return of the Elgin Marbles. He was a great European: he loved Italy; spoke Armenian so well he contributed to an English–Armenian grammar; he fought in the Greek war of independence against the Ottoman Empire, dying from sepsis in the struggle.† During that conflict, into which he sank what would now be millions of pounds, he was brave and unwavering, tolerant to Muslims and Christians alike, even adopting a Muslim girl when her parents died. But he neglected his own illegitimate daughter in a convent, and she died young, a tragedy for which it is hard to forgive him.

He is a modern figure of ambivalence and contradiction, of colour and contrast, in an age where ebullience and extravagance were more achievable and desirable than they are now. This is Shelley on Byron's home in Italy:

> Lord B.'s establishment consists, besides servants, of ten horses, eight enormous dogs, three monkeys, five cats, an eagle, a crow,

---

* At the Villa Diodati in Switzerland, when Mary Shelley came up with the tale that became *Frankenstein*, their doctor friend John Polidori produced 'The Vampyre', based on Byron. It went on to inspire Bram Stoker to create Dracula. So one night of storytelling produced both *Frankenstein* and *Dracula*, which is incredible when you think of it.

† He is still regarded as a hero in Greece, and a suburb of Athens (Vyronas) is named after him.

and a falcon; and all these, except the horses, walk about the house, which every now and then resounds with their unarbitrated quarrels, as if they were the masters of it . . . [P.S.] I find that my enumeration of the animals in this Circean Palace was defective. I have just met on the grand staircase five peacocks, two guinea hens, and an Egyptian crane. I wonder who all these animals were before they were changed into these shapes.

It is impossible not to want to meet Byron, although not all of his partners would agree. His mistress Lady Caroline Lamb called him, famously, 'mad, bad and dangerous to know', and wrote a novel called *Glenarvon* (1816) in which he was travestied as Lord Ruthven. Byron's marriage to Annabella was truly unhappy, and he behaved badly (to say the least): one story goes that during her pregnancy – perhaps even when she was giving birth – he would sit in a room below hers and throw bottles at the ceiling to stop her sleeping; he called their honeymoon a 'treaclemoon'.* Of course, we might now see that he was unable to express his true sexuality due to the constraints of the age. One of the reasons for his travel to the Mediterranean and beyond was to find a place in which he could express his same-sex desires: when he wrote home he used the code 'pl & opt Cs', which is *'coitum plenum et optabilem'* or 'full and desired sex', for his assignations with men.

---

* It was one of the worst marriages in the history of literature. Two others spring to mind. Evelyn Waugh's honeymoon with his wife, also called Evelyn, was so unsuccessful he published a book about it called *A Bachelor Abroad*. The Carlyles were no better: 'It was very good of God to let Carlyle and Mrs Carlyle marry one another,' Samuel Butler quipped, 'and so make only two people miserable and not four.'

Byron wrote a memoir of his fantastic life, which was destroyed – in an act often called 'the greatest crime in literary history' – on his death by his publisher John Murray,* two of his friends, and lawyers representing his half-sister and widow. What scenes, what depravity of body and soul, did those pages contain before they were dumped on the fire? We will never know.

Both Dickens and Larkin were determined to destroy material that might stain their posthumous reputations; both were largely unsuccessful. Dickens set on fire some 10,000 pages of letters and papers: 'They sent up a smoke like the Genie when he got out of the casket on the seashore,' he recalled, 'and as it was an exquisite day when I began, and rained very heavily when I finished, I suspect my correspondence of having overcast the face of the Heavens.'

Sometimes, posterity has been fortunate in preserving works of actual art, rather than personal effects, which would otherwise have been doomed to destruction. Franz Kafka famously asked his closest friend Max Brod to burn all his papers, including what would become *The Trial* (1925). Brod nodded and did not. Nabokov wished his last work, written in a fever after a bad fall (Davos, insect-hunting), to be burned. It was published earlier this century as *The Original of Laura* (2009), a set of notes towards a novel that contained plenty of Nabokovian touches, but nothing much of substance. As I said at the time, history should generally outweigh an author's wishes in favour of preservation: it is always better to read a work than see it destroyed. The burning question is not really much of a burning question.

You cannot account for error, though. Thomas Carlyle had loaned his friend John Stuart Mill the unpublished, and only

---

* And indeed my publisher, come to think of it.

manuscript copy, of his *History of the French Revolution* (1837), and the story goes that the latter's maid accidentally thought it was waste paper for the fire.* Carlyle, presumably with much chuntering and cursing, had to rewrite it from scratch. He was not a very nice man, so don't feel too sorry for him.

20 September

On this day exactly 200 years ago, John Keats – young at twenty-four, his body already destroying itself with the tuberculosis that would claim his life a year or so later – wrote 'To Autumn', his meditation upon the changing season. This is what he recorded on the day:

> How beautiful the season is now – How fine the air. A temperate sharpness about it. Really, without joking, chaste weather – Dian skies – I never liked stubble-fields so much as now – Aye better than the chilly green of the Spring. Somehow, a stubble-field looks warm – in the same way that some pictures look warm. This struck me so much in my Sunday's walk that I composed upon it.

That warm stubble-field makes it into the poem itself: 'While barred clouds bloom the soft-dying day, / And touch the stubble-plains with rosy hue'. This is in the final stanza, where for all the largesse of the countryside, there is more than a hint of things 'soft-dying' (like a man slowly being drowned by the fluid in his lungs): 'in a wailful choir the small gnats mourn', 'sinking as the light wind lives or dies', and so on.

---

* This event was transposed directly into the third *Blackadder* series, in which Baldrick destroys Samuel Johnson's *Dictionary*, 'the big papery thing tied up with string', by starting a fire with it.

It is impossible when thinking about Keats not to reflect on his early death, at the age of twenty-five in Rome. In 1819 he composed all his famous Odes, saturated as he was by foreboding. Like 'On Melancholy', with its telling idea of the dying 'fit' that 'shall fall / Sudden from heaven like a weeping cloud'. Its first verse, like an answer to Hamlet's 'To be or not to be' soliloquy, is a caution against self-slaughter, preferring instead the 'wakeful anguish of the soul'. What a phrase that is to ponder, anxious at night: is it better to die, to sleep, or linger in sorrowful distraction?

These Odes often return to the same sounds and ideas, as if Keats that year could not clear his mind of something nagging at him. That 'wailful choir of gnats' is striking a similar note to the 'murmurous haunt of flies' in 'Ode to a Nightingale'. Here the blessed release of non-existence is pondered once more, but more favourably, 'half in love with easeful Death', the temptation is 'to cease upon the midnight with no pain'.

Reputationally speaking, death served Keats well. He did not think it would: the epitaph on his tomb was 'Here lies One / Whose Name was writ in Water'. The critics of his day had been cruel and negligent, perhaps correctly about some of his later works. Byron, ever keen to lard his own writing with poetic commentary, suggested that literary criticism had indeed contributed to Keats's collapse:

> 'Tis strange the mind, that very fiery particle
> Should let itself be snuffed out by an article.

But as we have so often seen this year, neglected artists are often preferred by posterity. Plus, Keats's death was romantic, in the haunting sense of unfulfilled potential. Instead of another thirty years of plugging away at effortful epics like *Endymion* (1818), Keats died having written a series of almost perfect short poems, soaked in those everlasting ideas of death and beauty.

He is part of a pantheon of artists whose early work was never tainted by later excrescence; a grouping that is huge, possibly because greatness can tolerate little taint. I immediately start a list of the young dead creators, and it stretches out: all the Brontës, Stephen Crane, Sylvia Plath, Kurt Cobain, Jim Morrison, Sam Cooke, Georges Seurat, Van Gogh. Our friend John Kennedy Toole. Byron himself, who never saw forty. Maybe true genius resides, though, in Michelangelo or Shakespeare: who achieved wonder and repeated it over the years, and did not rely upon only a couple of seasons in the sun.

Byron is, predictably, rather beautiful on the subject, suggesting that 'mere breath' is not the only thing a person should be worried about losing:

> 'Whom the gods love die young,' was said of yore,
> And many deaths do they escape by this:
> The death of friends, and that which slays even more –
> The death of friendship, love, youth, all that is,
> Except mere breath; and since the silent shore
> Awaits at last even those who longest miss
> The old archer's shafts, perhaps the early grave
> Which men weep over may be meant to save.

22 September

Byron wrote *Don Juan* three years into his self-imposed exile when he was already a huge celebrity.* The first two Cantos of this 'epic satire' were published in 1819, and he went on working on the poem until his death (a further fourteen stanzas were found in his bag when he died). And, as I am now discovering,

---

* Thanks to his 1814 poem *Childe Harold's Pilgrimage*, as well as the pungency of his private life: 'I awoke one morning,' he said, 'and found myself famous.'

it is a fizzing, clever, funny, charming tour de force of the imagination. Virginia Woolf – with whose critical judgements throughout this year I feel I have been oddly in tune – said it was 'the most readable poem of its length ever written', thanks to 'the springy random haphazard galloping nature of its method'. And that is almost exactly right. The *Edinburgh Magazine* review of 1819 reacted to both the 'filthy and impious poem' and its author, the 'unrepenting, unsoftened, smiling, sarcastic, joyous sinner'. That is also right, but no reason for dispraise.

The poem begins with the misleading phrase: 'I want a hero'. What we know immediately is that the hero is not Don Juan, whom Byron has re-cast as a beautiful boy himself regularly seduced, rather than as a Byronic seducer. No, the hero is Byron himself, who bursts forth irrepressibly into the story, despite his disavowing jokes that he is only a 'moderate-minded bard'. As if. The dedication to the poem has already revealed his immoderate ability; it is a cannonade of abuse of his peers; poetry as rap battle, *8-Mile* in eight-line stanzas:

> And Coleridge, too, has lately taken wing,
> But like a hawk encumbered with his hood,
> Explaining metaphysics to the nation –
> I wish he would explain his explanation.

The Poet Laureate, Robert Southey, is mercilessly mocked too: 'Gasping on deck, because you soar too high, Bob, / And fall, for lack of moisture quite a-dry, Bob!'. Please bear in mind that a 'dry Bob' is an orgasm without ejaculation.* The whole Romantic movement led by Wordsworth gets it as well:

---

* Don't feel too sorry for Southey, though. He once told Charlotte Brontë that 'literature cannot be the business of a woman's life'. She had the last laugh in the end, what with the tremendous amount of business done by her books in the centuries since.

> There is a narrowness in such a notion,
> Which makes me wish you'd change your lakes for ocean.

We know immediately that we are in the presence of an ebullience, but while Woolf felt it was 'random haphazard galloping', it is actually matched by acute precision. *Donny Johnny* – as Byron charmingly called it – is 16,000 lines all in rigid rhythm and rhyme: a version of *ottavo rima*, in the scheme of *abababcc*. One of the examples of Byron's genius was in the sheer skill of his versification, his bold use of feminine rhymes,* ambitious soundings:

> There's not a sea the passenger e'er pukes in,
> Turns up more dangerous breakers than the Euxine.

Or:

> She snatch'd it, and refused another morsel,
> Saying, he had gorged enough to make a horse ill.

Indeed, the concluding couplet of each stanza is so often a phrase pitched between smart resolution and ironic punchline. I sigh each day, and underline with a smile things like:

> What men call gallantry, and gods adultery,
> Is much more common where the climate's sultry.

> Christians have burnt each other, quite persuaded
> That all the Apostles would have done as they did.

---

* Very important to Byron: it means rhymes not based on concluding stressed monosyllables (breath/death) but on an unstressed syllable, often part of a larger phrase: (morsel / horse ill).

If you think 't was philosophy that this did,
I can't help thinking puberty assisted.

23 September

I could go on just quoting memorable lines. But the joy of *Don Juan* is not simply in its tightness, its poetic focus. It is a poem in the sense that *Tristram Shandy* or *Don Quixote* are novels: full of switches of focus, musings, false starts, loss of concentration. And it knows it:

But let me to my story: I must own,
If I have any fault, it is digression –
Leaving my people to proceed alone,
While I soliloquize beyond expression.

This metafictionality is not dry or sterile, but part of the influx of broader life into the story. And Byron, despite his fault of digression, knows how to rattle things along in the story itself. So Don Juan gets into all sorts of romantic scrapes, picaresque adventures, like a dramatic shipwreck, which descends into cannibalism:*

And such things as the entrails and the brains
Regaled two sharks, who follow'd o'er the billow –
The sailors ate the rest of poor Pedrillo.

What makes me smile each morning is the sense of gliding naughtiness, of joyfulness in all this. This is poetry as hedonism,

---

* Before which it naturally descends into dog-eating: 'So Juan's spaniel, spite of his entreating, / Was kill'd and portion'd out for present eating.' Can you hear a bit of Roald Dahl's revolting rhymes here? I can.

the Byronic pleasure principle; life seen as no more or less than 'A little breath, love, wine,* ambition, fame, / Fighting, devotion, dust – perhaps a name'. Here is the moment Juan and Donna Inez, the older woman, finally get it on:

> But who, alas! can love, and then be wise?
> Not that remorse did not oppose temptation;
> A little still she strove, and much repented
> And whispering 'I will ne'er consent' – consented.

It is easy to enjoy the mock seriousness, the poetic pose – the lofty rhetorical question in the first line – that soon dissolves into a joke, made perfect by that rhyme at the end.

Reading *Don Juan* these last few days has been like reading a historical novel, rapped out by the wittiest person in the room. It is the variety, the freedom that is so winning, and which feels so fresh. But let me end on a view from Byron's own century, which still seems correct. Walter Scott said the poem 'has embraced every topic of human life, and sounded every string of the divine harp, from its slightest to its most powerful and heart-astounding tones'. It is good to be heart-astounded sometimes.

26 September

I grab a collection by Emily Dickinson as I leave the house. I know, I know: I should have got out of the nineteenth century in poetry terms by now. But it is impossible to cover everything, and I had a hankering for the real Dickinson after the

---

* Byron is the laureate of booziness: the 'best of life is but intoxication', he says, and ''Tis pity wine should be so deleterious, / For tea and coffee leave us much more serious.'

travesty of the TV series. There is a lot to be said for poetry of the next two centuries, but I am going to end the month in the company of a poet whose precise, self-sufficient, trembling and troubling verses are important to me.

It is fitting that, around her home town of Amherst, Emily Dickinson was nicknamed 'the myth': this slight figure, dressed perennially in white after the death of her father in 1874, who slowly recused herself from the world, remaining close to home to recoil into her gardens and her poetry. Her life was both more and less mythical than that. She lived in wealthy comfort, 'keeping house' as the 1850 census had it, singing out the 'most emphatic things in the pantry', as her cousin recalled her. She never married, but was no old maid. She had sexually charged correspondence with an older man, Judge Otis Lord, who did try to marry her; she wrote letters to an unnamed 'Master', purring with a sense of masochistic sex. And she may have been in love with her sister-in-law Susan Gilbert Dickinson, too, whose friendship seems to have verged upon the physical:

> Susie, will you indeed come home next Saturday, and be my own again, and kiss me . . . I hope for you so much, and feel so eager for you, feel that I cannot wait, feel that now I must have you – that the expectation once more to see your face again, makes me feel hot and feverish, and my heart beats so fast . . . my darling, so near I seem to you, that I disdain this pen, and wait for a warmer language.

That idea of 'warmer language' is so critical to Dickinson. She felt literally chilled by Susan's own verse: 'I always go to the fire,' she wrote, 'and get warm after thinking of it, but I never can again.' Dickinson is always pointing to something greater than reality when she is writing: the feelings of love or loneliness, the spectre of death, the meaning of nature. She is a poet of solitude and smallness, but also speaks of vast ideas.*

At her death, the world only knew a little of her genius, and that because she started a correspondence with war hero and man of letters Thomas Wentworth Higginson, who was half in love with her, as she was with him. This is how she introduced herself as a writer: 'Are you too deeply occupied to say if my verse is alive? . . . Should you think it breathes, and you had the leisure to tell me, I should feel quick gratitude.' Even in this tentative request for recognition we see the poet: that idea of the verse being alive and breathing; the two meanings of 'quick' as immediate, but also living. Her poems *are* quick: short, spiky and always with a sense of life. She knew that, too:

> A word is dead
> When it is said,
> Some say.
> I say it just
> Begins to live
> That day.

Each day I read her, I get the pulse of existence in her words, poetry that refuses to sit quietly. Indeed, she once wrote:

> They shut me up in Prose –
> As when a little Girl

* She once signed a letter with the name 'America'. And she is unquestionably one of its national poets. William Dean Howells once wrote that 'If nothing else had come out of our life but this strange poetry, we should feel that in the work of Emily Dickinson, America, or New England rather, had made a distinctive addition to the literature of the world, and could not be left out of any record of it.'

> They put me in the Closet –
> Because they liked me 'still' –

30 September

Dickinson's life is a testament to quickness amid self-imposed constraint, itself a good definition of poetry and why it is long-lasting: her family may have liked her still, but she wanted others still to like her. Dickinson left the world almost 1,800 poems, but published fewer than ten in her lifetime. It was a typically contrary position to take. She was not shy about her work (who possibly could be?): after all, she sent verses to Higginson, and some 500 other poems to her trusted correspondents. And while she wrote furiously on waste paper and chocolate wrappers, seemingly appeasing an urge inside her, she also carefully sewed together forty booklets, or 'fascicles', as if for posterity. 'If fame belonged to me,' she once said to Higginson, 'I could not escape her.' Well it did, and she did not.

Dickinson famously urged herself to 'tell all the truth but tell it slant – / Success in Circuit lies', and that resistance towards orthodoxy is heartening to read each morning. 'Slant rhyme' is another word for half rhyme, at which Dickinson excelled; sounds that come together but refuse quite to resolve themselves that easily:

> Remorse is cureless, – the disease
> Not even God can heal;
> For 't is his institution, –
> The complement of hell.

There is nothing consoling about the shift from 'heal' to 'hell', just a stubborn refusal to recognise that some things cannot be cured, or fixed that easily. Here is another:

> This world is not conclusion;
> A sequel stands beyond,
> Invisible, as music,
> But positive, as sound.

This is a poem about afterlife, and again the slant rhyme resists its own sense of 'conclusion': 'beyond' is not resolved by 'sound', in fact that shift in sound lingers in our minds; we want to hear one thing and we are left waiting. Something 'invisible' persists.

So it is there, when you look for it, the very tremble of existence. Dickinson heard it everywhere, which makes her a fine poet of the natural world:[*] 'A bird broke forth and sang / And trilled, and quivered, and shook his throat'; 'The lightning skipped like mice / the thunder crumbled like a stuff'. There is a breeze that crops up, lively as breath, in many of her poems: it 'quivered through the grass', it has a 'phraseless melody' or 'dateless melody', is a 'fleshless chant', a 'rapid, footless guest'. Dickinson's father bought her books to occupy her, but always worried that they would, as she said, 'joggle my mind'. He was right to notice that. His daughter is a poet of joggles, of quick movements in our brains.

But she is more than that. There is a heft, a denseness to her writing, what she termed 'condensed despatch'. This is not just living, physical poetry, it is poetry preoccupied with metaphysics too:

> Could mortal lip divine
> The undeveloped freight
> Of a delivered syllable,
> 'T would crumble with the weight.

---

[*] 'Inebriate of air am I, / And debauchee of dew', as she herself puts it.

That idea that words carry with them an 'undeveloped freight' is critical, recalling Chesterton when he said that 'The aim of good prose words is to mean what they say. The aim of good poetical words is to mean what they do not say.' Dickinson seems to do both. And her sense of heaviness means that I do not spend my journey simply sighing wistfully over a fleeting image of sunset or butterflies or grass, but also furrowing my brow in thought. I notice that several poems conclude with abstract nouns of complexity and multiple syllables. Taken together they seem to provide a grounding in the poetics of Dickinson: honesty, cordiality, immortality, plausibility, ecstasy, perfidy, simplicity, eternity, extremity.

She is also a poet of solidity. Even a beam of light is not allowed to flit about the place:

> There's a certain slant of light,
> On winter afternoons,
> That oppresses, like the weight
> Of cathedral tunes.

The physical meets the metaphysical once more: the way that particles of light and sound make us feel has its own reality to it, and a heavy, even morbid one at that. Dickinson knew that this was the very essence of poetry, bringing sensation and life to words. Her first letter to Higginson has her own definition of the form, which may well be unimprovable: 'If I read a book and it makes my whole body so cold no fire ever can warm me I know that is poetry. If I feel physically as if the top of my head were taken off, I know that is poetry.'

I cannot quite meet these sensations myself, because I am not a poet, just a reader, chuntering along insensitively in the daily course of life. But I have spent my time being enlivened by poetry this month, by finding energy within phrases and condensed sentences. The restrained force of Dickinson and Blake (so similar, as I now see, in so many respects), the ebullient control of Byron.

And today this figure from another country and another century still speaks to me. September is ending, summer is over, darkness is looming once more. Here is a poem from Dickinson fit to finish the season:

> As imperceptibly as grief
> The summer lapsed away, –
> Too imperceptible, at last,
> To seem like perfidy.
>
> A quietness distilled,
> As twilight long begun,
> Or Nature, spending with herself
> Sequestered afternoon.
>
> The dusk drew earlier in,
> The morning foreign shone, –
> A courteous, yet harrowing grace,
> As guest who would be gone.
>
> And thus, without a wing,
> Or service of a keel,
> Our summer made her light escape
> Into the beautiful.

∼

Further Reading

The Poems of Sappho (late sixth century BC)
Carmina (early first century BC) by Catullus
The Aeneid (19 BC) by Virgil
Selected Poems (*c.*750) by Li Bai
The Canterbury Tales (1387–1400) by Geoffrey Chaucer
Sir Gawain and the Green Knight (late fourteenth century)
Selected Poems (*c.*1620) by John Donne
Paradise Lost (1667) by John Milton
The Rape of the Lock (1712) by Alexander Pope
Lyrical Ballads (1798) by William Wordsworth
Lamia, Isabella, the Eve of St Agnes and Other Poems (1820) by
    John Keats
Dramatic Lyrics (1842) by Robert Browning
Selected Poems (1844) by Elizabeth Barrett Browning
In Memoriam A.H.H. (1850) by Alfred, Lord Tennyson
Leaves of Grass (1855) by Walt Whitman
A Shropshire Lad (1896) by A.E. Housman
The Ballad of Reading Gaol (1898) by Oscar Wilde
Satires of Circumstance (1914) by Thomas Hardy
The Penguin Book of First World War Poetry (1914–18)
The Waste Land (1922) by T.S. Eliot
Harmonium (1923) by Wallace Stevens
The Weary Blues (1926) by Langston Hughes
The Tower (1928) by W.B. Yeats
In Parenthesis (1937) by David Jones
The Age of Anxiety (1947) by W.H. Auden
Ariel (1965) by Sylvia Plath
Death of a Naturalist (1966) by Seamus Heaney
Briggflatts (1966) by Basil Bunting
Complete Poems (1967) by Marianne Moore
The Complete Poems (1969) by Elizabeth Bishop

High Windows (1974) by Philip Larkin
And Still I Rise (1978) by Maya Angelou
Chosen Poems Old and New (1982) by Audre Lorde
Omeros (1990) by Derek Walcott
Autobiography of Red (1998) by Anne Carson
Dart (2002) by Alice Oswald

AUTUMN

October

Modern Literary Fiction

Offshore (1979) by Penelope Fitzgerald
The Unconsoled (1995) by Kazuo Ishiguro
The Corrections (2001) by Jonathan Franzen

I realise that I need to tackle a category question here: does the phrase 'literary fiction' have any real meaning? Can you really quantify literariness? Better simply to say the true and only distinction in fiction is between 'good' and 'bad' books. I think, in reality, that everybody more or less knows what you mean when you talk about literary fiction. But, as the old French joke goes, it is all fine in practice, what about in theory?

To my mind, literary fiction denotes a novel for which the advance of the plot is not the primary purpose. Genre fiction – whether it be crime, SF, Westerns or whatever – is primarily about telling a story in a certain context, often according to certain rules. There are grey areas here: some literary fiction has a plot that zips along emphatically (*The Corrections*, as we will see, or *The Handmaid's Tale*, 1985); just as some genre fiction offers stylistic pleasure beyond its storytelling (*American Tabloid*, 1995, being my especial poster child here).

But I regard literary fiction as something written not within a specific genre, which seeks to create pleasures or provocations incidental to the plot. Here's guidance from Steinbeck's *Sweet Thursday* (1954):

> I like a lot of talk in a book and I don't like to have nobody tell me what the guy that's talking looks like. I want to figure out what he looks like from the way he talks . . . figure out what the guy's thinking from what he says. I like some description but not too much of that . . . Sometimes I want a book to break loose with a bunch of hooptedoodle . . . Spin up some pretty words maybe or sing a little song with language. That's nice. But I wish it was set aside so I don't have to read it. I don't want hooptedoodle to get mixed up with the story.

So I would say, as a good rule of thumb, that if there is more hooptedoodle than story (or at least as much), that's a good definition of literary fiction. Does it matter? Not really, but it is as good an attempt at distinction as any. This month I will read books judged as literary, but too recent to become argued over as possible classics. Hopefully, I might hear someone singing a little song with language along the way.

3 October

Penelope Fitzgerald was a late starter. She was sixty-one when she published her first novel, written to occupy and entertain her terminally ill husband, who died before it appeared. Novelists who begin their writing careers as their life has passed its midpoint are not that uncommon, perhaps because experience is rather useful to the creative imagination. If artists who died young are impossibly romantic, novelists who begin late feel justified, pragmatically matured.

The canon is full of good examples. George Eliot had been a journalist, and a notably unconventional lover, before publishing *Adam Bede* (1859) at thirty-nine. Raymond Chandler only started writing when he lost his job as an oil company executive at the age of forty-four. Richard Adams, of *Watership Down* (1972) fame, was fifty-four; Laura Ingalls Wilder was ten years older before beginning the *Little House on the Prairie* series (1932–43), motivated by the penury of the Great Depression, albeit with a successful journalistic career behind her. The biggest book in Britain in 2017 – including cookbooks and children's fiction – was a novel called *Eleanor Oliphant is Completely Fine*, whose author Gail Honeyman was forty-five.

William Burroughs was immersed in the literary movements of his day, companion to authors like Jack Kerouac. But he did not start writing fiction until after the death of his wife, whom he accidentally killed in a game of William Tell (she had a glass of water on her head; he apparently was trying to shoot it off): 'So the death of Joan brought me in contact with the invader,' he recalled, 'the Ugly Spirit, and maneuvered me into a lifelong struggle, in which I have had no choice except to write my way out.'

Fitzgerald's motivation is a rather more affecting version of this. She came from a family of public intellectuals: one uncle, Dillwyn Knox, was a mathematical genius and cryptographer at Bletchley Park; another was Ronald Knox, whom we met earlier, the cleric who wrote mystery novels, and whose biography was written by no less than Evelyn Waugh; her father Edmund was the editor of *Punch*. Penelope herself was brilliantly clever, one of the first women allowed into Oxford University, where she was a vast academic success. In these circumstances, it is surprising that her life was so often touched by poverty, unalleviated by her wealthy and influential family.

Perhaps she never asked for help.* When her husband, Desmond, was disbarred from his legal practice for stealing cheques, money was – and remained for years – in very short supply. The Fitzgeralds lived on a houseboat before it sank,† and then in a homeless shelter, before being granted a council flat.

Happily, the riverside location gave Fitzgerald the inspiration for *Offshore*, which won the Booker Prize in 1979. It is – as I see already – a kind of British *Cannery Row*, short and slight, but mesmerising; a tale of the lives of the colourful few who scratch out a living on old barges at Battersea Reach, those for whom 'a certain failure, distressing to themselves, to be like other people caused them to sink back, with so much else that drifted or was washed up, into the mud moorings of the great tideway'. This is a novel of human flotsam, rendered with love and beauty.

6 October

Fitzgerald said herself that she was drawn to 'people who seem to have been born defeated or even profoundly lost . . . they are ready to assume the conditions the world imposes on them, but they don't manage to submit to them, despite their courage and best efforts . . . when I write it is to give these people a voice'. That tenderness is ultimately affecting: a sensitive rendering of the strugglers and the seekers. She called *Offshore* a 'tragi-farce', and it is in its very ambivalence that its power lies: there is no

---

* They were, in common with many of their times, a buttoned-up bunch. When her brother Rawle was released after three years in a Japanese POW camp, he announced his liberation by posting a crossword clue. He subsequently made clear he would talk about his experiences; but nobody in his family ever asked him.

† Giving her the unimprovable line for showing up at her teaching job a few hours after she should have: 'I'm sorry I'm late, but my house sank.'

weight of tragedy, or release of comedy, just characters living on the margins, 'halfway between the need for security and the doubtful attraction of danger'.

Those characters are drawn from Fitzgerald's recollection of her own life on the boat: Nenna, her surrogate self, with her two children Martha and Tilda; the retired captain Richard, the kind of man who 'has two clean handkerchiefs on him at half past three in the morning';* the penurious painter Willis; Maurice, the rent boy and winsome philosopher, who 'told the sombre truths of the light-hearted'. The latter knows how marginalised they all are: 'It's right for us to live where we do, between land and water. You, my dear, you're half in love with your husband, then there's Martha who's half a child and half a girl, Richard who can't give up being half in the Navy, Willis who's half an artist and half a longshoreman, a cat who's half alive and half dead.'

This repeated sense of ambivalence is key to the novel. Fitzgerald is aware of the possibility of heavy symbolism here – the river, the drifting, the sense of life's losses and longings – but never allows it to become too pronounced. Look at this, for example: 'The river's edge, where Virgil's ghosts held out their arms in longing for the farther shore, and Dante, as a living man, was refused passage by the ferryman, the few planks that mark the meeting point of land and water, there, surely, is a place to stop and reflect, even if, as Father Watson did, you stumble over a ten-gallon tin of creosote.'

We do 'stop and reflect', think of an old Latin poet for a moment, but then are made to stumble back upon reality. We might see 'the river as a powerful god', but we then consider that he is actually 'bearded with the white foam of detergents'.

* According to Fitzgerald's real daughter Tina, reliable Richard was 'what my mother wanted my father to be'.

Indeed, we are endlessly reminded of the sheer workaday Britishness* of the novel's setting, the Britain of post-war hunger and genteel shabbiness. We cannot muse too much about river gods, or the mysterious workings of fate, when we linger so memorably in the reaches of lower-middle-class struggles: sandwiches that 'contained a substance called Spread, and, indeed, that was all you could do with it'; a museum attendant 'hoping that she would get a little closer to the picture, so that he could relieve the boredom of his long day by telling her to stand back'; a marital row based on where Nenna 'had put his squash rackets while he was away'.

9 October

Dickens is an irresistible comparison at various points in *Offshore*, and indeed we briefly see a Havisham-like character in an antique shop to remind us: 'perhaps she had been cruelly deserted on her wedding day, and had sat there ever since, refusing to have anything touched.' Fitzgerald has that Dickensian charm, as Nabokov once observed, of animating the solid, letting 'things participate': doors that 'stood open, breathing out incense and heavy soul'; anchors like 'specimens of some giant type long since discarded by Nature, but still clinging to their old habitat'. Above all, the 'crazy old vessels', which 'develop emotions to a fine pitch' and sink 'with a sound like a sigh', with 'groans that seem human'.

But Fitzgerald succeeds because of her non-Dickensian restraint. I am moved by the sheer *quietness* of this novel. Its hard-earned wisdom: 'all distances are the same to those who

---

* At one point, someone uses cheese straws from Fortnum & Mason as fuel for a rickety old stove, an act so British I nearly started singing the national anthem.

don't meet.' Its sensitivity to the atmosphere of people and place: the taxi 'reeking of tobacco and ancient loves', or the burning driftwood that 'gave out a villainous smell, the gross spirit of salt and fire'. Its celebration of sisterly devotion, the 'love of a pure kind, proof against many trials', and the inventive spirit of young children.

I admire a novel that conjures the very large and the very small, the mystical and the real. As when Nenna, who has lost her shoes and is struggling in a sleet-filled London thoroughfare, desperate and alone, and tries to find God, realises 'Prayer should be beyond self, and so Nenna repeated a Hail Mary for everyone in the world who was lost in Kingsland Road without their bus fares.' And I admire very much the fact that Fitzgerald changed the tragic fate of one of her friends when she fictionalised him as Maurice: 'I couldn't bear to let him kill himself. That would have meant he had failed in life, whereas, really, his kindness made him the very symbol of success in my eyes.'

You can call me a feeble sentimentalist, and you would – of course – be right. *Offshore* was a surprise winner of the Booker, and is probably not even Fitzgerald's greatest novel.* But it is charming and thoughtful and meaningful. Its reach never exceeds its grasp, and its very modesty is its greatest trait, because it matches the modesty of everyday existence. This is Willis, this is you and me, this is everybody, who 'had come to doubt the value of all new beginnings and to put his trust in not much more than the art of hanging together'.

---

* Her final book, *The Blue Flower* (1995), is one of the historical novels you should read, telling the story of the early German Romantic Friedrich von Hardenberg, who became known as Novalis. It is typically unusual that Fitzgerald would write about him.

10 October

I get a momentary glimpse of the Thames on my train each morning, which feels like a happy coincidence this month. And obviously I start to think about rivers as they appear in works of art, written or otherwise. The Thames itself is there, glinting and shimmering, in paintings: Monet and Turner spring immediately to mind. Then there is Whistler, who said this fine thing about 'when the evening mist clothes the riverside with poetry, as with a veil, and the poor buildings lose themselves in the dim sky, and the tall chimneys become campanile, and the warehouses are palaces in the night, and the whole city hangs in the heavens.'

Clothing the riverside in poetry is what, in her modest way, Fitzgerald does a little. And plenty of other authors have tried the same: Dickens on this same stretch of water, say, or Mark Twain on the Mississippi. Jerome K. Jerome's modestly comic account of *Three Men in a Boat* (1889). Eliot's *The Mill on the Floss*. Cormac McCarthy's *Suttree* (1979).

I always think of Mole from *The Wind in the Willows* (1908) by Kenneth Grahame, trotting 'as one trots, when very small, by the side of a man who holds one spellbound by exciting stories; and when tired at last, he sat on the bank, while the river still chattered on to him, a babbling procession of the best stories in the world, sent from the heart of the earth to be told at last to the insatiable sea'. The poet Alice Oswald heard less chatter and more of a poetic hymn in her book *Dart* (2002), about the river of the same name, with its 'water's soliloquy', or the 'sound map of the river, a songline from the source to the sea'.

13 October

We have a piece this week in the *TLS* by Sam Leith on semicolons, a vital piece of punctuation in my eyes, and perhaps the minutest speck in the world's ongoing culture war too. Kurt Vonnegut once said this: 'Here is a lesson in creative writing. First rule: do not use semicolons. They are transvestite hermaphrodites representing absolutely nothing. All they do is show you've been to college.' Let's leave to one side the fact that, surely, being transvestite or hermaphrodite must represent *something*, it is that latter charge that is often levied: semicolons are superfluous, prissy, braggart; they are a needless way of fusing sentences together for no benefit.* That is, I am afraid, bollocks. Milan Kundera has taken the anti-Vonnegut position: 'I once left a publisher,' said he, 'for the sole reason that he tried to change my semicolons to periods.' I learn today that the semicolon is a product of Renaissance humanism, that great attempt to instil the order of learning on the chaos of the world. Which makes me feel a bit better about my fondness for them.

Here is a real-life example of why they might matter. In 1927 the question of the death sentence hung on the interpretation of this actual sentence from a judge: 'We find the defendant, Salvatore Merra, guilty of murder in the first degree, and the defendant, Salvatore Rannelli, guilty of murder in the first degree and recommend life imprisonment at hard labour.' Is life imprisonment the fate of both men or merely the lucky Rannelli? A semicolon after the first reference to 'degree' would mean death; after the second 'degree' it would mean life. In the end, Merra was executed after a series of appeals. O bloody period.

A quick check of my manuscript so far shows I have used more than 620 semicolons, at a rate of about one every 180 words. Herman Melville would be scoffing right now: he used one every 52. The final word, though, on all this (as it does in

---

* See how I sneaked one in and you didn't even notice: that's the job of the semicolon right there.

the *TLS* article) must go to Irvine Welsh, a fine exponent of the semicolon: 'I've no feelings about it – it's just there. People actually get worked up about that kind of thing, do they? I don't fucking believe it. They should get a fucking life or a proper job. They've got too much time on their hands, to think about nonsense.'

All right Irvine; fucking hell.

14 October

I am now a few days into *The Unconsoled* by literary darling Kazuo Ishiguro, and things are not looking up. It takes me back to a question I have asked before: how long do I stick with reading something I am not enjoying? I am being demoralised every day by *The Unconsoled*, its pitch-perfect, repetitive, dreamy monotone, its cleverly crafted weirdness, its relentless neatness. Should I take my own advice for once?

I am reading it on the recommendation of the *TLS* Fiction Editor, Toby Lichtig, who does know a thing or two about books: he said, when Ishiguro won the Nobel Prize in Literature in 2017, that this one 'just about nails the human condition'. Others have leaped to love it, too:* it was named the joint third-best novel between 1980 and 2005 in a survey in the *Observer*, tied with *Earthly Powers* by Anthony Burgess, *Atonement* by Ian McEwan, and our old friend Penelope Fitzgerald's *The Blue Flower*.† Anita Brookner said it was 'almost certainly a masterpiece'. That 'almost certainly' feels a bit like Toby's 'just about'

---

* Not the critic James Wood, who said it 'invented its own category of badness'. He recanted later; some reputations are too strong to stand against.
† The winner was *Disgrace* (1999) by Coetzee, a profitable comparison point for Ishiguro; second was *Money* (1984) by Martin Amis, which seems a rather silly choice to me but there you go.

to me: this is not an unequivocal snorter of a book. Even being joint third in a list is a qualification in both senses of the word.

I have been looking at critical responses to it, which I never normally do in the middle of reading. I get the novel's brilliance, in the sense of its consistent application of tone and touch, but I just do not like it. I see that Michael Wood, in the *New York Review of Books*, went out of his way to praise *The Unconsoled*, yet called it 'hard work', noting that 'its determined equanimity of tone makes you drowsy, and sometimes you wonder if you'd notice if you dropped off to sleep while you were reading.' Why would I want a book to make me sleepy, or – really – to make me work?

That is the problem it seems to me with self-consciously 'literary' fiction: it values difficulty as a quality, where it is really a disadvantage. What I call the 'eat your vegetables' approach to writing, publishing and criticism: yes, the prose is hard to get through, but you'll feel the benefits later. Fiction should never be merely fibrous. Greatness, it seems to me, is always readily accessible to the mind.

Ishiguro clearly wanted *The Unconsoled* to be difficult from the start. He wrote it after publishing *The Remains of the Day* in 1989, which won the Booker, became a film and enjoys both acclaim and heartfelt devotion. He called it an 'over-perfect novel', though: too straightforward and easy, 'a bit like pushing a button all the time'. And its success was liberating; it freed him to be more cagey: 'If I was ever going to write something strange and difficult that was the time.'

The result is this vast unremitting narration by a man called Ryder, 'not only the world's finest living pianist, but perhaps the very greatest of the century', who is visiting an unnamed city to give a performance. His memory is incomplete and confused, so he does not know quite why he is there, or what his past connections to the city are. As a result, he moves around as if in a dream, nagged by endless connections and coincidences. And the novel is magnificently faithful to dream logic, where events make both deep near-sense and no sense at all: Ryder wanders in the downtown of a city, yet finds himself next to 'the edge of a vast grassy field'; he loses his companion even though she is a few feet away; waits for a bus that never comes. It is full of those eerie feelings we get in dreams where we have a combination of attempted movement and frustrated agency.

The first hundred pages or so painstakingly chart one bemusing night, in which Ryder picks up a mother and son, visits a cinema, and attends a formal dinner in the small hours wearing only a dressing gown (which naturally falls open when he stands up), at which the death of a composer's pet, 'the greatest dog of his generation', is announced. This is anxiety dream as novel. But I am reading it just minutes removed from my own anxiety dreams. I crave the consolation of fiction; this novel – as is clear, in fairness, from its title – is not going to give it to me.

15 October

Harold Bloom died today. He was a bestselling literary critic at the end of the last century, writing at a time when literary criticism was still just about considered culturally central and important.[*] His major book, *The Western Canon* (1994), was an attempt to consider the twenty-six 'crucial' writers in literature: Dante to Beckett, Kafka to Pynchon. Shakespeare was always at the centre, the literary giant of all giants.

His other famous book, *The Anxiety of Influence* (1973), contained the – to me – rather inflated idea that major writers were murderously wrestling with their forebears in a version of the Freudian family romance (Keats wanting to 'kill' Milton, his

---

[*] And no, I am not bitter.

poetic father, and the like). One thing I do agree strongly with him about is this: 'The great poems, plays, novels, stories teach us how to go on living, even submerged under forty fathoms of bother and distress . . . Rise up at dawn and read something that matters as soon as you can.'

Amen to that.

18 October

There is no colour in *The Unconsoled*: it is bloodless, expertly drained of life with the sterile precision of a mortician preparing a corpse. There is no writing for the sake of beauty, for the establishment of memorable metaphor. Characters talk only in rehearsed formalities: 'I live not so far from here. Unfortunately I can't ask you in just now because I'm very tired and have to go to sleep.'

And the narration is full of deliberate clichés, those miniature examples of the artificially smoothed, the creepily lingering, the purposely inelegant: 'I'll make a completely clean breast of it'; 'I decided to throw caution to the wind'; 'both openings had their pros and cons'. This is good writing wearing the cloak of bad writing. Why? First, because Ishiguro wants to refuse us any consolation; he wants to place us – confused and grasping – within the dreamscape he has created. This is a novel about feeling estranged, feeling foreign even in a recognisable place. Ryder is both clueless and also, at moments, strangely omniscient: he can suddenly understand the histories of people he meets, or record their conversations despite not being in the room, or read their thoughts ('I realised he was turning over in his mind a particular incident from several years ago').

It strikes me that *The Unconsoled* is a meditation on foreignness, by an author who knows what it feels to be transplanted to another culture. Ishiguro learned English by copying other boys when he moved to this country at the age of six. He was subject to the heedless racism of the post-war playground: called 'Ish da wog', shortened to 'Ishdar', as he grew up. He is known in literary circles as 'Ish' now. Perhaps you never forget formative dismay. Ryder is someone who struggles to be understood despite having all the tools of communication, a common existential condition.

Like the Sofia Coppola movie *Lost in Translation*, the novel is also acute on the feeling of the displacement, the unease, that can come with travel. This feels like something written by a man on an endless book tour, shunted from faceless place to place, disorientated and jet-lagged, alternatively pandered to and forgotten.

The location, however, is fully furnished in our minds. Ryder is lodging in a place worthy of the pantheon of literary hotels: the Overlook in *The Shining* (1977); the Bates motel from *Psycho* (1959); *The Hotel New Hampshire* (1981) by John Irving; *Hotel Honolulu* (2001) by Paul Theroux; Bertram's Hotel, where Miss Marple takes a holiday in which – unsurprisingly – some complicated, murderous crimes take place. Hotels are prime fictional assets: they bring together disparate people who behave differently away from the restraints of home; they hum with the savour of mystery and sex.

Not in *The Unconsoled*. The only hum is the persistent monotone of the prose, never rising or falling, just – with brilliantly controlled restraint – remaining ever consistent. 'Tell a dream, lose a reader,' said Henry James, himself no stranger to lengthy consistency. And I am lost; I cannot continue reading this book each day. It may be great, but it grates; it wearies, it withholds pleasure. It is admirable, but unhuggable. When I read, I clearly need sentiment, the action of plot, or something that sings a little song with a language. For all its musical references, its composers and piano movements, this never sings at all. At page 180, I close the book, return it to my shelf and look for another.

20 October

The Corrections is a correction to the Ishiguro: busy, funny, distracting, moving. Elmore Leonard once referred to the idea that 'being a good author is a disappearing act'; Franzen on the page seems to be the anti-bashful antithesis of it.

There is nothing wrong with that. Franzen wrote this book full of 'despair about the American novel' and saw himself as the saviour of the form, emitting a positive cry against the 'deafening silence of irrelevance'. And he was, largely, proved right. *The Corrections* sold like Ritalin. He became so big he could afford to disavow an endorsement by Oprah Winfrey (the devout desire of every other author on the planet) on the grounds it might put off a male audience to his book. The controversy added yet more lustre to publication, and the market boomed.

The Corrections was inspired by *The Recognitions* (1955) by William Gaddis, 'by a comfortable margin, the most difficult book I ever voluntarily read', according to Franzen. But *The Corrections* itself isn't difficult to read. Tom Wolfe is a clear influence and better point of reference:* he wrote about a similar 'information compulsion', his desire in *A Man in Full* (1998) 'to cram the world into that novel, all of it'. Greatness, in American fiction, is often a measure of quantity as well as quality: it was Sinclair Lewis who, in his Nobel acceptance speech, urged writers to give America 'a literature worthy of its vastness'. Decades later, Franzen (as well as Wolfe) obliged.

---

* Franzen shares Wolfe's relish – which he got from Dickens – for silly, satirical names: in *The Corrections* we meet Eden Procuro; Dick Hevy; Daffy Anderson; Dale Driblett; Don Armour and others. In *Freedom* (2010), he called a journalist Tom Aberant.

At one level, though, *The Corrections* is a small-scale family drama with no broader focus than the Lamberts: the patriarch Alfred succumbing to dementia; his son Chip, a failed academic, fired for 'an offence involving a female undergraduate which had fallen just short of the legally actionable'; Gary, a successful banker, grappling with depression and an inability to please his own, whiny family; and Denise, a bisexual chef – by far the warmest character in the book – seeking to balance love and a career. Against all this battles Enid, the mother whose simple desire is to achieve a 'miracle of niceness', to have the whole family back for one last Christmas before Alfred disintegrates into the meaningless abyss of incommunicative existence.

Franzen takes this core story and surrounds it with heavily researched detail. This is an exceptionally busy novel, loaded with information about, say, the financial markets, the economic viability of restaurants, prescription medicine, the Mid-West railroad system. Each sentence seems to be packed beyond bursting point: 'The sun was blazing in a pollen-filled sky, all the angiosperms in the newly rechristened Viacom Arboretum blooming hard'; or 'Under low-level radio stimulation at certain resonant frequencies the molecules may spontaneously polymerize.' The critic James Wood called this type of writing 'hysterical realism': a desire for authenticity revealed by an overload of factual data.

But Franzen writes with lyricism too. He has Updike's tight grasp on the short phrase, squeezing every drop of possible meaning from a handful of carefully chosen words: Enid, 'clotted with disapproval'; 'the seismic whomp of ball colliding with garage'; the basement with its 'necrosis of clutter'. How about: 'the ocean's skin of wakefulness' or 'the pineapple's jaundiced belly'. Or you might ponder 'the genital intensity of certain fragrant shrubs', 'the bradykinetic* languor of Enid's electric stove', 'the sickishness, the invalid waiting, of a major holiday'.

It is easy to see this as over-written, an exaggerated attempt at succinct wisdom. But many of those phrases punch at least their own weight, and maybe more: they give pause amid the clutter, a sense of timing, a nugget of clarity. This all can topple into ridiculousness, though: when I read about 'a butt of fascinating tininess' I found it hard not to smile. Just how small does a bottom have to be to be fascinating? And sex, inevitably, brings out the worst in Franzen's quest for exactitude: 'Julia's grapy smell of lecherous pliability'; 'her pussy like a seasoned baseball glove'; 'the fugitive afterscent of quim'; a penis† as 'the rapidly growing boy, the faintly urinary dumpling'. Sex may or may not be well cast as 'the jismic grunting butt-oink. The jiggling frantic nut-swing', but that description reveals a tendency to be unashamedly declarative, to catalogue life in all its forms.

28 October

I realise that I have struggled to convey the sense of sheer enjoyment I feel reading *The Corrections*. Its generosity of scale is entertaining and enriching. It is funny, too. Chip visits Scotland at one point, and feels close to 'regaining a sense of self and purpose, only to find himself at four in the afternoon drinking beer at a train station, eating chips and mayonnaise, and hitting on Yankee college girls'. Or, later, 'While killing some hours by circling in blue ballpoint ink every uppercase M in the front

---

* I had to look this up: it comes from Franzen's research into Parkinson's disease, and means the slowing of the body's ability to move. The metaphor, typically, has come from Alfred's actual condition: a neat Franzen trick by which he manages to be both realist and symbolist in the same sentence.
† Finally!

section of a month-old *New York Times*, Chip had concluded that he was behaving like a depressed person.'

The Corrections was ahead of its time in its assessment of issues like the opioid crisis and the problem of over-medication. And it still rings true in its exploration – which I certainly experience myself – of the over-pathologisation of mental unrest. Chip and Gary not only become depressed, but they worry about depression itself, making them spiral further. I have felt, like Gary, like this: 'as if, in his chest and head, worn-out gears were falling off their axles, chewing into other parts of his internal machinery, as he demanded of his body a bravado, an undepressed energy, that it was simply not equipped to give'. This is painful realism, not hysteria.

The Corrections came out in 2001 and is, like me, just about the child of the pre-digital period. It shows its age: Denise is able to consider 'cell phones the vulgar accessories of vulgar people'; Gary's most appealing quality is his success as a banker; the internet is there but clumsily used, non-pervasive and lacking social media; 9/11 was weeks away, but unimaginable. The novel benefits from this timing: already cluttered with information, it would have been overwhelmed with more. Franzen writes movingly about Alfred's dementia and its eviscerating impact on family life. 'It was hell to get old' is an unvarnished view, not primped with fancy language, and one of the things that linger as I close the book. Enid is a vivid case study in marital disappointment that thickens as the couple age together. She is mourning her husband while he still is alive, grieving for his failures as a man, husband and father: 'How wrong not to love her more, how wrong not to cherish her and have sex at every opportunity, how wrong not to trust her financial instincts, how wrong to have spent so much time at work and so little with the children, how wrong to have been so gloomy, how wrong to have run away from life, how wrong to have said no, again and again, instead of yes.'

This is a novel of incessant 'yes'. And I am thankful for it. It ends on the word 'life' and is proudly, sometimes perilously, full of it. *The Corrections* consoled me; and fiction should always do that, I think.

31 October

Franzen himself thought there were two models of fiction: Status and Contract. In the former, a writer need not trouble with comprehensibility, but can live on ambition alone: 'The value of any novel, even a mediocre one, exists independent of how many people are able to appreciate it.' In the latter, writing is based on communication: 'Every writer is first a member of a community of readers, and the deepest purpose of reading and writing fiction is to sustain a sense of connectedness, to resist existential loneliness.' The former means difficulty is a virtue, a pleasure prolonged; the latter means difficulty is a fault: 'If you crack a tooth on a hard word in a novel, you sue the author.' I am, in the end, a believer in the Contract model: I want to be brought to a pitch of 'connectedness'. And I found it this month with *Offshore* and *The Corrections*.

~

Further Reading

Midnight's Children (1981) by Salman Rushdie
Money (1984) by Martin Amis
The Handmaid's Tale (1985) by Margaret Atwood
Bonfire of the Vanities (1987) by Tom Wolfe
Breathing Lessons (1988) by Anne Tyler
A Prayer for Owen Meany (1989) by John Irving
The Wind-Up Bird Chronicle (1995) by Haruki Murakami

Atomised (1998) by Michel Houellebecq
Disgrace (1999) by J.M. Coetzee
White Teeth (2000) by Zadie Smith
The Kite Runner (2003) by Khaled Hosseini
The Line of Beauty (2004) by Alan Hollinghurst
On Chesil Beach (2007) by Ian McEwan
My Brilliant Friend (2012) by Elena Ferrante
A Death in the Family (2012) by Karl Ove Knausgaard
Dear Life (2012) by Alice Munro
A Girl is a Half-Formed Thing (2013) by Eimear McBride
How to Be Both (2014) by Ali Smith
The Little Red Chairs (2015) by Edna O'Brien
Sing, Unburied, Sing (2017) by Jesmyn Ward
Normal People (2018) by Sally Rooney

November

Autodidact Non-Fiction

Silent Spring (1962) by Rachel Carson
Sapiens (2014) by Yuval Noah Harari
Against Interpretation (1966) by Susan Sontag

1 November

This month I am reading what I call autodidact books, my only non-fiction period during this year of commuting. I have a modest theory that a new era of self-learning is upon us, the greatest since Victorian times. Then, it was because information was becoming more available from a position of scarcity: the old authorities* (the very wealthy and the Church) were losing their narrative monopoly; novelists were emerging, newspapers becoming dominant, literacy approaching universality. In such circumstances, people – including the formerly disenfranchised – could get access to the means of learning more about the world and their part in it. Political and intellectual enfranchisement, both of which really accelerate in this period, are connected.

Today, we drown in a superfluity of detail. The great online democratisation of information has been wonderful, but also

---

* The cognate connection between 'author' and 'authority' is not accidental: the ability to dictate a narrative is one of society's founding powers.

perilous. It is more possible to learn more, to be lied to more, to be enriched and baffled more, than at any other point in human civilisation. And that may come at a cost. As T.S. Eliot presciently asked in 1934: 'Where is the knowledge we have lost in information?' Well, everywhere.

But since then, and the advent of postmodernism, authority has been corroded further: we have healthily questioned the workings behind every structure to the point where we collectively doubt the validity of those structures at all. Experts have been dismissed; politicians who double down have prospered: we live in an age of assertion, in which, because all claims can now be questioned, all claims are theoretically equal. Tribes believe the facts that suit them, or are swayed by the volume and the confidence of the proclamation.

In such an environment, the autodidact must develop trusted sources, cling to expertise, find ways to learn how to navigate the stormy excess of information. Books can be a good way of doing that. And they provide that thrill of knowledge that is unmatchable: reading as a way of becoming – if only for a second – smarter or wiser.

2 November

This has been a year in which the environmental crisis has been demanding attention more keenly than ever. And yet the attention is still disproportionately small to the scale of the problem. In 1988 President Bush said this: 'Those who think we are powerless to do anything about the greenhouse effect forget about the "White House effect"; as President, I intend to do something about it.' Needless to say, he did not. What used to be one of the worst case scenarios – the planet increasing temperature by two degrees – is now its best, and the worst possible consequences – an increase of six degrees or more – threaten the very foundations of civilisation.

It is a tragedy that this existential issue is so political, and therefore so complicated and resistant to simple solution. And yet the arguments are actually very straightforward. Rachel Carson noted in 1938 the self-evident truth that 'the home of the wildlife is also our home'. Twenty-five years later, she asked: 'Can anyone believe it is possible to lay down such a barrage of poisons on the surface of the earth without making it unfit for all life?' Carson was one of the most eloquent witnesses of something that is continually staring us in the face.

4 November

Rachel Carson wrote only four books, before dying of cancer at fifty-seven, just as *Silent Spring* was becoming famous. Before that, she was already well known for her writing about the wonders of the sea, as – in the words of historian Jill Lepore – 'the scientist-poet of the ocean'. At the beginning, she was probably more poet than scientist, and her specialism was wonder: 'Neither you nor I, with our earth-bound senses, know the foam and surge of the tide that beats over the crab hiding under the seaweed of his tide-pool home; or the lilt of the long, slow swells of mid-ocean, where shoals of wandering fish prey and are preyed upon, and the dolphin breaks the waves to breathe the upper atmosphere.'

Carson's two ocean books – *The Sea Around Us* (1951) and *The Edge of the Sea* (1955) – were bestsellers, and she was recognised as a major nature writer, a genre that now is a mainstay of publishing. And it has its weaknesses, not least a fondness for over-writing, for self-conscious metaphorical textures and whimsy, what I call the 'crows bickering in wintry trees' fallacy.*

---

* Virginia Woolf, as ever, said it better than me: 'Nature and letters seem to have a natural antipathy; bring them together and they tear each other to pieces.'

Carson was never like that, not least because she was a marine biologist first and a writer second; her gift was imbuing science with clarity and poetry, not poetry with a bit of factual support. She ended up at the *New Yorker*, though, because her first magazine home, the *Atlantic*,* found her too poetic: it turned out to be a good move for her and her writing.

Carson was inspired to write *Silent Spring* following a letter to the *Boston Herald* about the death of birds on a friend's property due to DDT spraying. She began to investigate the widespread misuse of chemicals, and turned her detailed research into a quiet, fact-based polemic that became a milestone in environmental literature. Few books can point to such a significant and obvious impact on the world. It led to the creation of the Environment Protection Agency in 1970, the banning of agricultural DDT in 1972. It saved the bald eagle, which was on the endangered species list due to pesticide poisoning. It gave profile and empowerment to women in science, whose work was so often overlooked or commandeered. David Attenborough has said it was the book that changed the world the most since Darwin discovered evolution. Al Gore called Carson 'one of the reasons that I became so conscious of the environment and so involved with environmental issues'. William Douglas, a Supreme Court Justice, called it 'the most revolutionary book since *Uncle Tom's Cabin*'. It should clearly be part of my autodidact curriculum.

6 November

The impact of a book can be charted clearly by the spluttering outrage of its opponents. When *Silent Spring* was published,

---

* And yes, there is an irony about a publication called the *Atlantic* thinking a writer was too whimsical about oceans.

with some fanfare, the chemical lobby was militant in response. One chemist was quoted in full apocalyptic fury: 'If man were to follow the teachings of Miss Carson, we would return to the Dark Ages, and the insects and diseases and vermin would once again inherit the earth.' A former Secretary of Agriculture said she was 'probably a Communist'. But the more people railed against her publicly, the more her message was heard.*

The message – that we should think carefully before introducing poisons into our environment – not only remains relevant today, but feeds an ongoing controversy. Carson never called for a total ban on pesticides or insecticides, and yet she is often criticised for doing so to the cost of human life. In 2009 a think tank argued that 'Millions of people around the world suffer the painful and often deadly effects of malaria because one person sounded a false alarm. That person is Rachel Carson.' Even the sedate letters page of *Nature* magazine, as late as 2012, was roiled by Carson-shaming with a letter more or less blaming her for '60 or 80 million premature and unnecessary deaths'. As far as I can see, the book at no point is calling for the end to all chemicals for any purposes, or to end chemical spraying to stop malaria at all.† So what is it doing?

---

* Welcome to the Streisand effect, by which loud objections to something merely increase its visibility. It's named for the singer who sued to stop an image of one of her properties being published on the internet. At the time of the objection, it had been downloaded six times (twice by her lawyers); it subsequently went viral. In a further example of the awfulness of modernity, political parties now try to get people to object to their content (by making it rubbish) in order for people to spread it by criticising it. That's postmodern Streisanding and I will now set myself on fire.

† Carson was no hippy. She appealed regularly in the book to the hunting and fishing community. And she praised the introduction of chemical or genetic sterilisation, and other intrusive meddling. She simply did not believe that indiscriminate chemical spraying was a good thing.

Early on Carson notes that 'everywhere was a shadow of death'. This was sadly true for her: her bird-loving, burdensome mother had just died, and her own life was already waning after a discovery of virulent cancer in her breasts. She was writing a text soaked in morbidity. And it gives the prose an elegiac note from its very opening:

> There was once a town in the heart of America where all life seemed to live in harmony with its surroundings. The town lay in the midst of a checkerboard of prosperous farms, with fields of grain and hillsides of orchards where, in spring, white clouds of bloom drifted above the green fields. In autumn, oak and maple and birch set up a blaze of color that flamed and flickered across a backdrop of pines. Then foxes barked in the hills and deer silently crossed the fields, half hidden in the mists of the fall mornings.

We know the dying fall is coming: this Edenic image has already been lost by the time you are reading about it. Something has 'silenced the voices of spring', and that something is actually someone: 'No witchcraft, no enemy action had silenced the rebirth of new life in this stricken world. The people had done it themselves.' *Silent Spring* is an indictment of man-made environmental crisis, an early warning about the arrival of what we now call the Anthropocene, the epoch in which the biggest impact on the world is caused by one species alone.

7 November

I have been reading a little about Rachel Carson's family. In 1953 she met a woman called Dorothy Freeman with whom she was to build the closest connection of her life. 'I love you beyond expression. My love is boundless as the sea,' Freeman once wrote to her. And indeed their relationship was mainly to exist in the form of correspondence, or snatched summers together by the ocean. Many of their letters have been destroyed, so the impertinent question of the romantic nature of their relationship must go unproved. It is likely that they were, to all intents and purposes, lovers and soulmates.

It strikes me again and again this year how many of the authors I am reading were denied the opportunity fully to express their sexuality. This societal obstruction to the fulfilment of love for arbitrary reasons is one of the tragedies of human history, a sorrowful tale that keeps being rewritten in literature. We saw it in du Maurier, Shakespeare, Byron, Wilde, Renault and it is there in others I have read recently too (Robert Graves, Sylvia Townsend Warner and so on).

I wonder whether there is any connection between the thwarting of romantic energy and its subsequent outpouring in art. As if desire and love must find a voice, and – if it cannot be your own – proxies must be found. It seems a plausible thought to be getting along with.

9 November

The list of *100 Books That Shaped Our World* – which I did with the BBC over the summer – was released this week: a panel of literary types, and me, offering our thoughts on important books that mattered to us. There was mild outcry from middlebrow literary journalists because it featured novels like *Riders* (1985) by Jilly Cooper, the *Discworld* and the *Twilight* series, and not *Moby Dick* or *Ulysses* or *Jane Eyre*. The point was, though, not to re-imagine the canon like the ghost of Bloom (Harold, not Leopold), but to pick books that shaped us, that made us think or act or be different. Readers of this book thus far will be able to pick out my shouted recommendations, of course (*Mr Standfast*, *Sherlock Holmes*, *American Tabloid*, *The Shipping News*, *Rebecca*).

I am pretty relaxed about some of the 'non-literary' texts on the list. I cannot abide snobbishness, that vast mask for intellectual insecurity, especially based on people's often misleading accounts of their own reading. Unlike some of the critics, I have actually read *Moby Dick* and *Ulysses* in recent memory and, while happy to testify to their greatness, their importance in shaping literature, I could not quite argue that they had shaped me as a person. *Riders* was not one of my proposed books, but it is clear how it might mean something to many people as a formative, sex-inflected text, consumed as an adolescent. I can remember it being passed around my school, along with *Lady Chatterley's Lover* (another omission; I can never quite bring myself to argue for Lawrence), with the smutty pages folded down. There are not many other books from twenty-five years ago where I can remember so much: breasts 'like two poached eggs' or 'like duffel bags'; or the moment when an insouciant gentleman lowers his boxer shorts, flicks them off with a foot and catches them nonchalantly on his towering erection. Writing like that lingers in the memory.

I did not get all my choices on the list: *The Portrait of a Lady*[*] was rejected, as was *Catch-22*. But that is fine. If this book has shown anything, I hope it is that reading and rereading form one of the great human acts to be celebrated, its very plurality[†] to be enjoyed, not to be ossified by pseudo-intellectual bores who want to show off about how clever they are.

---

[*] The recognition scene between Isabel and Madame Merle, in which the former sits by a dwindling fire and realises the treachery that has been played upon her, actually influenced the key scene of a novel I wrote in my twenties about a serial killer called Ernest. And no, it will never see the light of day.

[†] It's not a coincidence, but making the list the personal choices of a wide-ranging panel meant that fifty-one were by women, and twenty were by authors of colour. That is not the case of many lists, including that breadth of representation found in this book.

12 November

Silent Spring did shape our world. As I read it, I am struck by two competing qualities in the prose. Yes, there is poetry and elegy. Carson is a sensitive, visual chronicler of the life that surrounds us: 'the sight and sound of drifting ribbons of waterfowl across an evening sky'; or 'the sparrows that flit through the shrubby under-story of the woodlands and forage with rustling sounds amid the fallen leaves – the song sparrow and the white-throat'.

The book is a catalogue of creatures imperilled by mankind's presence, whose modest exoticness gives a mild thrill on a miserable London morning: 'primitive wingless insects called springtails'; 'the oven-bird whose call throbs in the May-time woods'; stonerollers, gizzard shad, river carpsuckers, laughing gulls. Carson has the great gift of amazement at the 'creative magic' of the natural world. Among other things, this is a clarion call to stop and consider what surrounds our self-centred existence: 'Most of us walk unseeing through the world, unaware alike of its beauties, its wonders, and the strange and sometimes terrible intensity of the lives that are being lived about us.'

But if *Silent Spring* was all poetry, it would have been lost to the ages, I think. 'Terrible intensity' in that last sentence is an indication of Carson's way of imposing a seriousness, a realistic weight to what she is describing. Nature writing so often has an ephemeral quality to it, a joyful primping and playing with words. Carson was also writing a work of scientific journalism. Her prose is characterised by clarity, summary, what Henry James called the 'solidity of specification'.

She is good, for example, at explaining both the science and politics of environmental catastrophe. Carson places the rise in pollution in recent historical context (the use of chemicals in the Second World War led to huge advances in destructive knowledge), and more long-term trends: the idea of farming monoculture disturbing the natural order, 'agriculture as an engineer might conceive it to be'. Her declarations are apt: 'As man proceeds toward his announced goal of the conquest of nature, he has written a depressing record of destruction, directed not only against the earth he inhabits but against the life that shares it with him.' She can boil down the debate to its essence – still the central issue today – of 'whether any civilization can wage relentless war on life without destroying itself, and without losing the right to be called civilized'. Her chapter headings are like miniature expostulations of justified anger: 'Elixirs of Death'; 'Rivers of Death'; 'And No Birds Sing'*; 'Beyond the Dreams of the Borgias'; 'Needless Havoc'.

In some ways, then, *Silent Spring* is a model of non-fiction writing: it is unafraid of decisive statement; it has the heft of knowledge and research; and it has the momentary effervescence of poetry. It was to be Carson's last word on nature, alas. Her early death prevented her from returning to writing about the ocean as the next battleground for mankind's arrogant actions, where she would have likely proved the prophet: 'We live in an age of rising seas,' she once wrote. 'In our own lifetime we are witnessing a startling alteration of climate.' She was right about that too. Let's leave her speaking in a voice pitched somewhere between despair and hope. Remember that she said this more than fifty years ago, and that we merely have increased our speed on the road since then: 'The road we have long been traveling is deceptively easy, a smooth superhighway on which we progress with great speed, but at its end lies disaster. The other fork of the road – the one "less traveled by" – offers our last, our only chance to reach a destination that assures the preservation of our earth.'

---

* This is a bit of poetry: Keats in 'La Belle Dame Sans Merci': 'The sedge is wither'd from the lake, / And no birds sing.'

17 November

Human beings are hardwired for story. That is one of the conclusions of *Sapiens* – the global bestseller of 2014 by Yuval Noah Harari, translated from his own Hebrew version of three years before – and also the reason for its success. We crave narrative, the linking of things together to make a coherent argument. And, to Harari, that is what ultimately separated *Homo sapiens* from other similar species: a Cognitive Revolution took place that enabled us – nobody knows how – to talk about things that were not in front of us; to plan, to dream, to make things up. You are reading this because one of your distant antecedents learned to tell and listen to stories.

There are lots of thrills in Harari's book, but its main jolt comes from the chronological context it gives to human development. It tells you things you half knew, and then explains them. So, remember that from 2 million years ago to around 10,000 years ago there were lots of different species of humans (just like there are different species of, say, bears now): *Homo erectus*, *Homo neanderthalensis* and so on. Some of them had been around from the start: *Homo erectus* lasted for the full 2 million years before eventually falling out of the evolutionary record. And in that time period, it barely developed at all, not in two thousand millennia. In one hundred millennia, up to the present day, *Homo sapiens* went from stone flints to artificial intelligence. That is an incredible feat.

Harari is brilliant at framing that development. His central strength as a writer is his clarity of organisation. For Harari 'three important revolutions shaped the course of history: the Cognitive Revolution kick-started history 70,000 years ago. The Agricultural Revolution sped it up about 12,000 years ago. The Scientific Revolution, which got under way only 500 years ago, may well end history and start something completely different.' Go back 70,000 years and we are merely one of several species of the *Homo* genus, wandering around, scratching a living. And from then on we went on a killing spree that continues unabated. We drove out the other rival species: we either exterminated Neanderthal man, or absorbed them into our gene pool. As we entered new continents, we massacred countless other animals: we were, and are, an 'ecological serial killer', 'the deadliest species in the 4-billion-year history of life on earth'.

This is chastening stuff, and Harari at his best. And how did all this happen? Nobody knows. For all the information crammed into *Sapiens* (the book), the rise of *sapiens* (the species) will never be truly explained. How did humans start communicating better, sharing information that enabled them to become more successful than their peers? We may never find out. For all my lust for information, its irrevocable absence is still a source of wonder. For Harari too, I think; and my favourite parts of the book are those without glib answers. How did, say, *sapiens* pass over into Australia for the first time? We must believe that 45,000 years ago – well before sea travel was established – some men and women crossed the ocean to a continent they did not know existed, never left, and never communicated with their previous community. How? Impossible to say. We just know that mankind got there, and soon after almost all the big species already there died out. The serial killer had spread.

Or how about this poser, which is rather more relevant today? Why have women been so mistreated during human history? The argument about relative physical strength does not work, because history is filled with clever, bodily weak figures compelling the strong to perform menial labour for them. Brains have always governed brawn. The major religions – which have institutionalised misogyny – post-date the original acceptance of inequality; they have fixed it into society, but did not cause it. 'If the patriarchal system has been based on unfounded myths rather than on biological facts,' asks Harari, 'what accounts for the universality and stability of this system?' Like many good questions asked in his book, the answer is not straightforward.

Elsewhere, Harari can be straightforward, almost to a fault. This is a book of big ideas. Take the concept that evolution is a pathway towards increased happiness and wellbeing: that things only get better. Harari disagrees, arguing that the foraging life for early Man may have been – by some measurements – nicer than what has followed: it 'left them plenty of time to gossip, tell stories, play with their children and just hang out. Of course the tigers sometimes caught them, or a snake bit them, but on the other hand they didn't have to deal with automobile accidents and industrial pollution.' He suggests that the rise of farming proved the catalyst for inequality and poverty: it fixed us into specific locations, allowing hierarchies to rise, institutions to coalesce, a society of haves and have-nots to appear. As he puts it: 'This is the essence of the Agricultural Revolution: the ability to keep more people alive under worse conditions.'

This feels plausible, doesn't it? I think Rachel Carson would agree. Once we gathered around a food supply, rather than simply pursue nutrition where we could find it, we became essentially static. Agriculture has affected our morals, deeply and unconsciously: we avert our eyes from, say, the abuses of the dairy industry in which a cow is kept constantly pregnant, her calves removed from her, confined and stimulated for a product that is probably bad for us anyway. Thanks to settling down, we developed the concept of privacy, and therefore secrecy and mendacity. Thanks to the planning needed to grow crops, we learned anxiety and the fear of failure, and of the future.

Harari adds another, brilliant, notion to this. We have become what we are thanks to the evolutionary triumph of wheat: the rise of humanity has led to an innocuous species of grass, scattered pell-mell across the globe, developing into something that covers 215 million hectares. One way of looking at ourselves – and a healthily humbling one – is that we have been played by a plant: manipulated into making certain other species a global success. 'We did not domesticate wheat,' says he. 'It domesticated us.' More than 90 per cent of our calories come from food we selected between 9500 and 3500 BC; those foodstuffs have, through us, managed to conquer the world.

22 November

Appropriately enough, I have had a week filled with events based around non-fiction. We launched a new imprint, *TLS Books*, with titles by that inevitable literary couple, Lee Child and Virginia Woolf, both of whom are acutely convinced by the importance of *fiction*, and write well about it. To Child – really following the theory of Harari – storytelling is the great achievement of humanity, even the reason for our existence and success: the ability to share ideas that shift our perceptions away from reality to something larger and more communal. Woolf is also excited by that sinuous power of story, the fact that 'words do not live in dictionaries, they live in the mind' and do strange things to us.

I was also involved in awarding the Baillie Gifford Prize for non-fiction this week, to Hallie Rubenhold for her wonderful book on the victims of Jack the Ripper, *The Five*. I have read it three times in the judging process and was struck each time by its strength as a moral act in itself: it reclaims the narratives of five women, wrongly dubbed prostitutes by history, by dint of discovering and voicing the ordinary details of their existence.

It is a story, of course, about gender: these were women cast off by society, unable to find a place of refuge, and were thus on the streets of London when a psychopath was seeking bloody murder. But it is even more universal than that. The tragedies of the victims are also tragedies of class, poverty, denied opportunity. At some point in each tale, you feel hope that they might escape, even as you know they cannot, and could not even at the time. Tragedy is so often about the force of the inevitable: the treacherous illusion of agency, the sense – as we saw in Euripides and Shakespeare – that necessity overcomes hope or desire.

I think that the Baillie Gifford Prize is rather better than the Booker Prize,* not least because in any year it is possible to read several great works of non-fiction. It is sometimes possible to read no great new novels at all. The failure rate for fiction is heart-stoppingly high, and so often the Booker will go to something that is simply good, or just better than others. Look back at the last twenty years: what winner since Coetzee's extraordinary *Disgrace* (1999) has the power to last in the pantheon? Maybe *Wolf Hall* (2009) and *Bring Up the Bodies* (2012) by Hilary Mantel, but not many more.

24 November

As I have said before, one of the pleasures in life is learning new facts. And *Sapiens* is a treasure trove in that respect. Here are a few more I have foraged for you, shorn from their context to make them more intriguing:

- The world has a billion sheep and pigs, more than a billion cattle and 25 billion chickens.

---

* The prize for fiction was unforgivably botched this year, when they awarded it to two authors, Margaret Atwood and Bernardine Evaristo, for unclear reasons, and to the cost of the more deserving latter. Atwood's sequel to *The Handmaid's Tale* was not a great book, but it seems she was rewarded for a sort of lifetime achievement. In any event, the decision was met with widespread and deserving derision.

- The Sumerians (*c.*4500 BC) had a base-6 system of counting, which is why we talk about 24-hour days and 360 degrees. The first recorded name in history, Kushim the Sumerian, was an accountant.
- In the third century, the Mayan city of Tikal housed 250,000 people, the same size as its direct contemporary, Rome.
- In 1492 there were no horses in America.
- The sum total of money in the world is $60 trillion; the amount in cash is $6 trillion.
- In the 1860s Napoleon III commissioned aluminium cutlery to be used by his most distinguished guests; the less important had to make do with gold.

Each day I read *Sapiens*, I feel like my horizon has been expanded slightly. But I also feel that some of it does come too easy. This is unquestionably a book by a man in a desperate hurry to encapsulate and explain, as the *TLS* review noted: 'It is as if all the world's masses of tweets, blogs, academic papers and op-eds have entered into him, and re-emerged through his pen, distilled down to their essence and offered back to us in this book, neatly packed and branded.'

Charles Mann, of the *Wall Street Journal*, said that 'There's a whiff of dorm-room bull sessions about the author's stimulating but often unsourced assertions.' You do worry that Harari is a simplifier to a fault, as he half recognises himself: 'The better you know a particular historical period, the harder it becomes to explain why things happened one way and not another.' In his attempt to explain the whole of history, he is inevitably confessing to not knowing any of it in proper detail.

Unlike Carson, Harari is no prose stylist in English. The words slide by a little too effortlessly for my taste,* like they have

---

* Although he is self-translating an entire history of humanity from another language, so who am I to cavil?

been smoothed in the quest for universality of register: 'a jumbo brain is a jumbo drain on the body'; 'CEOs don dreary uniforms called suits that afford them all the panache of a flock of crows'; 'money has always tried to break through these barriers, like water seeping through cracks in a dam'.

25 November

But what I keep returning to, and what I think others have loved in this book,* is the boldness of its ideas, the spurs it provides to further thought. Why is it, for example, that Europeans developed the lust for empire, but other civilisations (Arabic, Chinese) had the means, but not the desire? In the fifteenth century there are records of a Chinese fleet of 30,000 people exploring the Indian Ocean, but not in search of colonisation. That was the ambition of the Europeans alone. An arresting thought.

Another is the huge shift in perspective undergone in humanity as a whole: the recognition of the very value of progress itself. Pre-Enlightenment thinking was based on the concept of authority, that the ancients knew more than us, and so increased knowledge could only come from a better understanding of past texts. The entirety of their thinking was based on the fact that the best days were behind us. Modern thinking is the exact opposite: we can only build upon, or disabuse, the work of the past by looking endlessly towards the future.

That is not an original idea, but Harari's modest genius comes from taking notions that should be obvious, and making you consider them afresh, which takes real cleverness. Like his observation that 'Since human and animal bodies were the only

* It is a huge favourite in Silicon Valley, whose inhabitants are endlessly seeking the singularity of total explanation. Bill Gates took it on holiday.

energy conversion device available, muscle power was the key to almost all human activities.' Or that, in the post-atomic age, 'while the price of war soared, its profits declined': a description of the Cold War in nine words.

Harari says at one point that all science is based on one word: '*ignoramus*', or 'we do not know'. And the prospering of humanity is based on our desire to find things out, to learn more. Lee Child makes a similar point in his book: 'Our species seems to be restless and curious to a degree that seems almost unhinged.' We keep finding things and breaking things; and we call it progress.

27 November

I finish *Sapiens* unexpectedly early, and grab something else to read on my way out of the door: *Against Interpretation and Other Essays* by Susan Sontag. She still looms large in the literary world (a massive biography of her was published in 2019), and is well known for her persona – black roll necks, cigarettes, a familiar face glowering beneath her fringe – as well as her writing. In the words of the feminist academic Elaine Showalter, Sontag was 'avid, ardent, driven, generous, narcissistic, Olympian, obtuse, maddening, sometimes loveable but not very likeable'. She was determined to be an intellectual titan, and felt that the world not only owed her a living, but a luxurious living at that.

The essays in this collection come from the 1960s and made Sontag's name; she became the go-to Europhile American woman of letters for the next fifty years. Here is Showalter again, talking about the 1970s:

> Sontag lived at a frenetic pace, barely sleeping, taking speed to write even faster, juggling affairs with gay men (Jasper Johns), notorious womanizers (Warren Beatty) and European lesbian

aristocrats* (Carlotta del Pezzo, Duchess of Caianello), winning fellowships and awards, travelling to Vietnam, China, Sweden, Cuba, Israel and France, publishing essays and books, directing two films, and becoming not just a star but a star-maker whose praise could transform an artist's career.

That's quite some life. Sontag died in 2004 from cancer, and I would like to consider the legacy she left, beyond tales of her clever, riotous living. These essays do not help that much. 'Against Interpretation' is an argument with herself about the value of literary criticism; 'On Style' an argument about whether style can be divorced from content (to which she unsurprisingly says no).

Sontag argues persuasively that art should not be over-thought, sterilised by academic musing. She is full of good lines to that end: 'interpretation is the revenge of the intellect upon art' or 'the compliment that mediocrity pays to genius'; 'the greatest art is secreted not constructed'; 'in place of a hermeneutics we need an erotics of art'. In the 1960s it must have seemed as though challenges to our collective responses to high culture were part of the spirit of the age: how we choose to read Kafka was a critical aspect of our civilisation as a whole. It no longer feels like that. Literary criticism, it pains me to say, was once important, but has been overwhelmed by postmodernism and an overall cheapening of culture.† Sontag provides me with diversion, impresses me still, but moves me not at all. I am not sure these essays, if published now, would raise much of a tremor, which is an indictment of them, and perhaps also of us.

* Sontag was never really forgiven by many in the gay community for being silent about her own sexuality. In 1980s America, with AIDS destroying lives, a refusal to be political was taken as a sign of complicity with a prejudicial system.

† Or, perhaps, a democratisation of culture: the idea of brainy elites like Sontag delivering judgements on art may no longer be politically tenable.

Death is much on my mind, as ever. Yesterday was the funeral of Clive James, the Australian broadcaster, writer and all-round wit. He was a regular contributor to the *TLS* for over fifty years, writing marvellous stuff, the sort of prose where every word feels hewn and polished for the occasion. My slightly sad job in the last two years has been shepherding away from publication some of his work – produced, amazingly, more than eight years since a terminal cancer diagnosis – that might not have sat well with his canonical excellence. He was always unfailingly upfront and polite about it.

James's late flowering of poetry really was something. Larkin-inflected, sparse and brooding intensely about mortality and – its corollary – life itself. One of his last poems we published, 'Anchorage International', concluded with these final seven lines, which are beautiful in their simplicity:

> In these last, feeble days I find it hard
> To fix a detail of the way things were
> And set it in its time. Soon there will be
> Only one final thing left to occur,
> One little thing. You need not fear for me:
> It can't hurt. Of that much I can be sure.
> I know this place. I have been here before.

The subtle insistence of that rhyme ('be' to 'me', and then 'occur', 'sure', 'before') hints at the inevitability of death, the irresistible flow towards it. But there is the tremor of life, and courage here too. That phrase 'it can't hurt', which is both true (death brings an absence of pain after years of endurance) and yet also a nod to colloquial conversation, in the sense that 'it can't hurt' to have another cup of tea or put on another jumper. What an achievement to stare death direct, to know of its imminent arrival, and to maintain a playful tone.

30 November

I end the month reading 'On Camp', one of the seminal essays of the sixties, which now feels something like a well-written blog post. It is a tour de force of quantity-surveying of what makes campness: 'Camp is a woman walking around in a dress made of three million feathers'; Gaudí's buildings are camp, Blake's drawings are not, 'weird and mannered as they are'; Dalí is 'on the barren edges' of camp; *La Traviata* is 'less campy' than *Il Trovatore*. Well, if you say so.

Sontag and Harari share a certain bracing self-confidence, which makes them capable of making large statements with ease. This is Sontag: 'The two pioneering forces of modern sensibility are Jewish moral seriousness and homosexual aestheticism and irony.' If this is true, it is unlikely to be wholly true. But perhaps that does not matter: the joy of reading the words of the wise comes from being challenged and provoked, given new information and prompted to find out more yourself. The work of an autodidact is never done.

~

Further Reading

Meditations (161–180) by Marcus Aurelius
The Wealth of Nations (1776) by Adam Smith
A Vindication of the Rights of Women (1792) by Mary
    Wollstonecraft
Essays: First Series (1841) by Ralph Waldo Emerson
Walden (1854) by Henry David Thoreau
Self-Help (1859) by Samuel Smiles
On the Origin of Species (1859) by Charles Darwin
On Liberty (1859) by John Stuart Mill
Das Kapital (1867) by Karl Marx

Married Love (1918) by Marie Stopes
A Room of One's Own (1929) by Virginia Woolf
A History of Western Philosophy (1945) by Bertrand Russell
Man's Search for Meaning (1946) by Viktor Frankl
The Second Sex (1949) by Simone de Beauvoir
The Origins of Totalitarianism (1951) by Hannah Arendt
The Selfish Gene (1976) by Richard Dawkins
Orientalism (1978) by Edward Said
The Tipping Point (2000) by Malcolm Gladwell
The Metaphysical Club (2001) by Louis Menand
Freakonomics (2005) by Steven Levitt and Stephen Dubner
Why I'm No Longer Talking to White People About Race (2017) by
   Reni Eddo-Lodge

December

Lucky Dip

The Three Musketeers (1844) by Alexandre Dumas
The Bloody Chamber (1979) by Angela Carter
Harry Potter and the Philosopher's Stone (1997) by J.K. Rowling

2 December

I had not realised this, but Alexandre Dumas père, the famously prolific author of *The Three Musketeers* and *The Count of Monte Cristo* (1846) with an output measuring more than 100,000 printed pages, was the victim of systemic prejudice throughout his life. He was mixed-race: the son of a Revolutionary general* and erstwhile favourite of Napoleon, whose own parents were a French marquis and a black slave from Haiti. Dumas is the family name of this grandmother; a slave name. When the Nazis occupied Paris they destroyed the monument to Dumas, because of his racial background. It has never been rebuilt.

He is firmly part, though, of the French canon. In 2002 he was enshrined in the Panthéon, the place where France honours

---

* A man who could lift up a horse with his bare hands, who lived his life filled with military bravery, and languished in an Italian prison so grim it probably inspired the account of the Chateau d'If in *The Count of Monte Cristo.*

and gives gratitude to its *grands hommes** such as Hugo, Rousseau and Voltaire. President Chirac noted the delay in the award, publicly apologised, and said he was 'repaying an injustice which marked Dumas from childhood, just as it marked the skin of his slave ancestors'.

But Dumas has also, from the beginning, transcended notions of race and nation, as Victor Hugo said in 1872: 'The name of Alexandre Dumas is more than French, it is European; it is more than European, it is universal.' In a list of the most frequently translated authors in the world, he appears in eighteenth place, between Pope John Paul II and Arthur Conan Doyle. They are fitting book-ends, really: Dumas is the arch genre novelist, a hack for all hacks, but also one with an elevated eye on the baroque world of European *haut monde*. He loved the swash-buckling grandeur of the past, in which morals were simpler, action was broader, the Church was a player, and swagger was swagger. This is from the beginning of *The Three Musketeers*: 'There were nobles, who made war against each other; there was the king, who made war against the cardinal; there was Spain, which made war against the king. Then, in addition to these concealed or public, secret or open wars, there were robbers, mendicants, Huguenots, wolves, and scoundrels, who made war upon everybody.' It is this world that Dumas is happiest inhabiting.

---

* For a long time, it was just *hommes*, as you might expect. Marie Curie was the first woman to get in, followed – in the last decade or so – by Germaine Tillion (anthropologist and resistance fighter); Geneviève de Gaulle-Anthonioz (resistance fighter and niece of Charles de Gaulle); and Simone Veil (politician and lawyer, not to be confused with Simone Weil, the philosopher who died during the Second World War). Camus's family turned down the honour in 2009.

6 December

Dumas took historical events and dramatised them enthusiastically; he was a 'novelising historian', as Tolstoy once put it, not a historical novelist, which perhaps unfairly suggests he was better on the facts than the fiction. Certainly, Dumas cannot be classed among *auteur* novelists at all: he wrote with a factory of up to seventy helpers. This is the recollection of one of them:

> I used to dress his characters for him and locate them in the necessary surroundings, whether in Old Paris or in different parts of France at different periods. When he was, as often, in difficulties on some matter of archaeology, he used to send round one of his secretaries to me to demand, say, an accurate account of the appearance of the Louvre in the year 1600 . . . I used to revise his proofs, make corrections in historical points and sometimes write whole chapters.

Dumas's primary helper was a man called Auguste Maquet, who played a large role in writing *Musketeers*, focusing especially on its ever-moving plot. In 1851 the partnership fragmented, and Maquet sued Dumas for absent royalties. He lost; the court averred that 'Dumas without Maquet would have been Dumas: what would Maquet have been without Dumas?'* Dumas was, as a *New Yorker* article once put it, the James Patterson† of his day: the owner of a brand, the driver of the story, the front-man standing over these vast swathes of prose.

---

* Not much according to the *TLS* of 1914, which called Maquet a 'second-rate writer and an invaluable assistant'.
† In 2010 one in every seventeen novels purchased in the US was written by Patterson and his team. He writes the outline, up to fifty pages, someone produces a draft, and then he edits and owns the result. It is astonishingly successful: in the twenty-first century he has outsold John Grisham, Stephen King and Dan Brown *together*.

In common with many people, Dumas's prolific approach to one area of his life was matched in various others. He certainly could have been enshrined in the shagger Panthéon, claiming to have fathered 500 children with forty mistresses. He earned millions and died broke. And yet through all that time he kept grinding out the books. As the *New York Times* said in 1884, he was a 'pleasure-seeker who might serve as a model to all industrious workers'.

8 December

The plot of *Musketeers* is instantly familiar, from the moment we meet d'Artagnan, 'a Don Quixote of eighteen', proudly looking for a scrap in the inn at Meung, glimpsing Milady for the first time, all 'pale and fair, with long curls falling in profusion over her shoulders . . . large, blue, languishing eyes, rosy lips, and hands of alabaster'. From films, cartoons, plays (including an adaptation by Dumas, and later by P.G. Wodehouse), and the sheer pervasiveness of the novel itself, we know what will follow: the duels with the Musketeers Porthos, Athos and Aramis; 'one for all and all for one'; the affair of the diamond studs; the picnic at the siege of La Rochelle; the final, Gothic conclusion.

This is a novel of straightforwardness, of moral absolutes. The Musketeers are sanctioned hoodlums, allowed to go broke, get hammered, fight and enjoy a life free generally from too much contemplation:

> Loose, half-drunk, imposing, the king's Musketeers, or rather M. de Treville's, spread themselves about in the cabarets, in the public walks, and the public sports, shouting, twisting their moustaches, clanking their swords, and taking great pleasure in annoying the Guards of the cardinal whenever they could fall in

with them; then drawing in the open streets, as if it were the best of all possible sports.

Dumas's prose is similarly brisk in its exploration of the action. He wastes little time on intricacies of personality, preferring instead schematic accounts that will not slow the story: 'The four countenances expressed four different feelings: that of Porthos, tranquillity; that of d'Artagnan, hope; that of Aramis, uneasiness; that of Athos, carelessness.'

The novel bears all the marks of fast writing, padding and little pause for restraint. It is full of cliché, that clear evidence of facility at the expense of felicity (one chapter actually begins, in my version, 'It was a dark and stormy night'), and summary wisdom: 'Love is the most selfish of all the passions'; 'A man of fifty cannot long bear malice with a wife of twenty-three'; and so on.

9 December

I never drink the night before I am working, which limits my possible consumption to just two evenings a week. I am not someone who luxuriates in booze, or who takes pleasure in losing control of myself. There is a moment in *The Three Hostages* (1924) by John Buchan when Sandy quotes an old Latin tag, '*Sit vini abstemius qui hermeneuma tentat aut hominum petit dominatum*', which – as we all know – means 'whoever seeks to interpret the world or to exercise power over men, should not drink wine'. I am more interested in the former (understanding things) than the latter (dominating anybody), but I think it is hard to get things done and drink a lot at the same time.*

---

* Counter-argument: the character who believes this in *The Three Hostages* is an evil megalomaniac who hypnotises people against their will and should not be trusted on anything.

But I do like reading about drinking. There is a lot of it in *The Three Musketeers*, for example. D'Artagnan does not want to go out on a 'hazardous expedition' unless he can 'have two or three bottles of old Burgundy mounting up into my head'. I am always amazed by the sheer scale of boozing described in books, and clearly attempted by many over the course of human history.

Has it ever struck you that most major historical events would have involved people who had drunk alcohol for breakfast, lunch and dinner? When an Italian ambassador was heading to the court of Queen Elizabeth I, he was cautioned under no circumstances to drink the water, but to confine himself only to wine and beer. Both were diluted, but still. I read recently that, in 1630s Venice, ship-workers were given access to a wine fountain, and managed to get through five litres every day. Even at 5 per cent, the strength of strong beer, that is a hell of a lot of booze to have at work. Nobody has quite been able to make clear to me the impact of alcohol on people's decision-making, or its effect on human civilisation, but it must be significant. Pitt the Younger was apparently a 'six-bottle man', and he had to decide about war with France and the introduction of income tax. Would he have acted differently sober?

In fiction, booze provides a spur to plotting, as reduced inhibition is ever the progenitor of interesting action. My most memorable drinking sessions in books? Gussie Fink-Nottle, 'tanked to the uvula' as Wodehouse would say, and addressing the prize-giving crowd at Market Snodsbury Grammar School with vim and vigour: 'I could chew holes in a steel door.' David Copperfield's 'dissipation' with Steerforth. The Porter in *Macbeth* struggles with the after-effects of his own bender, 'carousing till the second cock', and muses on wine's ability to 'provoke the desire', but 'take away the performance'. I was once tempted to try drinking along with the gang in Hemingway's *The Sun Also Rises*, but honestly believe it would have killed me. When they are not slurping wine from vast skins, pouring in without remission like water, they are mixing it up with absinthe, Pernod, fruit brandy and the like. Here's a line to leave on, from *Tender is the Night* (1934) by F. Scott Fitzgerald, himself an alcoholic: 'I want to give a party where there's a brawl and seductions and people going home with their feelings hurt and women passed out in the cabinet de toilette.'

I don't want to go to that party, but I do want to read about it.

15 December

I come to realise that the central hero of *The Three Musketeers* is not d'Artagnan, but Athos. It is his early marriage to Milady that provides the key to the whole story, and it is his character's complexity that best survives the broad strokes of the author's pen. He is the figure to whom Dumas shows the most fondness, dwelling on his many perfections: 'His head, with piercing eyes, a straight nose, a chin cut like that of Brutus, had altogether an indefinable character of grandeur and grace.' But more than that, Athos is the Hamlet of the Musketeers, endlessly questioning and moping, cursed by a brilliance that can drift towards depression and self-loathing, where 'in his hours of gloom – and these hours were frequent – he was extinguished as to the whole of the luminous portion of him, and his brilliant side disappeared as into profound darkness.' That is rather deftly put, and speaks to something desperate in all of us. Athos is, therefore, not just a cipher for martial acts, or a romantic turn, but a person of depth and contrast, 'an optimist when things were concerned, and a pessimist when men were in question'. Like Hamlet, he is conscious of the immensity of human life, its intricacy and complexity; but he also has the mental strength to set it at naught.

Disposed against him is the other great figure of the book: the gorgeous, evil, haunting Milady, 'with nothing of woman in her nature'. Dumas, like his characters, is clearly 'dazzled by the superhuman beauty of this woman who unveiled herself before him with an immodesty which appeared to him sublime'. She is one of the great villainesses in fiction, as compelling as Lady Macbeth, Mrs Danvers, or Cathy Ames in *East of Eden* (1952). The final pages are a morbid drama of which she is the sole figure on the stage, lit by a sanguinary moon, impossible to ignore. A happy link to my next book, actually: *The Bloody Chamber* by Angela Carter, itself full of promise of lush and mysterious wonder.

17 December

A good test of how you might feel about Angela Carter is your reaction to this passage, from 'The Lady of the House of Love', one of the stories in *The Bloody Chamber*:

> Wearing an antique bridal gown, the beautiful queen of the vampires sits all alone in her dark, high house under the eyes of the portraits of her demented and atrocious ancestors, each one of whom, through her, projects a baleful posthumous existence; she counts out the Tarot cards, ceaselessly construing a constellation of possibilities as if the random fall of the cards on the red plush tablecloth before her could precipitate her from her chill, shuttered room into a country of perpetual summer and obliterate the perennial sadness of a girl who is both death and the maiden.

We notice the intricate Gothic sensibility, the generosity of the description, the perilous flirtation with cliché. There is a sensuousness that never feels quite controlled. Look at the helpless pairing of adjectives, which adds a strange feel of uniform re-inforcement even in this fantasy world: 'dark, high', 'demented and atrocious', 'baleful, posthumous', 'red plush', 'chill shuttered'. These are stories, I see immediately, that are rather joyfully shorn of subtlety; they are ripe, fecund with descriptive force.

The Bloody Chamber is not, despite what you may read, simply a collection of feminised or grown-up fairy tales. Carter herself said that her 'intention was not to do "versions" or, as the American edition of the book said, horribly, "adult" fairy tales, but to extract the latent content from the traditional stories and to use it as the beginnings of new stories'. And, as she also noted, that latent content was already 'violently sexual'. Carter was an aficionado of fairy tales, the work of Charles Perrault from the seventeenth century (which she translated) and, later, from the Grimm Brothers or Isak Dinesen.[*] Although such folk narratives come from varied sources,[†] they were created in a time, generally, of child mortality, stepmothers being imposed upon existing family units, of unexplained accidents and super-stitious fears. Carter once reviewed some children's fiction for the *TLS*, and complained heartily about the sterilisation of the source material; she noted that 'this version robs the tale of the greatest punch line in the history of juvenile narrative, "and then the wolf gobbled her all Up!"'

Carter would never be so coy in her own work, and allowed herself a freedom to dramatise and to decorate what had gone before: 'The short story,' she said, is 'not minimalist, it is rococo'. What resulted was her own ebullient treatments of the 'Bluebeard'

---

[*] Best known for *Out of Africa* (1937), she was more relevantly the author of *Seven Gothic Tales* (1934), her own reimagining of the Scandinavian folk tradition.

[†] Carter once said that asking where a fairy tale came from was like asking who invented the meatball. As my Google history will now testify, you can't do it.

tale (in the title story), two versions of 'Beauty and the Beast', one of 'Puss in Boots' and three of 'Little Red Riding Hood'. In 'The Bloody Chamber', a young French woman is married off to a rich nobleman with a beautiful home and a vile secret: he murders his wives in a rather flamboyant torture chamber. This is, among other things, a sexed-up *Rebecca*, complete with its own cruel housekeeper with a 'bland, pale, impassive, dislikeable face'.

What was more or less restrained in du Maurier is given full vent by Carter and 'her world of sensuous intimacy'. The young narrator is a tingling bundle of sensation: her nightdress 'slipped over my young girl's pointed breasts and shoulders, supple as a garment of heavy water, and now teasingly caressed me, egregious, insinuating, nudging between my thighs as I shifted restlessly in my narrow berth'. Set against this vision of nubile pubescence is the absurdly masculine husband, with his cigar 'fat as a baby's arm',* his 'male scent of leather and spices'; the 'heavy, fleshy composure of his', his 'white, heavy flesh', his 'sheer carnal avarice'.

There is – as you may have noticed – a somewhat hefty flirtation with kitsch at work here: things happen in an 'eldritch half light' in which 'the day broke around me like a dream'. There is a lot of daunting redness: a ring is a 'bloody band of rubies', a rug with the 'red of the heart's dearest blood'. And how about the soapy glee behind this adversion: 'I ran to the telephone; and the line was, of course, dead. Dead as his wives.' I am enjoying all this furiously, of course.

---

* Carter was not shy of phallic imagery: 'the great pistons ceaselessly thrusting the train that bore me through the night' or his 'great black car, gouging tunnels through the shifting mist'.

18 December

I interview the actress Saoirse Ronan today, about her role in *Little Women*, Louisa May Alcott's ever-popular novel from 1868, now transformed by the talents of Greta Gerwig into a beautiful celebration of sisterliness. I saw it the day after the unseasonal general election in a room full of suppressed sobs, which *I think* were inspired by the on-screen happenings only. I try not to cry in films for reasons that are unclear when I analyse them: you are alone, in the dark, and free to respond viscerally for once. But some form of conditioning holds me back and I wince awkwardly to stop the tears coming.

The book – though not the film, which wryly messes with the chronology, just as it conflates the lives of the heroine Jo March with that of her creator – begins with a famously festive line: ' "Christmas won't be Christmas without any presents," grumbled Jo, lying on the rug.' It sets up the Dickensian scene of the impoverished Marches sharing their Christmas meal with an even poorer family from down the road, an event that is both sugary and yet still a little nourishing to the soul.

This scene qualifies *Little Women* as a 'Christmas book', at least, even though the narrative ranges widely afterwards. To me a Christmas book has to have at least one iconic festive scene, which affects the rest of the novel. My nomination is *LA Confidential* (1990) by James Ellroy,* a violent, curt and wonderful rendering of police corruption in the 1950s, beginning with the 'Bloody Christmas' beatings of prisoners, which ruptures the unanimity of the force, and spins off the central characters towards their eventual fatal reckonings. Maybe I am not getting

---

* For children, I will nominate the unforgettable *Cops and Robbers* (1978) by Allan and Janet Ahlberg; and for teenagers *The Hogfather* (1996) by Terry Pratchett.

this whole festive thing right. And yes, in the same spirit, my favourite Christmas film is *Die Hard*.

The aesthetic of Christmas, it is commonly said, was invented by the Victorians and their cultural bandleader Charles Dickens. As is so often the case, this is not quite the whole truth. St Francis of Assisi, around the turn of the thirteenth century, was the first person on record to construct a replica nativity scene; carols began in the sixteenth century; a decorated tree and mistletoe in the seventeenth century. And the widespread popularisation of some of these things actually post-dates Dickens, and has nothing to do with him: it is worth noting that the Cratchits in *A Christmas Carol* (1843) do not have a tree, send cards or give presents.

Dickens, though, was a champion of Christmas,* not only with his *Carol*, which began his annual tradition of a money-making festive story, but his novella *The Chimes* (1844), another attempt to make use of the emotional backdrop of the time of year to make a broader social point. His biographer John Forster explained it thus: 'When he came therefore to think of his new story for Christmas time, he resolved to make it a plea for the poor . . . He was to try and convert Society, as he had converted Scrooge, by showing that its happiness rested on the same foundations as those of the individual, which are mercy and charity not less than justice.'

Christmas charity pleas come straight from Dickens, as do Twitter gatherings for the lonely: the secularised moral weight of the season being used as inspiration for good.

---

* When his death was announced in June 1870, a barrow-girl in Drury Lane was said to ask: 'Dickens dead? Then will Father Christmas die too?' I am choosing to believe this.

Carter's tone wavers little across the stories. The female-centred narration was perhaps more striking forty years ago, but her fearless exploration of desire and sex from a woman's perspective remains vibrant and vital. Sometimes there is a curt masochism that brings you up short, with pornographic force: 'her cunt a split fig below the great globes of her buttocks'; or 'the candles dropped hot, acrid gouts of wax on my bare shoulders'. One story is merely 700 words long, and concludes more or less with this: 'Weeping, the Count got off his horse, unfastened his breeches and thrust his virile member into the dead girl.'

Elsewhere Carter is interested in a fluidity of sex and gender that feels very modern. This is a woman talking to a man: 'I should like to grow enormously small, so that you could swallow me, like those queens in fairy tales who conceive when they swallow a grain of corn or a sesame seed. Then I could lodge inside your body and you would bear me.'

If Carter can be kitsch, she is never drearily conventional. She would, one feels, be somewhat aghast at any attempts to compartmentalise her or fetishise her politics. Indeed, at the same time as *The Bloody Chamber*, she published a book-essay on the Marquis de Sade called *The Sadeian Woman*, which saw something in his 'moral pornography' and refused to condemn it entirely. Feminists were aghast, but Carter was undeterred.* Like du Maurier, she maintained an interest in a place where different worlds dreamily combine, including that of gender. Carter once wrote this to a friend:

> Somebody asked me who my favourite women writers were
> the other day, meaning, I guess, some kind of writers who

---

* For the rest of her life she got letters from guys wanting to be dominated by her. Men really are stupid sometimes.

expressed a specifically feminine sensibility – I said Emily Brontë, who's pure butch, and cursed myself afterwards because the greatest feminine writer who's ever lived is Dostoevsky, followed closely by Herman Melville, who has just the kind of relish of beautiful boys that emancipated ladies such as yourself express. And D.H. Lawrence is infinitely more feminine than Jane Austen, if one is talking about these qualities of sensitivity, vulnerability and perception traditionally ascribed by male critics to female novelists.

Beyond this, Carter is also a high priestess of the Ovidian imagination: the creator of constant metamorphoses. That is why fairy tales appealed to her so much, with their supernatural shifts and squishings; but it also represents her own creative response to them, as something to evolve and re-shape. 'The Tiger's Bride' is a reversioning of 'Beauty and the Beast', and ends with the former oddly becoming the latter, as the result of a rather passionate licking: 'And each stroke of his tongue ripped off skin after successive skin, all the skins of a life in the world, and left behind a nascent patina of shiny hairs. My earrings turned back to water and trickled down my shoulders; I shrugged the drops off my beautiful fur.'

24 December

I collapse into the end of the year, full of cold, phlegm, self-loathing and exhaustion. I suspect this happens to many of us: our bodies sustain ourselves right up until a holiday arrives, and then abandon all pretence at healthiness thereafter.

I come home to a house full of illness, a teething baby, and long days of holidays ahead of us. Phoebe, at eighteen months, doesn't understand Christmas, and has a routine that remains constant whatever else is going on: up at 6.30 a.m., nap at 12.30

p.m., bed at 7.30 p.m., endless supervision in between. She is a joyful presence when well, but has morphed into a shrieking, slobbering, monster in baby form just for the arrival of the festive season.

When she sleeps, I sag upon the sofa and go to my invalid books, the novels that give me succour when I feel terrible. You can probably guess some of them by now: this next couple of days I reread *Pride and Prejudice*, *The Shipping News*, a couple of Sherlock Holmes stories, some P.G. Wodehouse and *LA Confidential* (well, it is Christmas). You should always keep a sick shelf ready of your reliable treatment books, I think. I favour heavy plot-based novels, to lose myself in, and familiar set-pieces, to return to with pleasure.

The best novels* about the sensations of illness are harder to recall: *The Magic Mountain* is good on invalidism, as is *The Portrait of a Lady*, with whimsical, straggly old Ralph Touchett, as a stand-in for the author. Henry James himself had a mysterious ailment, what he called an 'obscure hurt', which kept him out of the American Civil War and bothered him afterwards. Nobody knows what it was, though some believe it was a groinal complaint that prevented him having much of a sexual life. It doesn't take a psychoanalyst to see the impact on his stories, which are full of lurkers, the pallid unwell, observers not doers, watchers not players. Inaction in action.

27 December

I cannot, off-hand, think of another serious writer so unafraid of unsubtlety as Angela Carter. And perhaps the great thrill of

---

* In non-fiction, there is the triptych of Sontag's *Illness as Metaphor* (1978), Elaine Scarry's *The Body in Pain* (1985), and – more recently – *The Undying: A Meditation on Modern Illness* (2019) by Anne Boyer. All by women, interestingly.

her work is its fearlessness, its unembarrassed desire to over-whelm the senses. The stories are muskier than a teenager's bedroom, stinking of 'the slumberous, pungent fumes of incense' or 'lush, insolent incense' or 'far too potent a reek of purplish civet'. Tales often start with the weather, always symbolically full of snow. And only Carter's Puss in Boots, you feel, would be seen 'tonguing my arsehole with the impeccable hygienic integrity of cats'.

Carter died in 1992 at the age of just fifty-one, and never lived truly to see herself, and what she called her 'batty kind of whim-sicality', in fashion. Today, I am told, *The Bloody Chamber* has more MA theses written about it than any other contemporary book. The idea of female-centred sexuality, or empowered female narrators, is far more established in the literary world than ever it was. She is a fitting figure to come to towards the end of my year of reading, this writer of metamorphosis who makes me think back to books of decisive imaginative shifts and self-transformations, like *Rebecca*, *Watchmen*, *Moby Dick*, *The King Must Die* and the *Sonnets*.

28 December

I am given, as part of a programme for Radio 4, the task of read-ing the first *Harry Potter* novel for the first time. I am entirely the wrong age for this epochal series: it came out when I was seven-teen and unlikely to bother reading a children's book,* and by the time my own children were old enough to understand it, they were old enough to read it for themselves. Indeed, Nelly still endlessly, restlessly rereads all the *Potter* books – a chip off

---

* Although consider this argument from Auden: 'There are good books which are only for adults, because their comprehension presupposes adult experiences, but there are no good books which are only for children.'

the old block in that respect – and the films are occasionally there in the background, all lush colours and explosions. But I have barely absorbed any of the lore or the imagery: I can name a few characters, am aware of cod-Latin like 'expelliamus', and vaguely know that someone significant dies at the end. What will encountering it for the first time be like? Over the next two journeys, I will find out.

29 December

Well, it is all right. I read it quickly, the story sliding past frictionlessly and happily enough. It feels like a compilation of familiar, well-written classics for children taken from the last century: the boarding school full of awe, history and magnificent food from Blyton and Wodehouse; Gothic-tinged magical lessons from *The Worst Witch* (1974) by Jill Murphy; the effortful mythology – dying unicorn, saviour centaurs – from C.S. Lewis. Harry Potter himself is the perfect amalgam of historic child heroes: his parents efficiently dispatched (Voldemort, explosion) before the story begins; the victim of a hateful step-family who refuse to recognise his individuality or potential; his believable valour immediately established.

Rowling's prose, in this first novel at least, is unexceptional but also unexceptionable, perfectly serviceable in the advancement of the plot, no obvious stubbed toes of inelegance. If it is hard to see how this book was rejected so many times (by all twelve publishing houses who first received it), it is perhaps not much easier to see how, upon publication, it has colonised the Anglophone world. The brand is now worth more than $15 billion, and the final four novels of the series each broke its predecessor's record for the fastest-selling books in history. It seems to have represented the perfect storm of franchisable fiction: a credible and likeable author, who achieves riches from rags in a heart-warming fashion; movie versions that enhance the original; a digital presence, in the Pottermore world, that provides both supplementation to the books and also a way of further monetising them; and a story that is familiar enough to grasp, with enough that is novel and inventive to prevent fatigue.

As I close the book, all that lingers in my memory is Quidditch – a fine update of the Wodehousian cricket match, in which the under-sized hero biffs his way to glory – and house points for Gryffindor. I am pleased finally to have experienced it, but I am not tempted to go further. I am thirty-nine, after all.

30 December

Today we release the decade's final *TLS* podcast, which is named – charmingly enough – *Freedom, Books, Flowers and the Moon*, after a line from Oscar Wilde. In it, we talk about changes in the cultural and intellectual world over the last ten years. The decade, which has no real name – 'the tens' or 'the twenty tens' being clearly sub-iconic as labels go – has been unequivocally dominated by issues of identity. Who you are is now at least as important as what you do or say.

This is not unequivocally a good or bad thing. We are living in an era in which opportunity is being expanded, somewhat slowly and painfully, for those who have historically been denied it. And to those in authority, this partial rise in equality feels like a denial of a right. It is not.* But one corollary of things changing is the rise of a culture of offence-taking, cancellation, hyper-sensitivity

---

* This year I had a long meeting with a senior broadcaster about ideas for television shows. It ended with him saying to me: 'Just to be clear, we're not commissioning any new shows presented by white men in the near future.' Something he could have said at the beginning of the meeting to have saved time.

and wokeness. This works in all directions: not only are some people prone to overstate issues of discrimination (taking offence at the term 'blind spot' as ableist, to pick one example), others are prone to overstate the existence of 'political correctness gone mad'. Our hurry to indignation is perhaps now our least attractive collective quality.

We talk on the podcast about the cultural high points of the decade, which are worth sharing. How about the musical *Hamilton*, by Lin-Manuel Miranda, an act of extraordinary imaginative alchemy, taking a doorstop of a biography and turning it into a hip-hop-inflected extravaganza, permanently altering the very make-up of musical theatre. Or the rise of translations in the book world – now amounting to more than 5 per cent of total sales in the UK – and thus the welcoming into the Anglophone world of Ferrante, Knausgaard, Svetlana Alexievich, Olga Togarczuk and so on. Ferrante is perhaps the novelist of the decade: her *Neapolitan Quartet* was first published in 2011, and a new book came out in Italian just before Christmas 2019. My favourite interviewee of the year, Maggie Gyllenhaal, is making a movie from another of Ferrante's books in 2020 too.

Or consider the success of the Marvel Cinematic Universe as a phenomenon of the age. When I was growing up, action movies had a certain right-wing aesthetic: macho, individualistic; a single white man set against a shadowy group of Others. It must be significant that the most money-making movies of the decade are not like that any more; instead they are those that celebrate concepts of equality, recognise difference but reflect essential similarity within human beings, contain diversity of hero and heroine, race and sexuality. And such politics are not added on for the sake of wokeness but are integral to the very essence of the story: *Black Panther*, with its vast African mythography; *X-Men*, who are themselves sustained metaphors for the different, the excluded; and the *Avengers* movies, with their conglomeration of variety. It must mean something that popular culture is becoming fairer-minded, mustn't it?

31 December

The year – and decade – ends, with one more day of work. I am bleary and exhausted. So here is an extract from one of the great poems by one of the great poets of the nineteenth century, *In Memoriam* (1850) by Tennyson. It is a glorious wallowing in noble sentiment. More and more this year, my sentimentalism has sustained me, so I am not going to apologise for it now.

> Ring out, wild bells, to the wild sky,
> The flying cloud, the frosty light:
> The year is dying in the night;
> Ring out, wild bells, and let him die.
> Ring out the old, ring in the new,
> Ring, happy bells, across the snow:
> The year is going, let him go;
> Ring out the false, ring in the true.
> Ring out the grief that saps the mind
> For those that here we see no more;
> Ring out the feud of rich and poor,
> Ring in redress to all mankind.
> Ring out a slowly dying cause,
> And ancient forms of party strife;
> Ring in the nobler modes of life,
> With sweeter manners, purer laws.

It seems a bit optimistic, doesn't it? Real life is not quite like that. Never mind, there will always be a book somewhere to console us.

~

Further Reading

The Duchess of Malfi (1614) by John Webster
The Awakening (1899) by Kate Chopin
The Souls of Black Folk (1903) by W.E.B. Du Bois
North of Boston (1914) by Robert Frost
Ulysses (1922) by James Joyce
The Well of Loneliness (1928) by Radclyffe Hall
Fahrenheit 451 (1953) by Ray Bradbury
Giovanni's Room (1956) by James Baldwin
Things Fall Apart (1958) by Chinua Achebe
The Deep Blue Good-by (1964) by John D. MacDonald
Do Androids Dream of Electric Sheep? (1968) by Philip K. Dick
The Left Hand of Darkness (1969) by Ursula Le Guin
Fear and Loathing in Las Vegas (1971) by Hunter S. Thompson
The Hour of the Star (1977) by Clarice Lispector
Rabbit is Rich (1981) by John Updike
Watermelon (1995) by Marian Keyes
Half of a Yellow Sun (2006) by Chimamanda Ngozi Adichie
The One from the Other (2006) by Philip Kerr
Faces in the Crowd (2011) by Valeria Luiselli
Drive Your Plow Over the Bones of the Dead (2018) by Olga
  Tokarczuk

Epilogue

The first journey of January is always burdened by gloom. I sit in an empty train carriage, well before daybreak, with night seeping away. But this time I feel a bit bereft: my morning reading is unplanned; I am without the comforting certainty of my next distraction. I'll probably go back to Dickens for something substantial.

Looking back on my year in literature, I am struck by the joy it has given me, and the solace. This diary documents the sense of unease and mental unrest I must be constantly feeling, the nagging, minor, effortfully endurable pain. It also shows the power of the printed word to oppose and relieve that existential throb.

I have read very little that has not brought me something memorable, diverting or analgesic. Big 'baggy monsters' of books – to use Henry James's phrase – like *Moby Dick*, *The Three Musketeers* or *The Radzetsky March* have provided something of measurable weight to which to moor myself. Then there have been the lighter, more insinuating achievements of *The Tiger in the Smoke* or *The King Must Die*. The colourful splurging of *The Bloody Chamber*. The self-conscious gloaming of *The Watchmen*. Rachel Carson and Yuval Noah Harari's explorations of the past and perilous future of the planet. Byron's rattling rhymes, set against those tiny, burrowing verses of Emily Dickinson. And that month of Shakespeare: from the unsettling navel-gazing of the sonnets to the vast, breathlessly magnificent achievements of the tragedies and histories.

Just as this book was being prepared for publication, the first warning signs of a virus began innocuously to make themselves clear in Britain. We all know what followed: lockdown, anxiety, heroic self-sacrifice from key workers, a nation holding itself together in mutual apprehension and consolation. And a profound advertisement for the value of reading. So, while my busy train – filled with unheeded miasma and now shocking proximity – might feel like a relic of a different world, the lessons from my journeys have never felt more relevant. The main thing I learned on the 6.28 is that I need reading to escape, to balance my mental state, to expand my horizons even when I feel circumstances closing in around me.

I am not the perfect reader. No such thing exists. I dwell on my prejudices too much, sometimes seek comfort more than challenge. I have tried to read more widely this year, but am still very much within the rutted path of tradition. Next year, I will broaden my horizons even more, an ambition I should always have, an ever-increasing circle to be drawn.

Henry James once said that 'Really, universally, relations stop nowhere, and the exquisite problem of the artist is eternally but to draw, by a geometry of his own, the circle within which they shall happily *appear* to do so.' All writing is a circling, just as all reading is. A happy metaphor for someone like me, locked into a routine, endlessly tracing the same elliptical route from home to work and back again, in the companionship of those who have circumscribed their own imaginations for me for a while. There will always be another book to read, or guiltily to reread. And that is a joy for all of us.

Acknowledgements

The idea for this book began in a conversation I had with Cathryn Summerhayes well before she became my agent (and subsequently the consensus greatest agent in publishing). I wanted to write about difficult books to help people find a way into them. As it turns out, I bravely broadened my horizons to write about easy books as well. I am endlessly grateful to Cathryn, even if she does spend most of her time telling me how well all her other clients are doing.

Mark Richards was the man who brought me to John Murray and convinced me to write books in the first place. It has been a pleasure doing this one for him. His colleagues Luke Brown and Morag Lyall have improved the text immeasurably and stopped me from writing only in the medium of footnotes.

I did have proper jobs while writing this book, two of which helped me enormously. Editing the *TLS* put me in contact every day with the cleverest writers in the world on the subject of reading, and their thoughts were always my guides. And presenting *Front Row* was the privilege of my broadcasting career: all of the producers were tireless and wise, and wonderful companions in discovering more about the arts every day. My thanks to Alice Feinstein for taking a chance on me.

Every writer needs readers; in my case, the following people helped with drafts of this book: Steve Kennedy, Roz Dineen, Ruth Scurr, Xand Van Tulleken, Jeanette Sanders, David Shriver and Robert Douglas-Fairhurst. Robert Potts made sure I covered poetry as properly as I could, and Toby Lichtig was a guru on fiction (even though he is totally wrong about *The Unconsoled*).

Every time I write about books, it is a reflection of my childhood and a house filled with the pleasure of reading. I owe so much to my parents, who are both great readers, though it is unlikely my mum will put up with the swearing in this one. My own children are, I hope, following me as book lovers; and they always provide the joyful, shouty, demanding backdrop to everything I do.

This book is dedicated to my only friend and wife, Nadine, from whom it is always a wrench to depart each morning and to whom I am always delighted to return.